# Taste of Home QUICK & EASY WEEKNIGHT DINNERS



TASTE OF HOME BOOKS • RDA ENTHUSIAST BRANDS, LLC • MILWAUKEE, WI

Visit us at **tasteofhome.com** for other Taste of Home books and products.

**International Standard Book Number:**
979-8-88977-169-2

**Content Directors:** Ellie Martin Cliffe, Mark Hagen
**Creative Director:** Raeann Thompson
**Associate Creative Director:** Jami Geittmann
**Senior Editor:** Christine Rukavena
**Senior Art Director:** Courtney Lovetere
**Manager, Production Design:** Satyandra Raghav
**Senior Print Publication Designer:** Bipin Balakrishnan
**Print Production Artist:** Akash Christopher
**Deputy Editor, Copy Desk:** Ann M. Walter
**Senior Copy Editors:** Elizabeth Pollock Bruch, Suchismita Ukil
**Contributing Art Director:** Julie Wagner
**Contributing Copy Editor:** Nancy J. Stohs

**Cover Photography**
**Photographer:** Mark Derse
**Set Stylist:** Melissa Franco
**Contributing Food Stylist:** Sue Draheim

**Pictured on front cover:**
Black Bean & Beef Tostadas, p. 70

**Pictured on back cover:**
Chicken Pasta Caesar Salad, p. 163; Muffin-Tin Lasagnas, p. 223; Copycat Fried Chicken Sandwich, p. 133; Shortcut Minestrone, p. 34; Mississippi Mud Pie, p. 295

Printed in China
3 5 7 9 10 8 6 4

SHRIMP SCAMPI SPINACH SALAD, PAGE 197

# CONTENTS

## QUICK & EASY ...

SOUPS, 6

BEEF, 36

PORK, 84

POULTRY, 126

SEAFOOD, 170

MEATLESS, 208

DINNER ADD-ONS, 240

SWEETS, 272

## INDEXES

ICON, 306

PROTEIN SOURCE, 311

ALPHABETICAL, 315

SLOW-COOKER PORK CHOPS, PAGE 102

# FAST. FRESH. FAMILY-FRIENDLY.

At *Taste of Home*, we've always believed that dinner does not have to be complicated to be delicious. That's the inspiration behind ***Quick & Easy Weeknight Dinners***, a new cookbook guaranteed to bring comfort, creativity and convenience to your table.

Inside this mouthwatering collection, you'll find hundreds of dishes that make the most of your time—quick skillet suppers, hearty soups and stews, satisfying sheet-pan meals and even irresistible desserts. Whether you're feeding a crowd, cooking for two or creating weekly menu plans, these recipes are here to help you win on weeknights.

When you're craving comfort, turn to Chicken Biscuit Potpie (p. 147) or Creamy Taco Soup (p. 10). Need something fresh yet fast? Try Mediterranean Shrimp Orzo Salad (p. 195) or zesty BLT Quinoa Bowls (p. 107). When you're looking for hands-off ease, put your slow cooker to work with "Secret's in the Sauce" BBQ Ribs (p. 98) or Easy Slow-Cooker Pot Roast (p. 54).

Don't forget about sides, breads and desserts! You'll love the simplicity of Quick Green Beans with Bacon, (p. 242), Air-Fryer Cornbread (p. 244), Mississippi Mud Pie (p. 295) and more than 70 other tasty bites that round out menus in a flash.

You'll also find shortcuts, substitutions and make-ahead ideas that beat the clock as well as smart indexes to help you find the recipes that fit your schedule best.

Because at the end of the day, meals should be rewarding—not rushed. With ***Quick & Easy Weeknight Dinners*** by your side, you'll save time while still serving warm, satisfying suppers made from the heart.

CHEESEBURGER CUPS, PAGE 38

## ICONS IN THIS BOOK

Icons make it easy to find a recipe for your needs.

These fast-fix dishes are table-ready in just 30 minutes or less.

Grab your air fryer to enjoy crispy foods without the added fat from frying in oil.

Get both flavor and efficiency with recipes made in an electric pressure cooker. Alternate directions are provided in case you don't have one.

These recipes demonstrate why the slow cooker is a favorite kitchen tool.

5i Save time in the kitchen and supermarket! These recipes use five or fewer ingredients (plus salt, pepper and/or cooking oil).

SHORTCUT MINESTRONE, PAGE 34

# QUICK & EASY SOUPS

AMISH CHICKEN CORN SOUP, PAGE 32

## SLOW-COOKER CHICKEN & RICE SOUP

Using the slow cooker takes some of the effort out of making from-scratch chicken soup. The long cook time helps develop superb homemade flavor.
*—Kevin Bruckerhoff, Columbia, MO*

**Prep:** 15 min. • **Cook:** 7 hours
**Makes:** 16 servings (4 qt.)

- 3 qt. water
- 4 bone-in chicken breast halves (about 3 lbs.)
- 1½ tsp. salt
- ¼ tsp. pepper
- ¼ tsp. poultry seasoning
- 1 tsp. chicken bouillon granules
- 3 medium carrots, chopped
- 2 celery ribs, chopped
- 1 small onion, chopped
- ½ cup uncooked parboiled (converted) rice
- Minced fresh parsley, optional

1. In a 6-qt. slow cooker, place water, chicken, salt, pepper and poultry seasoning. Cover and cook on low 6-7 hours or until chicken is tender.
2. With a slotted spoon, remove chicken from broth. When cool enough to handle, remove meat from bones; discard skin and bones. Cut chicken into bite-sized pieces. Skim fat from broth; add chicken and next 5 ingredients. Cover and cook on high 1-2 hours or until vegetables and rice are tender. If desired, sprinkle each serving with parsley.

**1 CUP** 202 cal., 6g fat (2g sat. fat), 66mg chol., 513mg sod., 10g carb. (1g sugars, 1g fiber), 25g pro.

## FAVORITE HAMBURGER STEW

I got this recipe from a woman at our church when I needed a way to use up our bounty of home-canned tomatoes. My husband loves it, and I like that it's easy to warm up for a carefree dinner in the winter months.
*—Marcia Clay, Truman, MN*

**Prep:** 20 min. • **Cook:** 65 min.
**Makes:** 16 servings (4 qt.)

- 2 lbs. ground beef
- 2 medium onions, chopped
- 4 cans (14½ oz. each) stewed tomatoes, undrained
- 8 medium carrots, thinly sliced
- 4 celery ribs, thinly sliced
- 2 medium potatoes, peeled and cubed
- 2 cups water
- ½ cup uncooked long grain rice
- 3 tsp. salt
- 1 tsp. pepper

1. In a Dutch oven, cook beef and onions over medium heat until meat is no longer pink, breaking it into crumbles; drain. Add the tomatoes, carrots, celery, potatoes, water, rice, salt and pepper; bring to a boil. Reduce heat; cover and simmer 30 minutes or until vegetables and rice are tender.
2. Uncover; simmer 20-30 minutes longer or until thickened to desired consistency.

**FREEZE OPTION** Freeze cooled stew in freezer containers. To use, partially thaw in refrigerator overnight. Heat through in a saucepan, stirring occasionally; add a little water if necessary.

**1 CUP** 191 cal., 7g fat (3g sat. fat), 35mg chol., 689mg sod., 21g carb. (8g sugars, 2g fiber), 12g pro.

**TEST KITCHEN TIP**

Stir in a can or two of rinsed, drained beans for a little more heft in each bite. We suggest kidney, pinto, great northern, white or cannellini beans.

## CREAMY TACO SOUP

This quick and easy recipe is one of our favorite meals for cold winter nights.
*—Sue Burton, Frankfort, KS*

**Takes:** 20 min. • **Makes:** 3¼ qt.

- 1½ lbs. ground beef
- 1 large onion, chopped
- 1 can (15 oz.) pinto beans, rinsed and drained
- 1 can (14½ oz.) stewed tomatoes
- 1 can (10 oz.) diced tomatoes and green chiles
- 1 can (10 oz.) chili without beans
- 1 lb. Velveeta, cubed
- Salt, pepper and garlic powder to taste
- 2 cups sour cream, divided

In a Dutch oven or soup kettle, cook beef and onion over medium heat until meat is no longer pink; drain. Add the beans, tomatoes, chili, Velveeta and seasonings. Reduce heat to low; cook and stir until Velveeta is melted. Stir in 1 cup sour cream; heat through (do not boil). Garnish with remaining sour cream.
**1 CUP** 333 cal., 20g fat (12g sat. fat), 76mg chol., 746mg sod., 15g carb. (7g sugars, 2g fiber), 21g pro.

### ADD A SPICY ACCENT

To spice things up a bit, cook the beef and onion with taco seasoning, chili powder, or ground cayenne pepper or cumin.

## SPRING SALMON CHOWDER

This creamy chowder really hits the spot. Enjoy it with a side salad and oven-fresh bread for a complete meal.
*—Pat Waymire, Yellow Springs, OH*

**Takes:** 30 min. • **Makes:** 8 servings (2 qt.)

- 2 cups cauliflowerets
- 1 Tbsp. water
- 2 Tbsp. butter
- 2 celery ribs, thinly sliced
- 8 green onions, thinly sliced
- 2 Tbsp. all-purpose flour
- ½ tsp. salt
- ½ tsp. dill weed
- 4 cups 2% milk
- 1 can (14¾ oz.) salmon, drained, skin and bones removed
- 1 pkg. (9 oz.) frozen peas, thawed
- ½ cup shredded Swiss cheese
- ½ cup shredded cheddar cheese

1. In a microwave-safe bowl, combine cauliflower and water. Microwave, covered, on high for 4-5 minutes or until tender, stirring once.
2. In a large saucepan, heat butter over medium-high heat. Add celery and green onions; cook and stir until tender. Stir in flour, salt and dill until blended; gradually whisk in milk. Bring to a boil, stirring constantly; cook and stir 2 minutes or until thickened.
3. Stir in salmon, peas and cauliflower; heat through. Stir in cheeses until melted. Serve immediately.

**1 CUP** 256 cal., 11g fat (5g sat. fat), 67mg chol., 558mg sod., 15g carb. (9g sugars, 3g fiber), 23g pro.

## CAZUELA

I learned to make this dish while we were living in Chile for a few months. We grow extra butternut squash in our garden just for this recipe.
*—Louise Schmid, Marshall, MN*

**Prep:** 20 min. • **Cook:** 30 min.
**Makes:** 6 servings

- 6 chicken drumsticks or thighs
- 3 cups cubed peeled butternut squash (1-in. cubes)
- 6 small potatoes, peeled
- 6 pieces of fresh or frozen corn on the cob (2 in. each)
- 3 carrots, cut into 1-in. chunks
- 3 cans (14½ oz. each) chicken broth
- Hot cooked rice
- Hot pepper sauce to taste
- Salt and pepper to taste
- Minced fresh cilantro or parsley

1. In a Dutch oven, place the chicken, squash, potatoes, corn, carrots and broth; bring to a boil. Reduce heat; cover and simmer for 25 minutes or until chicken is done and vegetables are tender.
2. Serve over rice in a shallow soup bowl. Serve with hot pepper sauce, salt, pepper and cilantro or parsley.

**1 SERVING** 416 cal., 8g fat (2g sat. fat), 52mg chol., 968mg sod., 67g carb. (12g sugars, 8g fiber), 23g pro.

## SO-EASY GAZPACHO

My daughter got this recipe from a friend a few years ago. Now I serve it often as an appetizer, and it certainly is the talk of any party!
*—Lorna Sirtoli, Cortland, NY*

**Prep:** 15 min. + chilling
**Makes:** 5 servings

- 2 cups tomato juice
- 4 medium tomatoes, peeled and finely chopped
- ½ cup chopped seeded peeled cucumber
- ⅓ cup finely chopped onion
- ¼ cup olive oil
- ¼ cup cider vinegar
- 1 tsp. sugar
- 1 garlic clove, minced
- ¼ tsp. salt
- ¼ tsp. pepper

In a large bowl, combine all ingredients. Cover and refrigerate until chilled, at least 4 hours.

**1 CUP** 146 cal., 11g fat (2g sat. fat), 0 chol., 387mg sod., 11g carb. (8g sugars, 2g fiber), 2g pro.

**ZUCCHINI GAZPACHO** Substitute 2 large tomatoes for the 4 medium. Add 1 can (15 oz.) drained rinsed black beans, 2 chopped medium zucchini and ¼ tsp. cayenne.

**REFRESHING GAZPACHO** Increase tomato juice to 4½ cups. Add 2 chopped celery ribs, 1 finely chopped red onion, 1 each chopped medium green and sweet red peppers, ¼ cup minced fresh cilantro, 2 Tbsp. lime juice, 2 tsp. sugar and 1 tsp. Worcestershire sauce. Serve with cubed avocado if desired.

### TEST KITCHEN TIP

For the freshest flavor, use fully ripe, juicy tomatoes—ideally from a local garden—for your gazpacho.

"Fast and easy. Hubby and I both really enjoyed it. I used shredded rotisserie chicken. Much more flavor than I expected."
—KELLYWILLIG, TASTEOFHOME.COM

## EASY WHITE CHICKEN CHILI

Chili is one of our favorite cold-weather foods. We use chicken and white beans for a twist on the regular bowl of red. This is wonderful comfort food.
*—Rachel Lewis, Danville, VA*

**Takes:** 30 min. • **Makes:** 6 servings

- 1 Tbsp. vegetable oil
- 1 lb. lean ground chicken
- 1 medium onion, chopped
- 2 cans (15 oz. each) cannellini beans, rinsed and drained
- 1 can (4 oz.) chopped green chiles
- 1 tsp. ground cumin
- ½ tsp. dried oregano
- ¼ tsp. pepper
- 1 can (14½ oz.) reduced-sodium chicken broth
- Optional toppings: Sour cream, shredded cheddar cheese and chopped fresh cilantro

1. Heat oil In a large pan; add chicken and onion and cook over medium-high heat until chicken is no longer pink, 6-8 minutes, breaking up chicken into crumbles.
2. Pour 1 can of beans in a small bowl; mash slightly. Stir mashed beans, remaining can of beans, chiles, seasonings and broth into chicken mixture; bring to a boil. Reduce heat; simmer, covered, until flavors are blended, 12-15 minutes. Serve with toppings as desired.

**FREEZE OPTION** Freeze cooled chili in freezer containers. To use, partially thaw in refrigerator overnight. Heat through in a saucepan, stirring occasionally; add broth if necessary.

**1 CUP** 228 cal., 5g fat (1g sat. fat), 54mg chol., 504mg sod., 23g carb. (1g sugars, 6g fiber), 22g pro.

## PRESSURE-COOKER CORN CHOWDER

Enjoy this chowder's slow-simmered, rich flavor in record time by using a pressure cooker. Corn chowder is a classic staple, with its hearty flavors of creamy sweet corn, bacon crumbles and shredded cheddar cheese.
—Taste of Home *Test Kitchen*

**Prep:** 15 min. • **Cook:** 15 min.
**Makes:** 8 servings (2 qt.)

- 4 medium red potatoes, peeled and cut into ½-in. cubes (about 2½ cups)
- 2 cans (14½ oz. each) chicken broth
- 3 cups fresh or frozen corn
- 1 medium onion, chopped
- 3 garlic cloves, minced
- ½ tsp. salt
- ½ tsp. pepper
- 2 Tbsp. cornstarch
- 1 cup half-and-half cream
- 1 cup shredded cheddar cheese
- 6 bacon strips, cooked and crumbled
- Chopped fresh parsley
- Optional: Additional shredded cheddar cheese and crumbled bacon

1. Place first 7 ingredients in a 6-qt. electric pressure cooker. Lock lid; close pressure-release valve. Adjust to pressure-cook on high for 15 minutes. Quick-release pressure.
2. Select saute setting and adjust for low heat. Mix cornstarch and cream until smooth; stir into soup. Cook and stir until slightly thickened, 6-8 minutes. Stir in cheese and bacon. Heat through until cheese is melted. Press cancel. Sprinkle servings with parsley and, if desired, additional cheese and bacon.

**1 CUP** 191 cal., 9g fat (5g sat. fat), 31mg chol., 709mg sod., 21g carb. (5g sugars, 2g fiber), 7g pro.

**STOVETOP CORN CHOWDER** Bring first 7 ingredients to a boil in a Dutch oven. Reduce heat; simmer for 20-25 minutes or until vegetables are tender. Combine cornstarch and cream; stir into soup. Proceed as directed.

## GUMBO IN A JIFFY

This is a yummy dish. My husband loves the spicy kick that the sausage gives this quick gumbo, and it's a cinch to assemble.
*—Amy Flack, Homer City, PA*

**Takes:** 20 min. • **Makes:** 6 servings

- 1 pkg. (12 oz.) smoked sausage, sliced
- 1 can (14½ oz.) diced tomatoes with green peppers and onions, undrained
- 1 can (14½ oz.) chicken broth
- ½ cup water
- 1 cup uncooked instant rice
- 1 can (7 oz.) whole kernel corn, drained
- Sliced green onions, optional

In a large saucepan, cook sliced sausage until browned on both sides. Stir in the tomatoes, broth and water; bring to a boil. Stir in rice and corn; cover and remove from the heat. Let stand for 5 minutes. If desired, top with green onions.

**1 CUP** 279 cal., 16g fat (7g sat. fat), 40mg chol., 1197mg sod., 22g carb. (6g sugars, 2g fiber), 11g pro.

## SHRIMP BISQUE

This bisque combines the perfect blend of seafood and Mexican spices. You'll for sure want seconds!
*—Karen Harris, Littleton, CO*

**Takes:** 30 min. • **Makes:** 3 cups

- 1 small onion, chopped
- 1 Tbsp. olive oil
- 2 garlic cloves, minced
- 1 Tbsp. all-purpose flour
- 1 cup water
- ½ cup heavy whipping cream
- 1 Tbsp. chili powder
- 2 tsp. sodium-free chicken bouillon granules
- ½ tsp. ground cumin
- ½ tsp. ground coriander
- ½ lb. uncooked shrimp, peeled and deveined
- ½ cup sour cream
- Optional: Fresh cilantro, cubed avocado and additional shrimp

**1.** In a small saucepan, saute onion in oil until tender. Add garlic; cook 1 minute longer. Stir in flour until blended. Stir in water, cream, chili powder, bouillon, cumin and coriander; bring to a boil. Reduce heat; cover and simmer 5 minutes.
**2.** Cut shrimp into bite-sized pieces; add to soup. Simmer 5 minutes longer or until shrimp turn pink. Gradually stir ½ cup hot soup into sour cream; return all to pan, stirring constantly. Heat through (do not boil). If desired, garnish with fresh cilantro, cubed avocado and additional shrimp.

**1 CUP** 317 cal., 23g fat (11g sat. fat), 141mg chol., 206mg sod., 11g carb. (4g sugars, 2g fiber), 17g pro.

**"Excellent—my wife says it's better than her favorite restaurant (and cheaper). I boiled the shrimp shells in half water and half vegetable stock and used this liquid in the soup. I added ¼ tsp. cayenne and 1 tsp. Old Bay. To cut fat, I used a 50-50 mix of heavy cream and fat-free half-and-half."**
—FRED MARCLEY, TASTEOFHOME.COM

## EASY SPINACH BISQUE

This creamy, easy-to-make soups turns an ordianry meal into extra-special dinner.
*—Patricia Tuckwiller, Lewisburg, WV*

**Takes:** 20 min. • **Makes:** 6 servings

- ½ cup chopped onion
- 2 Tbsp. butter
- ⅓ cup all-purpose flour
- ½ to 1 tsp. salt
- ⅛ tsp. ground nutmeg
- 2½ cups milk
- 1 cup water
- ¾ cup cubed Velveeta
- 1 pkg. (10 oz.) frozen chopped spinach, thawed and drained
- Oyster crackers, optional

In a large saucepan, saute onion in butter until tender. Stir in the flour, salt and nutmeg until blended. Gradually whisk in milk and water. Bring to a boil. Cook and stir for 2 minutes or until thickened. Reduce heat to medium; add the Velveeta and stir until melted. Stir in spinach; heat through. Serve with crackers if desired.

**1 CUP** 184 cal., 11g fat (7g sat. fat), 33mg chol., 488mg sod., 14g carb. (7g sugars, 2g fiber), 8g pro.

### SPICE SURPRISE

Usually associated with sweet recipes, nutmeg is the secret ingredient in flavorful bechamel and white sauces. Be careful not to overdo it, as a small amount of the spice goes a long way.

## SOUTHWEST CHICKEN STEW

This dish needs just 15 minutes of prep, so you'll be out of the kitchen in no time. The delicious low-fat chicken gets even better with a garnish of reduced-fat sour cream and fresh cilantro.
*—Brandi Castillo, Santa Maria, CA*

**Prep:** 15 min. • **Cook:** 3 hours
**Makes:** 6 servings

- 2 cans (15 oz. each) black beans, rinsed and drained
- 1 can (14½ oz.) reduced-sodium chicken broth
- 1 can (14½ oz.) diced tomatoes with mild green chiles, undrained
- ½ lb. boneless skinless chicken breast
- 1 jar (8 oz.) chunky salsa
- 1 cup frozen corn
- 1 Tbsp. dried parsley flakes
- 1 tsp. ground cumin
- ¼ tsp. pepper
- 3 cups hot cooked rice
- Optional: Lime wedges and fresh cilantro leaves

1. In a 2- or 3-qt. slow cooker, combine the beans, broth, tomatoes, chicken, salsa, corn and seasonings. Cover and cook on low 3-4 hours or until a thermometer inserted in chicken reads 165°.
2. Shred chicken with 2 forks and return to slow cooker; heat through. Serve over rice. If desired, serve with lime wedges and fresh cilantro.

**FREEZE OPTION** After shredding chicken, freeze cooled mixture in freezer containers. To use, partially thaw in refrigerator overnight. Heat through in a saucepan, stirring occasionally; add a little broth or water if necessary.

**1 CUP** 320 cal., 1g fat (0 sat. fat), 21mg chol., 873mg sod., 56g carb. (7g sugars, 8g fiber), 19g pro.

## VEGETABLE LENTIL SOUP

Here's a healthy soup that's ideal for vegetarians and anyone watching their weight. Butternut squash and lentils make it filling, while herbs and other veggies round out the flavor.
*—Mark Morgan, Waterford, WI*

**Prep:** 20 min. • **Cook:** 4½ hours
**Makes:** 6 servings (2 qt.)

- 3 cups cubed peeled butternut squash
- 1 cup chopped carrots
- 1 cup chopped onion
- 1 cup dried lentils, rinsed
- 2 garlic cloves, minced
- 1 tsp. dried oregano
- 1 tsp. dried basil
- 4 cups vegetable broth
- 1 can (14½ oz.) Italian diced tomatoes, undrained
- 2 cups frozen cut green beans (about 8 oz.)

1. Place the first 8 ingredients in a 5-qt. slow cooker. Cook, covered, on low until lentils are tender, about 4 hours.
2. Stir in tomatoes and beans. Cook, covered, on high until heated through, about 30 minutes.

**1⅓ CUPS** 217 cal., 1g fat (0 sat. fat), 0 chol., 685mg sod., 45g carb. (11g sugars, 8g fiber), 11g pro.

## SAUCY INDIAN-STYLE CHICKEN & VEGETABLES

This easy Indian dish will be loved by all. Feel free to add more or less tikka masala sauce according to your taste.
*—Erica Polly, Sun Prairie, WI*

**Prep:** 15 min. • **Cook:** 4 hours
**Makes:** 8 servings (2½ qt.)

- 2 medium sweet potatoes, peeled and cut into 1½-in. pieces
- 2 Tbsp. water
- 2 medium sweet red peppers, cut into 1-in. pieces
- 3 cups fresh caulifloweret s
- 2 lbs. boneless skinless chicken thighs, cubed
- 2 jars (15 oz. each) tikka masala curry sauce
- ¾ tsp. salt
- Minced fresh cilantro, optional
- Naan flatbreads, warmed

1. Microwave sweet potatoes and water, covered, on high just until potatoes begin to soften, 3-4 minutes.
2. In a 5- or 6-qt. slow cooker, combine sweet potatoes, peppers, cauliflowerets and chicken; add sauce and salt. Cook, covered, on low 4-5 hours or until meat is tender. If desired, top with cilantro. Serve with warmed naan.

**FREEZE OPTION** Omitting cilantro, freeze cooled chicken and vegetable mixture in freezer containers. To use, partially thaw in refrigerator overnight. Microwave, covered, on high in a microwave-safe dish until heated through, stirring gently; add water if necessary. If desired, sprinkle with cilantro. Serve with warmed naan.

**1¼ CUPS** 334 cal., 15g fat (4g sat. fat), 80mg chol., 686mg sod., 25g carb. (12g sugars, 5g fiber), 25g pro.

## KIDS' FAVORITE CHILI

This sweet and easy chili is sure to warm the whole family up on those chilly fall nights. The recipe has been in my family for three generations.
*—Terri Keeney, Greeley, CO*

**Takes:** 25 min. • **Makes:** 4 servings

- 1 lb. ground turkey
- ½ cup chopped onion
- 1 can (15¾ oz.) pork and beans
- 1 can (14½ oz.) diced tomatoes, undrained
- 1 can (10¾ oz.) condensed tomato soup, undiluted
- 1 Tbsp. brown sugar
- 1 Tbsp. chili powder
- Oyster or saltine crackers and shredded cheddar cheese

In a large saucepan, cook turkey and onion over medium heat until meat is no longer pink; drain. Stir in the next 5 ingredients. Bring to a boil. Reduce heat; cover and simmer until heated through, 15-20 minutes. Serve with crackers and cheese.

**1½ CUPS** 359 cal., 10g fat (2g sat. fat), 75mg chol., 908mg sod., 43g carb. (20g sugars, 9g fiber), 30g pro.

### CUSTOMIZE IT

- Add drained, rinsed pinto or black beans for extra protein.
- Stir in bell peppers, zucchini, butternut squash or corn for more nutrients.
- Offer toppings like cheese, sour cream, guacamole, crackers or tortilla chips.

STAUB

## SPINACH & SAUSAGE LENTIL SOUP

During the cooler months, this soup makes regular appearances on our dinner table. It is approved by all, including my picky 6-year-old.
*—Kalyn Gensic, Ardmore, OK*

**Prep:** 5 min. • **Cook:** 45 min.
**Makes:** 6 servings (2 qt.)

- 1 lb. bulk spicy pork sausage
- 1 cup dried lentils, rinsed
- 1 can (15 oz.) cannellini beans, rinsed and drained
- 1 carton (32 oz.) reduced-sodium chicken broth
- 1 cup water
- 1 can (14½ oz.) fire-roasted diced tomatoes, undrained
- 6 cups fresh spinach (about 4 oz.)
- Crumbled goat cheese, optional

1. In a Dutch oven, cook and crumble sausage over medium heat until no longer pink, 5-7 minutes; drain.
2. Stir in lentils, beans, broth and water; bring to a boil. Reduce heat. Simmer, covered, until lentils are tender, about 30 minutes. Stir in tomatoes; heat through.
3. Remove from heat; stir in spinach until wilted. If desired, serve with goat cheese.

**FREEZE OPTION** Freeze cooled soup in freezer containers. To use, partially thaw in refrigerator overnight. Heat through in a saucepan, stirring occasionally.

**1⅓ CUPS** 390 cal., 17g fat (5g sat. fat), 41mg chol., 1242mg sod., 37g carb. (3g sugars, 8g fiber), 22g pro.

## GINGER CHICKEN NOODLE SOUP

This is one of my favorite soup recipes to serve in the wintertime because it's easy and comforting, and it fills the entire house with a wonderful aroma. My whole family loves it!
*—Brandy Stansbury, Edna, TX*

**Prep:** 15 min. • **Cook:** 3½ hours
**Makes:** 8 servings (2½ qt.)

- 1 lb. boneless skinless chicken breasts, cubed
- 2 medium carrots, shredded
- 3 Tbsp. sherry or reduced-sodium chicken broth
- 2 Tbsp. rice vinegar
- 1 Tbsp. reduced-sodium soy sauce
- 2 to 3 tsp. minced fresh gingerroot
- ¼ tsp. pepper
- 6 cups reduced-sodium chicken broth
- 1 cup water
- 2 cups fresh snow peas, halved
- 2 oz. uncooked angel hair pasta, broken into thirds

1. In a 5-qt. slow cooker, combine the first 9 ingredients. Cook, covered, on low 3-4 hours or until chicken is tender.
2. Stir in snow peas and pasta. Cook, covered, on low until snow peas and pasta are tender, about 30 minutes longer.

**1¼ CUPS** 126 cal., 2g fat (0 sat. fat), 31mg chol., 543mg sod., 11g carb. (3g sugars, 2g fiber), 16g pro.

## HEARTY NAVY BEAN SOUP

Use thrifty dried beans and a ham hock to create this comfort-food classic. Bean soup is a family favorite that I make often.

*—Mildred Lewis, Temple, TX*

**Prep:** 30 min. + soaking
**Cook:** 1¾ hours
**Makes:** 10 servings (2½ qt.)

- 3 cups (1½ lbs.) dried navy beans
- 1 can (14½ oz.) diced tomatoes, undrained
- 1 large onion, chopped
- 1 meaty ham hock or 1 cup diced cooked ham
- 2 cups chicken broth
- 2½ cups water
- Salt and pepper to taste
- Minced fresh parsley, optional

**1.** Rinse and sort beans; soak according to package directions.
**2.** Drain and rinse beans, discarding liquid. Place in a Dutch oven. Add the tomatoes with juice, onion, ham hock, broth, water, salt and pepper. Bring to a boil. Reduce heat; cover and simmer until beans are tender, about 1½ hours.
**3.** Add more water if necessary. Remove ham hock and let it stand until cool enough to handle. Remove meat from bone; discard bone. Cut meat into bite-sized pieces; set aside. (For a thicker soup, cool slightly, then puree some of the beans in a food processor or blender and return to pan.) Return ham to soup and heat through. Garnish with parsley if desired.

**1 CUP** 244 cal., 2g fat (0 sat. fat), 8mg chol., 410mg sod., 42g carb. (5g sugars, 10g fiber), 18g pro.

### LONG-LASTING HERB BUNCH

To keep parsley fresh for up to a month, trim the ends of the stems and place the bunch in a tumbler with about an inch of water. Be sure no loose leaves are in the water. Tie a produce bag around the tumbler to trap humidity; store in the refrigerator.

## WATERMELON GAZPACHO

My refreshing gazpacho is a delightfully simple, elegant dish. Serve as a side or with pita and hummus for a meal.
*—Nicole Deelah, Nashville, TN*

**Takes:** 25 min. • **Makes:** 4 servings

- 4 cups cubed watermelon, seeded, divided
- 2 Tbsp. lime juice
- 1 Tbsp. grated lime zest
- 1 tsp. minced fresh gingerroot
- 1 tsp. salt
- 1 cup chopped tomato
- ½ cup chopped cucumber
- ½ cup chopped green pepper
- ¼ cup minced fresh cilantro
- 2 Tbsp. chopped green onion
- 1 Tbsp. finely chopped seeded jalapeno pepper
- Watermelon wedges, optional

1. Puree 3 cups watermelon cubes in a blender. Cut remaining 1 cup watermelon cubes into ½-in. pieces; set aside.
2. In a large bowl, combine pureed watermelon, lime juice and zest, ginger and salt. Stir in tomato, cucumber, green pepper, cilantro, green onion, jalapeno and reserved 1 cup watermelon pieces. Refrigerate until serving. If desired, serve with wedge of watermelon.

**NOTE** Wear disposable gloves when cutting hot peppers; the oils can burn skin. Avoid touching your face.

**1 CUP** 58 cal., 0 fat (0 sat. fat), 0 chol., 599mg sod., 18g carb. (15g sugars, 2g fiber), 1g pro.

## CHICKPEA TORTILLA SOUP

This vegan tortilla soup recipe is healthy, filling and family-friendly! We love how hearty and flavorful it is. We like to play around with the different toppings we add each time it's served.
*—Julie Peterson, Crofton, MD*

**Takes:** 30 min. • **Makes:** 8 servings (3 qt.)

- 1 Tbsp. olive oil
- 1 medium red onion, chopped
- 4 garlic cloves, minced
- 1 to 2 jalapeno peppers, seeded and chopped, optional
- ¼ tsp. pepper
- 8 cups vegetable broth
- 1 cup red quinoa, rinsed
- 2 cans (15 oz. each) no-salt-added chickpeas or garbanzo beans, rinsed and drained
- 1 can (15 oz.) no-salt-added black beans, rinsed and drained
- 3 medium tomatoes, chopped
- 1 cup fresh or frozen corn
- ⅓ cup minced fresh cilantro
- Optional toppings: Crushed tortilla chips, cubed avocado, lime wedges and additional chopped cilantro

Heat oil in a Dutch oven over medium-high heat. Add the red onion, garlic, jalapeno if desired, and pepper; cook and stir until tender, 3-5 minutes. Add broth and quinoa. Bring to a boil; reduce heat. Simmer, uncovered, until quinoa is tender, about 10 minutes. Add the chickpeas, beans, tomatoes, corn and cilantro; heat through. If desired, serve with optional toppings.

**NOTE** Wear disposable gloves when cutting hot peppers; the oils can burn skin. Avoid touching your face.

**1½ CUPS** 289 cal., 5g fat (0 sat. fat), 0 chol., 702mg sod., 48g carb. (5g sugars, 9g fiber), 13g pro.

## CHICKEN RAMEN NOODLE BOWL

This healthier take on ramen uses ingredients I usually have on hand. It is an easy, quick and satisfying lunch. You can also make this with leftover chicken or pork. Fresh lime and/or bean sprouts make a nice garnish.
*—Alicia Rooker, Milwaukee, WI*

**Takes:** 20 min. • **Makes:** 2 servings

- 1 pkg. (3 oz.) chicken ramen noodles
- 1 cup frozen stir-fry vegetable blend
- 1 can (5 oz.) chunk white chicken, drained
- 2 medium fresh mushrooms, thinly sliced
- 1 garlic clove, minced
- ½ tsp. Sriracha chili sauce
- 2 soft-boiled large eggs
- 1 green onion, thinly sliced

Cook noodles and stir-fry blend according to package directions. Stir chicken, mushrooms, garlic, chili sauce and cooked stir-fry blend into noodles; heat through. Divide between 2 bowls. Serve with soft-boiled eggs, green onion and additional chili sauce if desired.

**1½ CUPS** 368 cal., 14g fat (5g sat. fat), 230mg chol., 1199mg sod., 36g carb. (4g sugars, 3g fiber), 24g pro.

## RUSTIC FISH CHOWDER

For my version of this classic, I use halibut that my brother-in-law, a commercial fisherman, catches in Kodiak, Alaska. Top each serving with some grated Parmesan and minced green onions.
*—Diana Lassen, Eugene, OR*

**Prep:** 15 min. • **Cook:** 30 min.
**Makes:** 12 servings (3 qt.)

- ¼ cup butter, cubed
- 1 small onion, finely chopped
- 1 garlic clove, minced
- 3 lbs. potatoes (about 6 medium), cut into ½-in. cubes
- 1½ cups fresh or frozen corn
- 5 cups chicken broth
- 1½ tsp. salt
- ¾ tsp. celery salt
- ¾ tsp. pepper
- ½ tsp. dried thyme
- 1 lb. cod or halibut fillets, cut into ¾-in. pieces
- 1 cup heavy whipping cream

1. In a 6-qt. stockpot, heat butter over medium heat. Add onion; cook and stir until tender, 3-4 minutes. Add garlic; cook 1 minute longer. Add potatoes, corn, broth, salt, celery salt, pepper and thyme; bring to a boil. Reduce heat; simmer, covered, until potatoes are tender, 10-15 minutes. Mash potatoes slightly.
2. Stir in cod and cream; bring to a boil. Reduce heat; simmer, covered, until fish just begins to flake easily with a fork, 6-8 minutes.

**1 CUP** 242 cal., 12g fat (7g sat. fat), 49mg chol., 842mg sod., 25g carb. (3g sugars, 3g fiber), 10g pro.

## SPINACH & WHITE BEAN SOUP

For me, soup is love, comfort, happiness and memories. With all its veggies and beans, this one appeals to my "kitchen sink" style of cooking.
*—Annette Palermo, Beach Haven, NJ*

**Takes:** 30 min. • **Makes:** 6 servings

- 2 tsp. olive oil
- 3 garlic cloves, minced
- 3 cans (15 oz. each) cannellini beans, rinsed and drained, divided
- ¼ tsp. pepper
- 4 cups vegetable or reduced-sodium chicken broth
- 4 cups chopped fresh spinach (about 3 oz.)
- ¼ cup thinly sliced fresh basil
- Shredded Parmesan cheese, optional

1. In a large saucepan, heat oil over medium heat. Add garlic; cook and stir until tender, 30-45 seconds. Stir in 2 cans of beans. Add pepper and broth.
2. Puree mixture using an immersion blender. Or puree in a blender and return to pan. Stir in remaining can of beans; bring to a boil. Reduce heat; simmer, covered, 15 minutes, stirring occasionally.
3. Stir in spinach and basil; cook, uncovered, until spinach is wilted, 2-4 minutes. If desired, serve with cheese.

**1¼ CUPS** 192 cal., 2g fat (0 sat. fat), 0 chol., 886mg sod., 33g carb. (1g sugars, 9g fiber), 9g pro.

## EGG DROP SOUP

We start many stir-fry meals with this easy soup, which cooks in just minutes flat. There are many recipe variations, but we like the addition of cornstarch to thicken the soup and give it a rich, golden color. I got the recipe from my grandma's old cookbook.
*—Amy Beth Corlew-Sherlock, Lapeer, MI*

**Takes:** 15 min. • **Makes:** 4 servings

- 3 cups chicken broth
- 1 Tbsp. cornstarch
- 2 Tbsp. cold water
- 1 large egg, lightly beaten
- 1 green onion, sliced

1. In a large saucepan, bring broth to a boil over medium heat. Combine cornstarch and water until smooth; gradually stir into broth. Bring to a boil; cook and stir for 2 minutes or until thickened.
2. Reduce heat. Drizzle beaten egg into hot broth, stirring constantly. Remove from the heat; stir in onion.

**¾ CUP** 39 cal., 2g fat (0 sat. fat), 53mg chol., 714mg sod., 3g carb. (1g sugars, 0 fiber), 3g pro.

> **"Simple and to the point. This makes a great starter for a larger Asian meal or alone as a quick lunch! Occasionally, I add a drop or two of sesame oil to change things up."**
> —REDHEN1970, TASTEOFHOME.COM

## GREEK-STYLE LENTIL SOUP

This healthy, warming soup is a satisfying vegetarian recipe, but you can use chicken broth or add cooked meat if you like.
*—Mary E. Smith, Columbia, MO*

**Prep:** 20 min. • **Cook:** 5 hours
**Makes:** 12 servings (3 qt.)

- 4 cups water
- 4 cups vegetable broth
- 2 cups dried lentils, rinsed
- 2 medium carrots, chopped
- 1 small onion, chopped
- 1 celery rib, chopped
- 1 tsp. dried oregano, divided
- 1 cup chopped fresh spinach
- ½ cup tomato sauce
- 1 can (2¼ oz.) sliced ripe olives, drained
- 3 Tbsp. red wine vinegar
- 2 garlic cloves, minced
- ½ tsp. salt
- ¼ tsp. pepper
- Optional: Chopped red onion, chopped parsley and lemon wedges

1. Place water, broth, lentils, carrots, onion, celery and ½ tsp. oregano in a 5- or 6-qt. slow cooker. Cook, covered, on low 4-5 hours or until lentils are tender.
2. Stir in spinach, tomato sauce, olives, vinegar, garlic, salt, pepper and the remaining ½ tsp. oregano. Cook, covered, on low until spinach is wilted, about 1 hour longer. If desired, serve with red onion, parsley and lemon wedges.

**1 CUP** 134 cal., 1g fat (0 sat. fat), 0 chol., 420mg sod., 24g carb. (2g sugars, 4g fiber), 9g pro.

## SLOW-COOKER BEEF STEW

When there's a chill in the air, I love to make my slow-cooked stew. It's loaded with tender chunks of beef, potatoes and carrots.
*—Earnestine Wilson, Waco, TX*

**Prep:** 25 min. • **Cook:** 7 hours
**Makes:** 8 servings (2 qt.)

- 1½ lbs. potatoes, peeled and cubed
- 6 medium carrots, cut into 1-in. lengths
- 1 medium onion, coarsely chopped
- 3 celery ribs, coarsely chopped
- 3 Tbsp. all-purpose flour
- 1½ lbs. beef stew meat, cut into 1-in. cubes
- 3 Tbsp. canola oil
- 1 can (14½ oz.) diced tomatoes, undrained
- 1 can (14½ oz.) beef broth
- 1 tsp. ground mustard
- ½ tsp. salt
- ½ tsp. pepper
- ½ tsp. dried thyme
- ½ tsp. browning sauce, optional
- Minced fresh thyme, optional

1. Layer the potatoes, carrots, onion and celery in a 5-qt. slow cooker. Place flour in a large shallow dish. Add stew meat; turn to coat evenly. In a large skillet, brown meat in oil in batches. Place over vegetables.
2. In a large bowl, combine the tomatoes, broth, mustard, salt, pepper, thyme and, if desired, browning sauce. Pour over beef. Cover and cook on low for 7-8 hours, or until the meat and vegetables are tender. If desired, sprinkle with fresh thyme before serving.

**1 CUP** 272 cal., 12g fat (3g sat. fat), 53mg chol., 541mg sod., 23g carb. (6g sugars, 4g fiber), 19g pro.

## ONE-POT COCONUT CURRY LENTIL SOUP

This curry soup might be vegan, but it's still as creamy as ever. If you prefer a meatier bowl, toss some chicken and chicken broth into the recipe.
*—Kijan Zendi, San Diego, CA*

**Prep:** 10 min. • **Cook:** 25 min.
**Makes:** 8 servings (2 qt.)

- 1 pkg. (16 oz.) dried lentils, rinsed
- 1 carton (32 oz.) vegetable broth
- 1 garlic clove, minced
- 2 Tbsp. curry powder
- 2 cans (13.66 oz. each) coconut milk
- ½ tsp. kosher salt
- Chopped green onions

Place lentils, broth, garlic and curry powder in a Dutch oven. Bring to a boil; reduce heat. Add coconut milk; simmer, uncovered, until lentils are tender, 25-30 minutes. Stir in salt. Serve with green onions.

**FREEZE OPTION** Before adding green onions, freeze soup in freezer containers. To use, partially thaw in refrigerator overnight. Heat through in a saucepan, stirring occasionally; add broth or water if necessary. Sprinkle with green onions.

**1 CUP** 365 cal., 16g fat (16g sat. fat), 0 chol., 493mg sod., 40g carb. (4g sugars, 7g fiber), 16g pro.

### CUSTOMIZE IT

- Stir in sweet potato, butternut squash, carrots, bell pepper or tomatoes.
- Serve soup over jasmine rice or rice noodles.
- Sprinkle with fresh basil or cilantro.

## SLOW-COOKER SWEET POTATO SOUP

I love that I can top this creamy soup with anything my heart desires, which means I can eat it several days in a row without ever having to have it the same way twice. You can substitute fresh onions and celery in this recipe if you prefer, but using the dried versions makes it easy to throw together on a weekday morning.
*—Colleen Delawder, Herndon, VA*

**Prep:** 15 min. • **Cook:** 5 hours
**Makes:** 8 servings (2½ qt.)

- 3 lbs. sweet potatoes, peeled and cut into 1-in. cubes (about 8 cups)
- 2 Tbsp. butter
- 1 Tbsp. Worcestershire sauce
- 1 tsp. dried minced onion
- 1 tsp. dried celery flakes, optional
- ½ tsp. salt
- ½ tsp. pepper
- ¼ tsp. dried thyme
- ⅛ tsp. ground chipotle pepper
- 6 cups reduced-sodium chicken broth
- Optional: Sour cream and pepitas

1. In a 4- or 5-qt. slow cooker, combine all ingredients except sour cream and pepitas. Cook, covered, on low until potatoes are tender, 5-6 hours.
2. Puree soup using an immersion blender. Or, cool slightly and puree soup in batches in a blender; return to slow cooker and heat through. If desired, top servings with sour cream and pepitas.

**FREEZE OPTION** Freeze cooled soup in freezer containers. To use, partially thaw in refrigerator overnight. Heat through in a saucepan, stirring occasionally; add broth or water if necessary.

**1¼ CUPS** 215 cal., 3g fat (2g sat. fat), 8mg chol., 637mg sod., 43g carb. (18g sugars, 5g fiber), 5g pro.

## TEST KITCHEN TIP

Instead of doing the hot-soak method for beans described in step 1, you can soak the beans at least 8 hours or overnight in a bowl, covered with cool water. It just takes a little planning ahead.

## OLD-FASHIONED HAM & BEAN SOUP

This old-fashioned version of ham and bean soup starts with dried navy beans, but you could start with great northern beans instead. The first soak of the beans softens them, but they won't get tender until after they are simmered in the second step.
—Taste of Home *Test Kitchen*

**Prep:** 15 min. + soaking • **Cook:** 1½ hours
**Makes:** 10 servings (2½ qt.)

- 1 lb. dried navy beans
- 1 Tbsp. canola oil
- 2 medium onions, chopped
- 2 celery ribs, chopped
- 8 cups water
- 1 medium carrot, chopped
- 2 bay leaves
- 1 tsp. dried thyme
- ½ tsp. pepper
- 2 smoked ham hocks
- 2 cups cubed fully cooked ham
- ½ tsp. salt

1. Place beans in a Dutch oven; add water to cover by 2 in. Bring to a boil; boil for 2 minutes. Remove from the heat; cover and let stand for 1-4 hours or until beans are softened. Drain and rinse beans, discarding liquid.
2. In the same pan, heat oil over medium heat; add onions and celery. Cook and stir until crisp-tender, 3-5 minutes. Stir in softened beans, 8 cups water, carrot, bay leaves, thyme and pepper. Add ham hocks. Bring to a boil. Reduce heat; cover and simmer for 1¼-1½ hours or until beans are tender.
3. Discard bay leaves. Remove ham hocks; set aside until cool enough to handle. Remove ham from bones and cut into cubes; discard bones. Stir cubed ham and salt into soup; heat through.

**1 CUP** 230 cal., 4g fat (1g sat. fat), 25mg chol., 521mg sod., 31g carb. (3g sugars, 8g fiber), 20g pro.

## SPINACH & TORTELLINI SOUP

A simple tomato-enhanced broth is perfect for cheese tortellini and fresh spinach. Increase the garlic and add Italian seasoning to suit your taste.
*—Debbie Wilson, Burlington, NC*

**Takes:** 20 min.
**Makes:** 6 servings (2 qt.)

- 1 tsp. olive oil
- 2 garlic cloves, minced
- 1 can (14½ oz.) no-salt-added diced tomatoes, undrained
- 3 cans (14½ oz. each) vegetable broth
- 2 tsp. Italian seasoning
- 1 pkg. (9 oz.) refrigerated cheese tortellini
- 4 cups fresh baby spinach
- Shredded Parmesan cheese
- Freshly ground pepper

1. In a large saucepan, heat oil over medium heat. Add garlic; cook and stir 1 minute. Stir in tomatoes, broth and Italian seasoning; bring to a boil. Add tortellini; bring to a gentle boil. Cook, uncovered, just until tortellini are tender, 7-9 minutes.
2. Stir in spinach. Sprinkle servings with cheese and pepper.

**1⅓ CUPS** 164 cal., 5g fat (2g sat. fat), 18mg chol., 799mg sod., 25g carb. (4g sugars, 2g fiber), 7g pro.

## AMISH CHICKEN CORN SOUP

Creamed corn and butter make my chicken noodle soup homey and rich. This recipe makes a big batch, but the soup freezes well for future meals.

*—Beverly Hoffman, Sandy Lake, PA*

**Prep:** 15 min. • **Cook:** 50 min.
**Makes:** 12 servings (4 qt.)

- 1 medium onion, chopped
- 2 celery ribs, chopped
- 1 cup shredded carrots
- 2 lbs. boneless skinless chicken breasts, cubed
- 3 chicken bouillon cubes
- 1 tsp. salt
- ¼ tsp. pepper
- 12 cups water
- 2 cups uncooked egg noodles
- 2 cans (14¾ oz. each) cream-style corn
- ¼ cup butter
- Optional: Celery leaves and coarsely ground pepper

1. Place first 8 ingredients in a Dutch oven; bring slowly to a boil. Reduce heat; simmer, uncovered, until chicken is no longer pink and vegetables are tender, about 30 minutes.
2. Stir in noodles, corn and butter. Cook, uncovered, until noodles are tender, about 10 minutes, stirring occasionally. If desired, top with celery leaves and pepper.

**1⅓ CUPS** 201 cal., 6g fat (3g sat. fat), 57mg chol., 697mg sod., 19g carb. (3g sugars, 2g fiber), 18g pro.

## COOL AS A CUCUMBER SOUP

This chilled soup makes a wonderful appetizer or side on a hot summer day. Bright bursts of dill provide pleasant contrasts to the milder flavor of cucumber.

*—Deirdre Cox, Kansas City, MO*

**Prep:** 15 min. + standing
**Makes:** 5 servings

- 1 lb. cucumbers, peeled, seeded and sliced
- ½ tsp. salt
- 1½ cups fat-free plain yogurt
- 1 green onion, coarsely chopped
- 1 garlic clove, minced
- 4½ tsp. snipped fresh dill
- Additional chopped green onion and snipped fresh dill

1. In a colander set over a bowl, toss cucumbers with salt. Let stand for 30 minutes. Squeeze and pat dry.
2. Place the cucumbers, yogurt, onion and garlic in a food processor; cover and process until smooth. Stir in dill. Serve immediately in chilled bowls. Garnish with additional chopped onion and dill.

**⅔ CUP** 40 cal., 0 fat (0 sat. fat), 2mg chol., 279mg sod., 8g carb. (5g sugars, 1g fiber), 3g pro.

**"Fabulous soup, absolutely delicious. I substituted low-sodium chicken broth for the water and bouillon."**

—CAROL353, TASTEOFHOME.COM

## MINESTRONE TIPS

**How can I make this soup my own?** Add any veggies you like—zucchini, squash, potatoes, kale—and swap in your favorite pasta shape. For more heartiness, stir in cooked ground beef or Italian sausage.

**What do I serve with minestrone?** Pair with warm crusty bread or garlic bread and a crisp side salad.

**How do I store leftovers?** Refrigerate in a sealed container for up to 4 days, or freeze for up to 3 months.

## SHORTCUT MINESTRONE

This soup is hearty and makes a comforting lunch or dinner on a brisk day. The spaghetti sauce provides rich flavor without a long simmering time. I further cut the prep time by using my food processor to chop the vegetables.
*—Barbara Jellison, Bellevue, WA*

**Prep:** 20 min. • **Cook:** 15 min.
**Makes:** 10 servings (2½ qt.)

- 4 bacon strips, diced
- 1 large onion, chopped
- 3 medium carrots, chopped
- 3 garlic cloves, minced
- 1 jar (28 oz.) spaghetti sauce
- 1 carton (32 oz.) beef broth
- 1 can (16 oz.) kidney beans, rinsed and drained
- 1 can (15 oz.) garbanzo beans or chickpeas, rinsed and drained
- ⅔ cup uncooked small shell pasta
- 2 tsp. brown sugar
- ½ tsp. dried basil
- ½ tsp. dried oregano
- 1 cup frozen cut green beans
- Grated Parmesan cheese, optional

1. In a Dutch oven or soup kettle, cook bacon over medium heat until crisp. Using a slotted spoon, remove to paper towels. Drain, reserving 2 Tbsp. drippings; set bacon aside. In the drippings, saute onion and carrots until tender, 3-4 minutes. Add garlic; cook 2 minutes longer.
2. Stir in the spaghetti sauce, broth and beans. Bring to a boil. Add the pasta, brown sugar, basil and oregano. Cook, uncovered, until pasta is tender, 8-10 minutes, stirring occasionally. Add green beans; cook until heated through, about 5 minutes longer. Garnish with bacon and, if desired, Parmesan cheese.

**1 CUP** 188 cal., 3g fat (1g sat. fat), 2mg chol., 560mg sod., 31g carb., 7g fiber), 10g pro.

## BEAN COUNTER CHOWDER

This hearty chowder is one of our favorite vegetarian dishes. Loaded with beans, noodles and herbs, it's so comforting on a chilly day.
*—Vivian Haen, Menomonee Falls, WI*

**Takes:** 30 min.
**Makes:** 8 servings (2 qt.)

- ½ cup chopped onion
- 1 Tbsp. canola oil
- 2 garlic cloves, minced
- 1 medium tomato, chopped
- 2 cans (14½ oz. each) chicken or vegetable broth
- 1¾ cups water
- ½ tsp. each dried basil, oregano and celery flakes
- ¼ tsp. pepper
- 3 cans (15½ oz. each) great northern beans, rinsed and drained
- 1 cup uncooked elbow macaroni
- 1 Tbsp. minced parsley

1. In a large saucepan, saute onion in oil until tender. Add garlic; cook 1 minute longer. Add tomato; simmer for 5 minutes. Add broth, water and seasonings. Bring to a boil; cook for 5 minutes. Add beans and macaroni; return to a boil.
2. Reduce heat; simmer, uncovered, until macaroni is tender, about 15 minutes. Sprinkle with parsley.

**1 CUP** 196 cal., 3g fat (0 sat. fat), 2mg chol., 676mg sod., 33g carb. (2g sugars, 9g fiber), 10g pro.

GARLIC-BUTTER STEAK, PAGE 62

# QUICK & EASY BEEF

ONE-SKILLET LASAGNA, PAGE 76

## LI'L CHEDDAR MEAT LOAVES

I got this recipe from my aunt when I was a teen and have made these miniature loaves many times since. My husband and three children count this main dish among their favorites.
*—Kathy Bowron, Cocolalla, ID*

**Prep:** 15 min. • **Bake:** 25 min.
**Makes:** 8 servings

- 1 large egg
- ¾ cup 2% milk
- 1 cup shredded cheddar cheese
- ½ cup quick-cooking oats
- ½ cup chopped onion
- ½ tsp. salt
- 1 lb. ground beef
- ⅔ cup ketchup
- ½ cup packed brown sugar
- 1½ tsp. prepared mustard

**1.** In a large bowl, whisk egg and milk. Stir in the cheese, oats, onion and salt. Crumble beef over mixture and mix well. Shape into 8 loaves; place in a greased 13x9-in. baking dish. In a small bowl, combine the ketchup, brown sugar and mustard; spoon over loaves.
**2.** Bake, uncovered, at 350° until no pink remains and a thermometer inserted in center reads 160°, 25-30 minutes.
**1 MEAT LOAF** 279 cal., 13g fat (6g sat. fat), 81mg chol., 547mg sod., 25g carb. (20g sugars, 1g fiber), 17g pro.

## CHEESEBURGER CUPS

A terrific recipe for moms with young kids and busy lives, this simple, inexpensive dish is made with handy ingredients and takes just a short time. Best of all, kids go absolutely crazy for these darling dinner bites!
*—Jeri Millhouse, Ashland, OH*

**Takes:** 30 min. • **Makes:** 10 servings

- 1 lb. ground beef
- ½ cup ketchup
- 2 Tbsp. brown sugar
- 1 Tbsp. prepared mustard
- 1½ tsp. Worcestershire sauce
- 2 tubes (10½ oz. each) large refrigerated buttermilk biscuits
- ½ cup cubed Velveeta

**1.** In a large skillet, cook beef over medium heat until no longer pink, breaking it into crumbles; drain. Stir in the ketchup, brown sugar, mustard and Worcestershire sauce. Remove from the heat.
**2.** Press each biscuit onto the bottom and up the side of a greased muffin cup. Spoon beef mixture into cups; top with Velveeta cubes. Bake at 400° until cups are golden brown, 14-16 minutes.
**1 CHEESEBURGER CUP** 299 cal., 14g fat (5g sat. fat), 34mg chol., 910mg sod., 32g carb. (9g sugars, 1g fiber), 13g pro.

## MEXICAN BUBBLE PIZZA

This tasty pizza offers a new way to experience Mexican cuisine. Serve it at your next party and watch it disappear before your eyes.
*—Jackie Hannahs, Cedar Springs, MI*

**Prep:** 15 min. • **Cook:** 3 hours 5 min.
**Makes:** 6 servings

- 1½ lbs. ground beef
- 1 can (10¾ oz.) condensed tomato soup, undiluted
- ¾ cup water
- 1 envelope taco seasoning
- 1 tube (16.3 oz.) large refrigerated buttermilk biscuits
- 2 cups shredded cheddar cheese
- Optional toppings: Shredded lettuce, chopped tomatoes, salsa, sliced ripe olives, sour cream and thinly sliced green onions

1. Line a 6-qt. slow cooker with a double thickness of heavy-duty foil. Coat with cooking spray.
2. In a large skillet, cook beef over medium heat until no longer pink, 6-8 minutes, breaking it into crumbles; drain. Stir in soup, water and taco seasoning. Bring to a boil. Reduce heat; simmer, uncovered, until slightly thickened, 3-5 minutes.
3. Cut each biscuit into 4 pieces; gently stir into beef mixture. Transfer to slow cooker. Cook, covered, on low until dough is cooked through, 3-4 hours. Sprinkle with cheese. Cook, covered, until cheese is melted, about 5 minutes longer. Serve with toppings.

**1 SERVING** 643 cal., 35g fat (15g sat. fat), 109mg chol., 1870mg sod., 46g carb. (8g sugars, 2g fiber), 35g pro.

## CUBE STEAKS WITH GRAVY

Here's a hearty homestyle dinner your family will love after a busy day. The slow-cooked beef is wonderful served over mashed potatoes or noodles.
*—Judy Long, Limestone, TN*

**Prep:** 15 min. • **Cook:** 8½ hours
**Makes:** 6 servings

- ⅓ cup all-purpose flour
- 6 beef cube steaks (4 oz. each)
- 1 Tbsp. canola oil
- 1 large onion, sliced and separated into rings
- 3 cups water, divided
- 1 envelope brown gravy mix
- 1 envelope mushroom gravy mix
- 1 envelope onion gravy mix
- Hot mashed potatoes or cooked noodles

1. Place flour in shallow dish. Add steaks, 1 or 2 at a time, and turn to coat completely.
2. In a skillet, cook steaks in oil until lightly browned on each side. Transfer to a 3-qt. slow cooker. Add the onion and 2 cups water. Cover and cook on low for 8 hours or until meat is tender.
3. In a bowl, whisk together gravy mixes with remaining 1 cup water. Add to slow cooker; cook 30 minutes longer. Serve over mashed potatoes or noodles.

**1 SERVING** 245 cal., 7g fat (2g sat. fat), 64mg chol., 850mg sod., 16g carb. (4g sugars, 1g fiber), 29g pro.

## ALL-AMERICAN HAMBURGERS

We do a lot of camping and outdoor cooking. Hamburgers are on our menu more than any other food.
*—Diane Hixon, Niceville, FL*

**Takes:** 20 min. • **Makes:** 4 servings

- 1 lb. ground beef
- 2 Tbsp. finely chopped onion
- 2 Tbsp. chili sauce
- 2 tsp. Worcestershire sauce
- 2 tsp. prepared mustard
- 4 slices American cheese or cheddar cheese, halved diagonally
- 2 slices Swiss cheese, halved diagonally
- 4 hamburger buns, split and toasted
- Optional: Lettuce leaves, sliced tomato, sliced onion, cooked bacon strips, ketchup and mustard

1. Combine the first 5 ingredients, mixing lightly but thoroughly. Shape into 4 patties. Grill burgers, covered, on an oiled rack over medium direct heat until a thermometer reads 160° and juices run clear, about 6 minutes on each side.
2. During the last minute of cooking, top each patty with 2 triangles American cheese and 1 triangle Swiss cheese. Serve on buns. Top with lettuce, tomato, onion, bacon, ketchup and mustard as desired.

**1 HAMBURGER** 432 cal., 21g fat (9g sat. fat), 80mg chol., 681mg sod., 26g carb. (6g sugars, 1g fiber), 30g pro.

## GREEK-STYLE RIBEYE STEAKS

Because our children are grown, I often cook for just my husband and me. When I want to serve something special, this is the entree I often reach for. Seasonings, black olives and feta cheese give the steak such great flavor.
*—Ruby Williams, Bogalusa, LA*

**Takes:** 25 min. • **Makes:** 2 servings

- 1½ tsp. garlic powder
- 1½ tsp. dried oregano
- 1½ tsp. dried basil
- ½ tsp. salt
- ⅛ tsp. pepper
- 2 beef ribeye steaks (1½ in. thick)
- 1 Tbsp. olive oil
- 1 Tbsp. lemon juice
- 2 Tbsp. crumbled feta cheese
- 1 Tbsp. sliced ripe olives

In a small bowl, combine the first 5 ingredients; rub onto both sides of steaks. In a large skillet, cook steaks in oil for 7-9 minutes on each side or until meat reaches desired doneness (for medium-rare, a thermometer should read 135°; medium, 140°; medium-well, 145°). Sprinkle with lemon juice, cheese and olives. Serve immediately.

**1 STEAK** 1084 cal., 80g fat (31g sat. fat), 271mg chol., 897mg sod., 4g carb. (0 sugars, 1g fiber), 82g pro.

### TEST KITCHEN TIP

Common olive oil works better for cooking at high heat than virgin or extra-virgin olive oil. These higher grades have ideal flavor for cold foods, but they smoke at lower temperatures.

## BRISKET FOR A BUNCH

This makes tender slices of delicious beef with plenty of juices. To make it easy to cut very thin slices, chill the brisket before slicing, and then reheat in the juices.
*—Dawn Fagerstrom, Warren, MN*

**Prep:** 20 min. • **Cook:** 7 hours
**Makes:** 12 servings

- 1 fresh beef brisket (2½ lbs.)
- 1 Tbsp. canola oil
- ½ cup chopped celery
- ½ cup chopped onion
- ¾ cup beef broth
- ½ cup tomato sauce
- ¼ cup water
- ¼ cup sugar
- 2 Tbsp. onion soup mix
- 1 Tbsp. cider vinegar
- 12 garlic bread slices or split hamburger buns

1. In a large skillet, brown brisket in oil on both sides; transfer to a 3-qt. slow cooker. In the same skillet, saute celery and onion for 1 minute. Gradually add broth, tomato sauce and water; stir to loosen the browned bits from pan. Add sugar, soup mix and vinegar; bring to a boil. Pour over brisket.
2. Cover and cook on low until meat is tender, 7-8 hours. Let stand for 5 minutes before slicing. Skim fat from cooking juices. Serve with bread or buns and cooking juices.

**1 SERVING** 279 cal., 7g fat (2g sat. fat), 40mg chol., 458mg sod., 28g carb. (8g sugars, 1g fiber), 24g pro.

## CAST-IRON SKILLET STEAK

If you've never cooked steak at home before, it can be a little intimidating. That's why I came up with this simple steak recipe that's so easy, you could make it any day of the week.
*—James Schend, Pleasant Prairie, WI*

**Prep:** 5 min. + standing • **Cook:** 5 min.
**Makes:** 2 servings

- 1 beef New York strip or ribeye steak (1 lb.), 1 in. thick
- 3 tsp. kosher salt, divided

1. Remove steak from refrigerator and sprinkle with 2 tsp. salt; let stand 45-60 minutes.
2. Preheat a cast-iron skillet over high heat until extremely hot, 4-5 minutes. Sprinkle remaining 1 tsp. salt in bottom of skillet; pat beef dry with paper towels. Place steak in skillet and cook until easily moved, 1-2 minutes; flip, placing steak in a different section of the skillet. Cook 30 seconds and then begin moving steak, occasionally pressing slightly to ensure even contact with skillet.
3. Continue turning and flipping until cooked to desired degree of doneness (for medium-rare, a thermometer should read 135°; medium, 140°; medium-well, 145°), 1-2 minutes.

**6 OZ. COOKED BEEF** 494 cal., 36g fat (15g sat. fat), 134mg chol., 2983mg sod., 0 carb. (0 sugars, 0 fiber), 40g pro.

> **"Learned a new trick today about salting 45 minutes before. We've tried this with filets and strip steaks, and they turned out perfectly."**
> —LYNN7995, TASTEOFHOME.COM

## TACOS IN A BOWL

This easy skillet dish offers a tasty use for leftover taco meat. Garnish it with sour cream and salsa for added southwestern flavor.
*—Sue Schoening, Sheboygan, WI*

**Takes:** 25 min. • **Makes:** 2 servings

- ½ lb. lean ground beef (90% lean)
- 2 Tbsp. finely chopped onion
- ¾ cup canned diced tomatoes, drained
- 2 Tbsp. taco seasoning
- 1 cup water
- 1 pkg. (3 oz.) ramen noodles
- ¼ cup shredded cheddar or Mexican cheese blend
- Crushed tortilla chips, optional

1. In a small skillet, cook beef and onion over medium heat until meat is no longer pink, breaking beef into crumbles; drain. Stir in the tomatoes, taco seasoning and water. Bring to a boil. Add ramen noodles (discard seasoning packet or save for another use). Cook and stir until noodles are tender, 3-5 minutes.
2. Spoon into serving bowls; sprinkle with cheese and, if desired, tortilla chips.

**1 CUP** 480 cal., 21g fat (10g sat. fat), 85mg chol., 1279mg sod., 40g carb. (3g sugars, 2g fiber), 30g pro.

## ROAST BEEF & GRAVY

This is by far the simplest way to make roast beef and gravy. On busy days, I can put this main dish in the slow cooker and forget about it. My family likes it with mashed potatoes and fruit salad.

*—Abby Metzger, Larchwood, IA*

**Prep:** 15 min. • **Cook:** 8 hours
**Makes:** 10 servings

- 1 boneless beef chuck roast (3 lbs.)
- 2 cans (10¾ oz. each) condensed cream of mushroom soup, undiluted
- ⅓ cup sherry or beef broth
- 1 envelope onion soup mix
- Warm mashed potatoes

1. Place beef in a 3-qt. or 4-qt. slow cooker. In a large bowl, combine soup, sherry and onion soup mix; pour over beef.
2. Cover and cook on low 8-10 hours or until meat is tender. Serve beef with gravy and mashed potatoes.

**FREEZE OPTION** Place sliced pot roast in freezer containers; top with cooking juices. Cool and freeze. To use, partially thaw in refrigerator overnight. Heat through in a covered saucepan, gently stirring and adding water if necessary.

**1 SERVING** 267 cal., 14g fat (6g sat. fat), 90mg chol., 517mg sod., 4g carb. (0 sugars, 0 fiber), 27g pro.

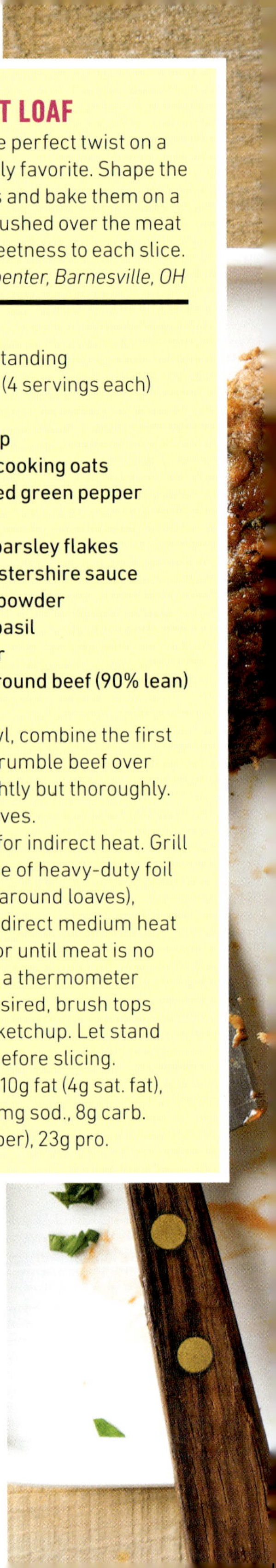

## GARLIC BEEF STROGANOFF

I am a mom and work full time, so I use my slow cooker whenever possible. This Stroganoff is perfect because I can get it ready in the morning before the kids get up and I head out the door for work.
*—Erika Anderson, Wausau, WI*

**Prep:** 20 min. • **Cook:** 7 hours
**Makes:** 6 servings

- 2 tsp. beef bouillon granules
- 1 cup boiling water
- 1 can (10¾ oz.) condensed cream of mushroom soup, undiluted
- 2 jars (4½ oz. each) sliced mushrooms, drained
- 1 large onion, chopped
- 3 garlic cloves, minced
- 1 Tbsp. Worcestershire sauce
- 1½ lbs. beef top round steak, cut into thin strips
- 2 Tbsp. canola oil
- 1 pkg. (8 oz.) cream cheese, cubed
- Hot cooked noodles
- Minced fresh parsley, optional

1. In a 3-qt. slow cooker, dissolve bouillon in boiling water. Add soup, mushrooms, onion, garlic and Worcestershire sauce. In a skillet, brown beef in oil.
2. Transfer to the slow cooker. Cover and cook on low until the meat is tender, 7-8 hours. Stir in cream cheese until smooth. Serve with noodles and, if desired, minced parsley.

**1 SERVING** 383 cal., 24g fat (10g sat. fat), 104mg chol., 991mg sod., 12g carb. (4g sugars, 2g fiber), 29g pro.

## GRILLED MEAT LOAF

This recipe is the perfect twist on a comforting family favorite. Shape the meat into loaves and bake them on a grill. Ketchup brushed over the meat lends a little sweetness to each slice.
*—Catherine Carpenter, Barnesville, OH*

**Prep:** 10 min.
**Grill:** 50 min. + standing
**Makes:** 2 loaves (4 servings each)

- ½ cup ketchup
- ½ cup quick-cooking oats
- ¼ cup chopped green pepper
- 1 large egg
- 1 tsp. dried parsley flakes
- 1 tsp. Worcestershire sauce
- ½ tsp. garlic powder
- ½ tsp. dried basil
- ¼ tsp. pepper
- 2 lbs. lean ground beef (90% lean)

1. In a large bowl, combine the first 9 ingredients. Crumble beef over mixture; mix lightly but thoroughly. Shape into 2 loaves.
2. Prepare grill for indirect heat. Grill loaves on a piece of heavy-duty foil (do not seal foil around loaves), covered, over indirect medium heat for 50 minutes or until meat is no longer pink and a thermometer reads 160°. If desired, brush tops with additional ketchup. Let stand for 10 minutes before slicing.

**1 PIECE** 223 cal., 10g fat (4g sat. fat), 94mg chol., 266mg sod., 8g carb. (4g sugars, 1g fiber), 23g pro.

## CALIFORNIA TAMALE PIE

When I serve this dish, I know I'll see smiles on the faces of everyone at the table. With this recipe, you'll enjoy the taste and texture of classic tamales, without the time and hassle.
*—Patricia Nieh, Portola Valley, CA*

**Prep:** 15 min. • **Cook:** 6 hours
**Makes:** 5 servings

- 1 cup beef broth
- ¾ cup cornmeal
- 1 lb. ground beef
- 1 tsp. chili powder
- ½ tsp. ground cumin
- 1 jar (16 oz.) chunky salsa
- 1 can (15¼ oz.) whole kernel corn, drained
- 1 can (15 oz.) black beans, rinsed and drained
- ¼ cup sliced ripe olives
- ½ cup shredded Monterey Jack cheese
- Optional toppings: Sour cream and fresh jalapeno pepper slices

1. In a 3-qt. slow cooker, combine broth and cornmeal. Let stand for 5 minutes. In a large skillet, cook beef over medium heat until no longer pink; drain. Stir in chili powder and cumin. Transfer to slow cooker. Stir in the salsa, corn, beans and olives. Cover and cook on low for 6-8 hours or until heated through.
2. Sprinkle with cheese. Cover and cook 5-10 minutes longer or until cheese is melted. If desired, top with sour cream and jalapeno slices.

**1⅓ CUPS** 455 cal., 16g fat (6g sat. fat), 66mg chol., 1112mg sod., 45g carb. (7g sugars, 7g fiber), 27g pro.

> **"A hit for the family, even with our more particular eaters. I added a taco seasoning packet in addition to the listed seasonings."**
> —AAA588, TASTEOFHOME.COM

## BEEF BROCCOLI STIR-FRY

My family asks for this tasty stir-fry over and over again. I love it because it comes together quickly, and it combines tender beef and good-for-you veggies in one dish.

*—Ruth Stahl, Shepherd, MT*

**Takes:** 25 min. • **Makes:** 4 servings

- ½ tsp. garlic powder
- 3 Tbsp. cornstarch, divided
- 2 Tbsp. plus ½ cup water, divided
- 1 lb. boneless beef top round steak, cut into thin 2-in. strips
- ¼ cup soy sauce
- 2 Tbsp. brown sugar
- 1 tsp. ground ginger
- 2 Tbsp. canola oil, divided
- 4 cups fresh broccoli florets
- 1 small onion, cut into thin wedges
- Hot cooked rice

1. Mix garlic powder, 2 Tbsp. cornstarch and 2 Tbsp. water; toss with beef. In a small bowl, mix soy sauce, brown sugar, ginger and remaining 1 Tbsp. cornstarch and ½ cup water until smooth.
2. In a large skillet, heat 1 Tbsp. oil over medium-high heat; stir-fry beef until browned, 2-3 minutes. Remove from pan.
3. In same pan, stir-fry broccoli and onion in remaining 1 Tbsp. oil over medium-high heat until crisp-tender, 4-5 minutes. Stir soy sauce mixture; add to pan. Cook and stir until thickened, 1-2 minutes. Return beef to pan; heat through. Serve with rice.

**1 CUP** 291 cal., 11g fat (2g sat. fat), 63mg chol., 974mg sod., 18g carb. (9g sugars, 2g fiber), 30g pro.

## AIR-FRYER REUBEN CALZONES

I love a Reuben sandwich, so I tried the fillings in a pizza pocket instead of on rye bread. This simple dinner is a big-time winner at our house.

*—Nickie Frye, Evansville, IN*

**Prep:** 15 min. • **Cook:** 10 min./batch
**Makes:** 4 servings

- 1 tube (13.8 oz.) refrigerated pizza crust
- 4 slices Swiss cheese
- 1 cup sauerkraut, rinsed and well drained
- ½ lb. sliced cooked corned beef
- Thousand Island salad dressing

1. Preheat air fryer to 400°. On a lightly floured surface, unroll pizza crust dough and pat into a 12-in. square. Cut into 4 squares. Layer 1 slice cheese and a fourth of the sauerkraut and corned beef diagonally over half of each square to within ½ in. of edges. Fold 1 corner over filling to the opposite corner, forming a triangle; press edges with a fork to seal. Place 2 calzones in a single layer on greased tray in air-fryer basket.
2. Cook until golden brown, 8-12 minutes, flipping halfway through cooking. Serve with salad dressing.

**NOTE** Cook times vary dramatically among brands of air fryers. Refer to your air fryer manual for general cook times and adjust if necessary.

**1 CALZONE** 430 cal., 17g fat (6g sat. fat), 66mg chol., 1471mg sod., 49g carb. (7g sugars, 2g fiber), 21g pro.

## REFRIED BEAN-TACO PIZZA

I like to make pizzas, and this one is my favorite. You can't beat ready-to-use pizza crust when time is tight. If you enjoy taco salad, you'll love this pizza.
*—Mary Detweiler, Middlefield, OH*

**Prep:** 30 min. • **Bake:** 10 min.
**Makes:** 8 servings

- 1¼ lbs. ground beef
- 1 small onion, chopped
- ½ cup water
- 1 envelope taco seasoning
- 1 prebaked 12-in. pizza crust
- 1 can (16 oz.) refried beans
- 2 taco shells, coarsely crushed
- 1 cup shredded cheddar cheese
- 1 cup shredded part-skim mozzarella cheese
- 2 cups torn iceberg lettuce
- 2 medium tomatoes, chopped
- 1 Tbsp. sliced ripe olives

1. Preheat oven to 450°. In a large skillet, cook beef and onion over medium heat, crumbling beef, until meat is no longer pink; drain. Stir in water and taco seasoning. Bring to a boil. Reduce heat; simmer, uncovered, for 5 minutes.
2. Meanwhile, place crust on an ungreased baking sheet. Spread with refried beans. Top with beef mixture, taco shell pieces and cheeses. Bake for 10-15 minutes or until cheese is melted. Top with lettuce, tomatoes and olives Cut into 8 pieces.

**1 PIECE** 420 cal., 17g fat (8g sat. fat), 62mg chol., 1051mg sod., 39g carb. (3g sugars, 5g fiber), 28g pro.

## ZESTY STEAK SALAD

Stir-fried steak and veggies give this salad a hearty kick. Add any of your favorite salad ingredients, such as shredded cheese, croutons, mushrooms or cucumber.
*—Leah Carrell, Quitman, TX*

**Takes:** 20 min. • **Makes:** 4 servings

- 1 lb. beef top sirloin steak, cut into strips
- ⅓ cup Worcestershire sauce
- 1 medium onion, julienned
- 1 medium green pepper, julienned
- 1 Tbsp. butter
- 6 cups torn lettuce
- 6 to 9 cherry tomatoes, halved
- Salsa, optional

1. In a large bowl, combine steak and Worcestershire sauce; cover and refrigerate.
2. Meanwhile, in a large skillet, saute onion and green pepper in butter until crisp-tender, 3-4 minutes. Add steak; stir-fry until meat is no longer pink. Spoon meat and vegetables over lettuce; garnish with tomatoes. Serve with salsa if desired.

**1 SERVING** 218 cal., 8g fat (4g sat. fat), 54mg chol., 314mg sod., 11g carb. (5g sugars, 2g fiber), 26g pro.

### DID YOU KNOW?

Green peppers are unripened versions of red, yellow or orange peppers. They are less expensive because they're quicker to get to market. Use colored peppers in recipes for more sweetness.

## BEEF & TATER BAKE

The entire family will enjoy this heartwarming, all-in-one dinner. Plus, it offers easy cleanup!
*—Mike Tchou, Pepper Pike, OH*

**Prep:** 10 min. • **Bake:** 35 min.
**Makes:** 8 servings

- 4 cups frozen Tater Tots
- 1 lb. ground beef
- ¼ tsp. garlic powder
- ⅛ tsp. pepper
- 1 can (10¾ oz.) condensed cream of broccoli soup, undiluted
- ⅓ cup 2% milk
- 1 pkg. (16 oz.) frozen chopped broccoli, thawed
- 1 can (2.8 oz.) french-fried onions, divided
- 1 cup shredded Colby-Monterey Jack cheese, divided
- 1 medium tomato, chopped

**1.** Preheat oven to 400°. Spread Tater Tots evenly in an ungreased 13x9-in. baking dish. Bake, uncovered, 10 minutes.
**2.** Meanwhile, in a large skillet, cook beef over medium heat until no longer pink, 5-7 minutes, breaking it into crumbles; drain. Stir in seasonings, soup, milk, broccoli, ¾ cup onions, ½ cup cheese and the chopped tomato; heat through. Pour over potatoes.
**3.** Bake, covered, 20 minutes. Sprinkle with the remaining onions and cheese. Bake, uncovered, until cheese is melted, 5-10 minutes.

**1 SERVING** 400 cal., 24g fat (9g sat. fat), 50mg chol., 805mg sod., 29g carb. (3g sugars, 4g fiber), 17g pro.

## FREEZER BURRITOS

I love burritos, but the frozen ones are high in salt and chemicals. So I created these. They're wonderful to have on hand for quick dinners or late-night snacks—I've even had them for breakfast!
*—Laura Winemiller, Delta, PA*

**Prep:** 35 min. • **Cook:** 15 min.
**Makes:** 12 servings

- 1¼ lbs. lean ground beef (90% lean)
- ¼ cup finely chopped onion
- 1¼ cups salsa
- 2 Tbsp. reduced-sodium taco seasoning
- 2 cans (15 oz. each) pinto beans, rinsed and drained
- ½ cup water
- 2 cups shredded reduced-fat cheddar cheese
- 12 flour tortillas (8 in.), warmed

1. In a large skillet, cook beef and onion over medium heat until meat is no longer pink, 5-7 minutes, breaking beef into crumbles; drain. Stir in salsa and taco seasoning. Bring to a boil. Reduce heat; simmer, uncovered, for 2-3 minutes. Transfer to a large bowl; set aside.
2. In a food processor, combine pinto beans and water. Cover and process until almost smooth. Add to beef mixture. Stir in cheese.
3. Spoon ½ cup beef mixture down the center of each tortilla. Fold ends and sides over filling; roll up. Wrap each burrito in waxed paper and foil. Freeze for up to 1 month.

**TO USE FROZEN BURRITOS** Remove foil and waxed paper. Place 1 burrito on a microwave-safe plate. Microwave on high until a thermometer reads 165°, 2½-2¾ minutes, turning burrito over once. Let stand for 20 seconds.

**1 BURRITO** 345 cal., 11g fat (4g sat. fat), 36mg chol., 677mg sod., 40g carb. (3g sugars, 3g fiber), 22g pro.

## EASY SLOW-COOKER POT ROAST

I love making this pot roast for a couple of reasons. First, it's delicious. Second, it's so easy! I can't describe the feeling of walking into my house after work and smelling this dish that's been simmering in the slow cooker all day. There's simply nothing better.
*—James Schend, Pleasant Prairie, WI*

**Prep:** 10 min. • **Cook:** 10 hours
**Makes:** 10 servings

- 1 boneless beef rump or chuck roast (3 to 3½ lbs.)
- 1 Tbsp. canola oil
- 6 medium carrots, cut into thirds
- 6 medium potatoes, peeled and quartered
- 1 large onion, quartered
- 3 tsp. Montreal steak seasoning
- 1 carton (32 oz.) beef broth
- 3 Tbsp. cornstarch
- 3 Tbsp. water

1. In a large skillet over medium heat, brown roast in oil on all sides. Place carrots, potatoes and onion in a 6-qt. slow cooker. Place roast on top of vegetables; sprinkle with steak seasoning. Add broth. Cook, covered, on low 10-12 hours or until beef and vegetables are tender.
2. Remove roast and vegetables from slow cooker; keep warm.
3. Transfer cooking juices to a saucepan; skim off fat. Bring juices to a boil. In a small bowl, mix cornstarch and water until smooth; stir into juices. Return to a boil, stirring constantly; cook and stir until thickened, 1-2 minutes. Serve with roast and vegetables.

**1 SERVING** 354 cal., 15g fat (5g sat. fat), 88mg chol., 696mg sod., 24g carb. (4g sugars, 3g fiber), 30g pro.

## LAYERED REUBEN CASSEROLE

This easy dish packs traditional Reuben taste without all the bread. Sauerkraut fans will love this hearty layered casserole. Round out the meal with dinner rolls and a light fruit dessert.
*—Agnes Golian, Garfield Heights, OH*

**Prep:** 15 min. • **Bake:** 25 min.
**Makes:** 2 servings

- 1 can (8 oz.) sauerkraut, rinsed and well drained
- ⅛ tsp. caraway seeds
- 1 small tomato, cut into thin wedges
- 2 Tbsp. Thousand Island salad dressing
- 1 pkg. (2 oz.) thinly sliced deli corned beef
- ¼ cup shredded Swiss cheese
- ¼ cup cubed rye bread
- 2 tsp. butter, melted

1. Place the sauerkraut in an ungreased 3-cup baking dish; sprinkle with caraway seeds. Layer with the tomato wedges, salad dressing, corned beef and Swiss cheese. Toss bread cubes and butter; sprinkle over the top.
2. Bake, uncovered, at 375° for 25-30 minutes or until heated through.

**1 SERVING** 166 cal., 8g fat (3g sat. fat), 36mg chol., 1403mg sod., 14g carb. (6g sugars, 4g fiber), 12g pro.

## HEARTY MEATBALL SUB SANDWICHES

Making the saucy meatballs in advance and reheating them saves precious time when I'm expecting company. These sandwiches are great for casual parties.
*—Deena Hubler, Jasper, IN*

**Takes:** 30 min. • **Makes:** 12 servings

- 2 large eggs, lightly beaten
- 1 cup dry bread crumbs
- 2 Tbsp. grated Parmesan cheese
- 2 Tbsp. finely chopped onion
- 1 tsp. salt
- ½ tsp. pepper
- ½ tsp. garlic powder
- ¼ tsp. Italian seasoning
- 2 lbs. ground beef
- 1 jar (28 oz.) spaghetti sauce
- 12 sandwich rolls, split
- Optional: Sliced onion, sliced green pepper and additional grated Parmesan cheese

1. In a large bowl, combine first 8 ingredients. Crumble beef over mixture and mix lightly but thoroughly. Shape into 1-in. balls. Place in a single layer in a 3-qt. microwave-safe dish.
2. Cover and microwave on high for 3-4 minutes. Turn meatballs; cook 3-4 minutes longer or until no longer pink. Drain. Add spaghetti sauce.
3. Cover and microwave on high for 2-4 minutes or until heated through. Serve on rolls. If desired, top with sliced onion, green pepper and additional grated Parmesan cheese.

**1 SANDWICH** 464 cal., 18g fat (7g sat. fat), 88mg chol., 1013mg sod., 49g carb. (10g sugars, 3g fiber), 26g pro.

## SAUCY BEEF WITH BROCCOLI

When I'm looking for a fast entree, I turn to this beef-and-broccoli stir-fry. It features a tantalizing sauce made with garlic and ginger.
*—Rosa Evans, Odessa, MO*

**Takes:** 30 min. • **Makes:** 2 servings

- 1 Tbsp. cornstarch
- ½ cup reduced-sodium beef broth
- ¼ cup sherry or additional beef broth
- 2 Tbsp. reduced-sodium soy sauce
- 1 Tbsp. brown sugar
- 1 garlic clove, minced
- 1 tsp. minced fresh gingerroot
- 2 tsp. canola oil, divided
- ½ lb. beef top sirloin steak, cut into ¼-in.-thick strips
- 2 cups small fresh broccoli florets
- 8 green onions, cut into 1-in. pieces

1. Mix the first 7 ingredients. In a large nonstick skillet, heat 1 tsp. oil over medium-high heat; stir-fry beef until browned, 1-3 minutes. Remove from pan.
2. Stir-fry broccoli in remaining 1 tsp. oil until crisp-tender, 3-5 minutes. Add green onions; cook just until tender, 1-2 minutes. Stir cornstarch mixture and add to pan. Bring to a boil; cook and stir until sauce is thickened, 2-3 minutes. Add beef and heat through.

**1¼ CUPS** 313 cal., 11g fat (3g sat. fat), 68mg chol., 816mg sod., 20g carb. (11g sugars, 4g fiber), 29g pro.

## BEEF & CHEESE WRAPS

These make-ahead wraps are delicious and portable, making them ideal for picnics and tailgates. You can enjoy them whole, cut them in half to share, or slice them into 1-inch pieces to serve as an appetizer. They also make an excellent lunch on the go.
*—Sue Sibson, Howard, SC*

**Prep:** 10 min. + chilling
**Makes:** 4 servings

- 4 flour tortillas (10 in.), warmed
- 1 carton (8 oz.) spreadable chive-and-onion cream cheese
- 1 cup shredded carrots
- 1 cup shredded Monterey Jack cheese
- 1 lb. thinly sliced cooked roast beef
- Leaf lettuce

Spread 1 side of each tortilla with cream cheese; layer with the carrots, cheese, beef and lettuce. Roll up tightly and cover. Refrigerate for at least 30 minutes. Cut in half or into 1-in. slices.

**1 WRAP** 657 cal., 35g fat (20g sat. fat), 143mg chol., 1431mg sod., 38g carb. (6g sugars, 7g fiber), 38g pro.

### SAUCY BEEF TIPS

**What should I serve with it?**
Spoon the beef and broccoli over fluffy rice or cauliflower rice so the delicious sauce doesn't go to waste.

**Can I use other cuts of beef?**
Yes—sirloin is ideal, but skirt steak, flank or chuck also work well.

**Can I marinate the beef?**
Yes. Reserve some of the sauce mixture to marinate the meat for about 30 minutes. Discard the marinade before cooking.

## FRENCH DIP

For a sandwich with more pizzazz than the traditional French dip, give this recipe a try. The seasonings give the broth a wonderful flavor, and the meat cooks up tender and juicy. This new version will soon be a favorite at your house too.
*—Margaret McNeil, Germantown, TN*

**Prep:** 15 min. • **Cook:** 5 hours
**Makes:** 8 servings

- 1 beef chuck roast (3 lbs.), trimmed
- 2 cups water
- ½ cup reduced-sodium soy sauce
- 1 tsp. dried rosemary, crushed
- 1 tsp. dried thyme
- 1 tsp. garlic powder
- 1 bay leaf
- 3 to 4 whole peppercorns
- 8 French rolls, split

**1.** Place roast in a 5-qt. slow cooker. Add water, soy sauce and seasonings. Cover and cook on high for 5-6 hours or until beef is tender.
**2.** Remove meat from broth; shred with 2 forks and keep warm. Strain broth; skim fat. Pour broth into small cups for dipping. Serve beef on rolls.

**1 SANDWICH** 467 cal., 19g fat (7g sat. fat), 111mg chol., 1300mg sod., 31g carb. (3g sugars, 2g fiber), 41g pro.

## FAVORITE MEXICAN LASAGNA

Tortillas replace lasagna noodles in this enchilada-inspired lasagna. With beef, refried beans, salsa, chiles and cheese, it's a fiesta of flavors.
*—Tina Newhauser, Peterborough, NH*

**Prep:** 25 min. • **Bake:** 40 min. + standing
**Makes:** 12 servings

- 1¼ lbs. ground beef
- 1 medium onion, chopped
- 4 garlic cloves, minced
- 2 cups salsa
- 1 can (16 oz.) refried beans
- 1 can (15 oz.) black beans, rinsed and drained
- 1 can (10 oz.) enchilada sauce
- 1 can (4 oz.) chopped green chiles
- 1 envelope taco seasoning
- ¼ tsp. pepper
- 6 flour tortillas (10 in.)
- 3 cups shredded Mexican cheese blend, divided
- 2 cups crushed tortilla chips
- Optional: Sliced ripe olives, guacamole, chopped tomatoes and sour cream

**1.** In a large skillet, cook beef and onion over medium heat, crumbling beef, until meat is no longer pink. Add garlic; cook 1 minute longer. Drain. Stir in the salsa, refried beans, black beans, enchilada sauce, chiles, taco seasoning and pepper; heat through.
**2.** Spread 1 cup meat mixture in a greased 13x9-in. baking dish. Layer with 2 tortillas, a third of the remaining meat mixture and 1 cup cheese. Repeat layers. Top with remaining tortillas and meat mixture.
**3.** Cover and bake at 375° for 30 minutes. Uncover; sprinkle with remaining 1 cup cheese and top with tortilla chips.
**4.** Bake 10-15 minutes longer or until cheese is melted. Let stand 10 minutes. Serve with toppings as desired.

**1 PIECE** 448 cal., 19g fat (9g sat. fat), 57mg chol., 1240mg sod., 43g carb. (3g sugars, 8g fiber), 22g pro.

# BEEF TENDERLOIN IN MUSHROOM SAUCE

When our kids are visiting Grandma, I make this recipe for just my husband and myself. It's a recipe my mother-in-law has been using for more than 30 years. I especially look forward to preparing it as part of a special Valentine's Day menu.
*—Denise McNab, Warminster, PA*

**Takes:** 25 min. • **Makes:** 2 servings

- 4 Tbsp. butter, divided
- 1 tsp. canola oil
- 2 beef tenderloin steaks (1 in. thick and 4 oz. each)
- 1 cup sliced fresh mushrooms
- 1 Tbsp. chopped green onion
- 1 Tbsp. all-purpose flour
- ⅛ tsp. salt
- Dash pepper
- ⅔ cup chicken or beef broth
- ⅛ tsp. browning sauce, optional

1. In a large skillet, heat 2 Tbsp. butter and oil over medium-high heat; cook steaks to desired doneness (for medium-rare, a thermometer should read 135°; medium, 140°), 5-6 minutes per side. Remove from pan, reserving drippings; keep warm.
2. In same pan, heat the drippings and the remaining 2 Tbsp. butter over medium-high heat; saute mushrooms and green onion until tender. Stir in flour, salt and pepper until blended; gradually stir in broth and, if desired, browning sauce. Bring to a boil, stirring constantly; cook and stir until thickened, 1-2 minutes. Serve with steaks.

**1 SERVING** 417 cal., 32g fat (17g sat. fat), 112mg chol., 659mg sod., 5g carb. (1g sugars, 1g fiber), 26g pro.

## SPINACH FLANK STEAK PINWHEELS

I wow family and friends with this impressive-looking dish that's as easy to make as it is delicious. Even those who don't like spinach seem to enjoy it!
*—Mary Ann Marino, West Pittsburgh, PA*

**Takes:** 30 min. • **Makes:** 4 servings

- 1 beef flank steak (1½ lbs.)
- 1 pkg. (10 oz.) frozen chopped spinach, thawed and squeezed dry
- ¼ cup grated Parmesan cheese
- ¼ cup sour cream
- Dash each salt and pepper

1. Cut steak horizontally from a long side to within ½ in. of opposite side. Open meat so it lies flat; cover with plastic wrap. Flatten to ¼-in. thickness. Remove plastic.
2. In a small bowl, combine the spinach, cheese and sour cream; spread over steak to within ½ in. of edges. With the grain of the meat going from left to right, roll up jelly-roll style from bottom or top. Slice beef across the grain into 8 slices.
3. Transfer to an ungreased baking sheet. Sprinkle with salt and pepper. Broil 4-6 in. from the heat for 5-7 minutes on each side or until meat reaches desired doneness (for medium-rare, a thermometer should read 135°; medium, 140°; medium-well, 145°).

**2 PINWHEELS** 320 cal., 16g fat (8g sat. fat), 96mg chol., 271mg sod., 4g carb. (1g sugars, 2g fiber), 37g pro.

**"I made this and it was yummy! I did change it a little—I used cheddar cheese instead. My husband loved it!"**
—MICKEYPOTWIN, TASTEOFHOME.COM

## STUFFED PEPPERS FOR TWO

My husband likes stuffed peppers, but my original recipe made too many servings. I cut it down to accommodate just the two of us. It helps to use a small casserole dish so the peppers won't tip over while they bake. I serve steamed carrots to round out the meal perfectly.
*—Elaine Carpenter, Horseshoe Bay, TX*

**Prep:** 20 min. • **Bake:** 50 min.
**Makes:** 2 servings

- 2 medium green peppers
- ½ lb. ground beef
- 1 can (8 oz.) tomato sauce, divided
- ¼ cup uncooked instant rice
- 3 Tbsp. shredded cheddar cheese, divided
- 1 Tbsp. chopped onion
- ½ tsp. Worcestershire sauce
- ½ tsp. salt
- ¼ tsp. pepper
- 1 large egg, beaten

1. Cut tops off peppers and discard; remove seeds. Blanch peppers in boiling water for 5 minutes. Drain and rinse in cold water; set aside.
2. In a bowl, combine beef, ¼ cup tomato sauce, rice, 2 Tbsp. cheese, onion, Worcestershire sauce, salt, pepper and egg; mix well. Stuff the peppers; place in an ungreased 1½-qt. baking dish. Pour the remaining tomato sauce over peppers. Cover and bake at 350° for 45-60 minutes or until meat is no longer pink and peppers are tender.
3. Sprinkle with remaining 1 Tbsp. cheese; return to oven for 5 minutes or until cheese is melted.

**1 STUFFED PEPPER** 405 cal., 20g fat (9g sat. fat), 193mg chol., 1277mg sod., 25g carb. (6g sugars, 3g fiber), 32g pro.

## GARLIC-BUTTER STEAK

This quick and easy skillet entree is definitely restaurant quality. It's sure to become a staple at your house too!
*—Lily Julow, Lawrenceville, GA*

**Takes:** 20 min. • **Makes:** 2 servings

- 2 Tbsp. butter, softened, divided
- 1 tsp. minced fresh parsley
- ½ tsp. minced garlic
- ¼ tsp. reduced-sodium soy sauce
- 1 beef flat iron steak or boneless top sirloin steak (¾ lb.)
- ⅛ tsp. salt
- ⅛ tsp. pepper

1. Mix 1 Tbsp. butter with parsley, garlic and soy sauce.
2. Sprinkle steak with salt and pepper. In a large skillet, heat remaining 1 Tbsp. butter over medium heat. Add steak; cook until meat reaches desired doneness (for medium-rare, a thermometer should read 135°; medium, 140°; medium-well, 145°), 4-7 minutes per side. Serve with garlic butter.

**4 OZ. COOKED BEEF WITH 2 TSP. GARLIC BUTTER** 316 cal., 20g fat (10g sat. fat), 124mg chol., 337mg sod., 0 carb. (0 sugars, 0 fiber), 32g pro.

## STOVETOP ITALIAN MACARONI

I love how tasty and quick this is. I've shared it with many friends over the years. This is a good meatless dish if you substitute vegetarian meat crumbles.
*—Laila Zvejnieks, Stoney Creek, ON*

**Takes:** 25 min. • **Makes:** 5 servings

- 1 lb. ground beef
- 1 can (28 oz.) diced tomatoes, undrained
- 2 cups water
- 1 envelope onion soup mix
- 1 tsp. Italian seasoning
- ¼ tsp. crushed red pepper flakes, optional
- 2 cups uncooked elbow macaroni
- ½ cup grated Parmesan cheese
- 1 cup shredded part-skim mozzarella cheese

1. In a Dutch oven, cook beef over medium heat until no longer pink; drain. Add the tomatoes, water, soup mix, Italian seasoning and, if desired, pepper flakes. Bring to a boil. Stir in macaroni. Reduce heat; cover and simmer for 8-9 minutes or until macaroni is tender.
2. Remove from the heat; stir in Parmesan cheese. Sprinkle with mozzarella cheese. Cover and let stand for 2 minutes or until cheese is melted.

**1⅓ CUPS** 410 cal., 17g fat (8g sat. fat), 76mg chol., 969mg sod., 34g carb. (7g sugars, 4g fiber), 30g pro.

> **"Easy to put together and tasted amazing! I did make a few tweaks. Instead of tomatoes, I used green chiles, and I also added bacon. My husband went back three times for more!"**
> —MADIZEN4, TASTEOFHOME.COM

## FLAVORFUL POT ROAST

On hectic days, this is so quick and easy to prep! Convenient packages of dressing and gravy combine to create a delicious sauce for a fall-apart roast.
*—Arlene Butler, Ogden, UT*

**Prep:** 10 min. • **Cook:** 7 hours
**Makes:** 15 servings

- 2 boneless beef chuck roasts (2½ lbs. each)
- 1 envelope ranch salad dressing mix
- 1 envelope Italian salad dressing mix
- 1 envelope brown gravy mix
- ½ cup water
- Chopped fresh parsley, optional

Place the chuck roasts in a 5-qt. slow cooker. In a small bowl, combine salad dressing mixes and gravy mix; stir in water. Pour over meat. Cover and cook on low for 7-8 hours or until tender. If desired, sprinkle with parsley and thicken cooking juices for gravy.

**4 OZ. COOKED BEEF** 142 cal., 7g fat (3g sat. fat), 49mg chol., 496mg sod., 3g carb. (1g sugars, 0 fiber), 15g pro.

## TANGY SWEET-AND-SOUR MEATBALLS

A fabulous sauce, green pepper and pineapple chunks transform premade meatballs into something special. Serving them over rice makes for a satisfying main dish.
*—Ruth Andrewson, Leavenworth, WA*

**Takes:** 30 min. • **Makes:** 6 servings

- 1 can (20 oz.) pineapple chunks
- ⅓ cup water
- 3 Tbsp. vinegar
- 1 Tbsp. soy sauce
- ½ cup packed brown sugar
- 3 Tbsp. cornstarch
- 30 frozen fully cooked Italian meatballs (about 15 oz.)
- 1 large green pepper, cut into 1-in. pieces
- Hot cooked rice

1. Drain pineapple, reserving juice. If needed, add enough water to juice to measure 1 cup; pour liquid into a large skillet. Add ⅓ cup water, vinegar, soy sauce, brown sugar and cornstarch; stir mixture until smooth.
2. Cook over medium heat until thick, stirring constantly. Add the pineapple, meatballs and green pepper.
3. Simmer, uncovered, until heated through, about 20 minutes. Serve with rice.

**5 MEATBALLS** 389 cal., 19g fat (8g sat. fat), 30mg chol., 682mg sod., 47g carb. (36g sugars, 2g fiber), 11g pro.

## AIR-FRYER SALISBURY STEAK

This dish can be made in 25 minutes, making it a perfect weeknight dinner. I often double the recipe and freeze a batch of cooked steaks and gravy for an even faster meal on an especially busy night.

*—Carol Callahan, Rome, GA*

**Takes:** 25 min. • **Makes:** 4 servings

- ⅓ cup chopped onion
- ¼ cup crushed saltines
- 1 large egg white, lightly beaten
- 2 Tbsp. 2% milk
- 1 Tbsp. prepared horseradish
- ¼ tsp. salt, optional
- ⅛ tsp. pepper
- 1 lb. lean ground beef (90% lean)
- 1 jar (12 oz.) beef gravy
- 1½ cups sliced fresh mushrooms
- 2 Tbsp. water
- Hot cooked noodles, optional

1. Preheat air fryer to 350°. In a large bowl, combine onion, saltines, egg white, milk, horseradish, salt if desired, and pepper. Crumble beef over mixture and mix lightly but thoroughly. Shape into 4 oval patties. Place patties in a greased tray in air-fryer basket. Cook until browned and thermometer reads 160°, 12-15 minutes, turning once.
2. Meanwhile, in a large skillet, stir together gravy, mushrooms and water; cook over medium high heat until heated through, 3-5 minutes. Serve patties with sauce and, if desired, noodles.

**NOTE** Cook times vary dramatically among brands of air fryers. Refer to your air fryer manual for general cook times and adjust if necessary.

**1 SERVING** 253 cal., 11g fat (4g sat. fat), 78mg chol., 582mg sod., 11g carb. (2g sugars, 1g fiber), 26g pro.

## SLOW-COOKER ASIAN SHORT RIBS

My slow cooker is my best friend, and I use it at least three times a week. This versatile recipe is one of my favorites. The sauce can be used for other cuts of meat too.

*—Carole Resnick, Cleveland, OH*

**Prep:** 15 min. • **Cook:** 6 hours
**Makes:** 6 servings

- ¾ cup sugar
- ¾ cup ketchup
- ¾ cup reduced-sodium soy sauce
- ⅓ cup honey
- ¼ cup lemon juice
- 3 Tbsp. hoisin sauce
- 1 Tbsp. ground ginger
- 2 garlic cloves, minced
- 4 lbs. bone-in beef short ribs
- Optional: Hot cooked ramen noodles, sesame seeds, julienned green onions and carrots, and sliced cucumber, radishes, mushrooms and red chili peppers

In a greased 4- or 5-qt. slow cooker, whisk together the first 8 ingredients. Add short ribs and turn to coat; cook, covered, on low 6-7 hours or until meat is tender. If desired, serve with ramen noodles and optional toppings.

**1 SERVING** 460 cal., 15g fat (6g sat. fat), 73mg chol., 1706mg sod., 56g carb. (51g sugars, 0 fiber), 27g pro.

## CHILI CONEY DOGS

From the youngest kids to the oldest adults, everyone in our family loves these hot dogs. They're so easy to throw together in the morning or even the night before.

*—Michele Harris, Vicksburg, MI*

**Prep:** 20 min. • **Cook:** 4 hours
**Makes:** 8 servings

- 1 lb. lean ground beef (90% lean)
- 1 can (15 oz.) tomato sauce
- ½ cup water
- 2 Tbsp. Worcestershire sauce
- 1 Tbsp. dried minced onion
- ½ tsp. garlic powder
- ½ tsp. ground mustard
- ½ tsp. chili powder
- ½ tsp. pepper
- Dash cayenne pepper
- 8 hot dogs
- 8 hot dog buns, split
- Optional toppings: Shredded cheddar cheese, relish, mustard and chopped onion

1. In a large skillet, cook beef over medium heat until no longer pink, 6-8 minutes, breaking it into crumbles; drain. Stir in tomato sauce, water, Worcestershire sauce, dried minced onion and seasonings.
2. Place hot dogs in a 3-qt. slow cooker; top with beef mixture. Cook, covered, on low 4-5 hours or until heated through. Serve on buns with toppings as desired.

**1 CHILI DOG** 371 cal., 20g fat (8g sat. fat), 53mg chol., 992mg sod., 26g carb. (5g sugars, 2g fiber), 21g pro.

## SWITCH UP THE PROTEIN

This salad is versatile: Substitute ground pork, chorizo or lean ground chicken or turkey for the beef. The well-seasoned base also accommodates shredded rotisserie or leftover chicken.

## CATALINA TACO SALAD

At the youth camp my husband directs, the teen campers love this quick and easy taco salad. Our daughter has requested it two years in a row for her birthday dinner.
*—Kay Curtis, Guthrie, OK*

**Takes:** 25 min. • **Makes:** 12 servings

- 1½ lbs. lean ground beef (90% lean)
- 3 cups shredded cheddar cheese
- 1 can (15 oz.) pinto beans, rinsed and drained
- 2 medium tomatoes, seeded and chopped
- 1 large onion, chopped
- 1 bunch romaine, torn
- 1 pkg. (9¼ oz.) corn chips
- 1 bottle (24 oz.) Catalina salad dressing

1. In a large skillet, cook beef over medium heat until no longer pink, breaking it into crumbles; drain. Transfer to a large serving bowl.
2. Add cheese, beans, tomatoes, onion, romaine and corn chips. Drizzle with dressing; gently toss to coat.

**1 CUP** 631 cal., 42g fat (12g sat. fat), 58mg chol., 1145mg sod., 39g carb. (16g sugars, 4g fiber), 21g pro.

## SKILLET STEAK SUPPER

With all the ingredients cooked in one skillet, this steak dish couldn't be quicker to prepare—or to clean up! But the wine-and-mushroom sauce makes it seem special.
*—Sandra Fisher, Missoula, MT*

**Takes:** 20 min. • **Makes:** 2 servings

- 1 beef top sirloin steak (¾ lb.)
- ½ tsp. salt, divided
- ½ tsp. pepper, divided
- 1 Tbsp. olive oil
- 1 to 2 Tbsp. butter
- ½ lb. sliced fresh mushrooms
- 2 Tbsp. white wine or chicken broth
- 3 Tbsp. chopped green onions
- 1 Tbsp. Worcestershire sauce
- 1 tsp. Dijon mustard

1. Sprinkle steak with ¼ tsp. salt and ¼ tsp. pepper. In a skillet, heat oil over medium-high heat; cook steak to the desired doneness (for medium-rare, a thermometer should read 135°; medium, 140°), 4-6 minutes per side. Remove from pan; keep warm.
2. In same skillet, heat butter over medium-high heat; saute mushrooms until tender. Stir in wine; bring to a boil, stirring to loosen browned bits from pan. Stir in green onions, Worcestershire sauce, mustard and the remaining ¼ tsp. salt and ¼ tsp. pepper. Cut steak in half; serve with mushroom mixture.

**1 SERVING** 368 cal., 20g fat (7g sat. fat), 85mg chol., 915mg sod., 6g carb. (3g sugars, 2g fiber), 40g pro.

## SO-EASY SLOPPY JOES

Everybody in the family will love the zesty flavor of this yummy comfort food. Try it on buns or spooned over warmed cornbread.
*—Karen Anderson, Cuyahoga Falls, OH*

**Takes:** 30 min. • **Makes:** 6 servings

- 1½ lbs. ground beef
- 1 can (10 oz.) diced tomatoes and green chiles, undrained
- 1 can (6 oz.) tomato paste
- ¼ cup ketchup
- 2 Tbsp. brown sugar
- 1 Tbsp. spicy brown mustard
- ¼ tsp. salt
- 6 sandwich buns, split
- Fresh arugula, optional

In a large skillet, cook beef over medium heat until no longer pink, 5-7 minutes, breaking it into crumbles; drain. Stir in the tomatoes, tomato paste, ketchup, brown sugar, mustard and salt. Bring to a boil. Reduce heat; simmer, uncovered, for 5 minutes. Serve on buns. Add arugula if desired.

**FREEZE OPTION** Freeze cooled meat mixture in freezer containers. To use, partially thaw in refrigerator overnight. Heat through in a saucepan, stirring occasionally; add water if necessary.

**1 SANDWICH** 478 cal., 18g fat (6g sat. fat), 70mg chol., 918mg sod., 49g carb. (15g sugars, 2g fiber), 30g pro.

## BLACK BEAN & BEEF TOSTADAS

You only need a handful of ingredients to make one of our family's favorites. Also easy to double for company!
*—Susan Brown, Kansas City, KS*

**Takes:** 30 min. • **Makes:** 4 servings

- ½ lb. lean ground beef (90% lean)
- 1 can (10 oz.) diced tomatoes and green chiles, undrained
- 1 can (15 oz.) black beans, rinsed and drained
- 1 can (16 oz.) refried beans, warmed
- 8 tostada shells
- Optional toppings: Pickled red onion, crumbled queso fresco, thinly sliced radishes, shredded cabbage, chopped tomato, cubed avocado, fresh cilantro leaves and lime wedges

1. In a large skillet, cook beef over medium-high heat until no longer pink, 4-6 minutes, breaking it into crumbles. Stir in tomatoes and chiles; bring to a boil. Reduce heat; simmer, uncovered, until liquid is almost evaporated, 6-8 minutes. Stir in black beans; heat through.
2. To serve, spread refried beans over tostada shells. Top with beef mixture; add toppings as desired.

**2 TOSTADAS** 392 cal., 14g fat (4g sat. fat), 35mg chol., 1011mg sod., 46g carb. (2g sugars, 10g fiber), 23g pro.

## CABBAGE ROLL CASSEROLE

I layer cabbage with tomato sauce and beef to create a hearty casserole that tastes like cabbage rolls—but without all the work.

*—Doreen Martin, Kitimat, BC*

**Prep:** 20 min. • **Bake:** 55 min.
**Makes:** 8 servings

- 2 lbs. ground beef
- 1 large onion, chopped
- 3 garlic cloves, minced
- 2 cans (15 oz. each) tomato sauce, divided
- 1 tsp. dried thyme
- ½ tsp. dill weed
- ½ tsp. rubbed sage
- ¼ tsp. salt
- ¼ tsp. pepper
- ¼ tsp. cayenne pepper
- 2 cups cooked rice
- 4 bacon strips, cooked and crumbled
- 1 medium head cabbage (2 lbs.), shredded
- 1 cup shredded part-skim mozzarella cheese
- Coarsely ground pepper, optional

1. Preheat oven to 375°. In a large skillet, cook beef and onion over medium heat until meat is no longer pink, breaking beef into crumbles. Add garlic; cook 1 minute longer. Drain. Stir in 1 can tomato sauce and next 6 ingredients. Bring to a boil. Reduce heat; simmer, covered, 5 minutes. Stir in the rice and bacon; remove from heat.

2. Layer a third of the cabbage in a greased 13x9-in. baking dish. Top with half the meat mixture. Repeat layers; top with remaining cabbage. Pour remaining can of tomato sauce over top.

3. Cover and bake 45 minutes. Uncover; sprinkle with cheese and bake until cheese is melted, about 10 minutes more. Let stand 5 minutes before serving. If desired, sprinkle with coarsely ground pepper.

**1⅓ CUPS** 384 cal., 19g fat (7g sat. fat), 83mg chol., 813mg sod., 26g carb. (6g sugars, 5g fiber), 29g pro.

## SLOW-COOKER BEEF AU JUS

It's easy to fix this roast, which has lots of onion flavor. Sometimes I also add cubed potatoes and baby carrots to the slow cooker to make a terrific meal with plenty of leftovers.

*—Carol Hille, Grand Junction, CO*

**Prep:** 20 min. • **Cook:** 6 hours + standing
**Makes:** 10 servings

- 1 beef rump roast or bottom round roast (3 lbs.)
- 1 large onion, sliced
- ¾ cup reduced-sodium beef broth
- 1 envelope (1 oz.) au jus gravy mix
- 2 garlic cloves, halved
- ¼ tsp. pepper

1. In a large skillet coated with cooking spray, brown meat on all sides over medium-high heat.
2. Place onion in a 5-qt. slow cooker. Top with meat. Combine the broth, gravy mix, garlic and pepper; pour over meat. Cover and cook on low for 6-7 hours or until meat is tender.
3. Remove meat to a cutting board. Let stand for 10 minutes. Thinly slice meat and return to the slow cooker; serve with cooking juices and onion.

**3 OZ. COOKED BEEF** 188 cal., 7g fat (2g sat. fat), 82mg chol., 471mg sod., 3g carb., 0 fiber), 28g pro.

> **"The leftovers make wonderful French dip sandwiches."**
> —NANCY GASTON, TASTEOFHOME.COM

## BACON CHEESEBURGER PASTA

I make foods that are kid friendly and easy to reheat since my husband works long hours and often eats later than our children. If you like, use reduced-fat cheese and ground turkey for a lighter version.

*—Melissa Stevens, Elk River, MN*

**Takes:** 30 min. • **Makes:** 6 servings

- 8 oz. uncooked penne pasta
- 1 lb. ground beef
- 6 bacon strips, diced
- 1 can (10¾ oz.) condensed tomato soup, undiluted
- ½ cup water
- 1 cup shredded cheddar cheese
- Optional: Barbecue sauce and prepared mustard

1. Cook pasta according to package directions. Meanwhile, in a large skillet, cook beef over medium heat until no longer pink; drain and set meat aside.
2. In the same skillet, cook bacon until crisp; remove with a slotted spoon to paper towels to drain. Discard drippings. Drain pasta; add to the skillet. Stir in the soup, water, beef and bacon; heat through.
3. Remove from the heat and sprinkle with cheese. Cover and let stand for 2-3 minutes or until the cheese is melted. Serve with barbecue sauce and mustard if desired.

**1 SERVING** 389 cal., 16g fat (8g sat. fat), 62mg chol., 565mg sod., 36g carb. (5g sugars, 2g fiber), 25g pro.

**TEST KITCHEN TIP**

Using lean ground beef (90% lean) in this meat loaf instead of beef that's 80% lean saves 45 calories per serving. Lean ground beef is also 29% lower in saturated fat.

## MOM'S MEAT LOAF

Mom made the best meat loaf, and now I do too. When I first met my husband, he wasn't a meat loaf guy, but this recipe won him over.
*—Michelle Beran, Claflin, KS*

**Prep:** 15 min.
**Bake:** 1 hour + standing
**Makes:** 6 servings

- 2 large eggs, lightly beaten
- ¾ cup 2% milk
- ⅔ cup finely crushed saltines
- ½ cup chopped onion
- 1 tsp. salt
- ½ tsp. rubbed sage
- Dash pepper
- 1½ lbs. lean ground beef (90% lean)
- 1 cup ketchup
- ½ cup packed brown sugar
- 1 tsp. Worcestershire sauce

1. Preheat oven to 350°. In a large bowl, combine the first 7 ingredients. Add beef; mix lightly but thoroughly. Shape into an 8x4-in. loaf in an ungreased 15x10x1-in. baking pan.
2. In a small bowl, combine remaining ingredients, stirring to dissolve sugar; reserve ½ cup for sauce. Spread remaining mixture over meat loaf.
3. Bake 60-65 minutes or until a thermometer inserted in meat loaf reads 160°. Let stand 10 minutes before slicing. Serve with reserved sauce.

**1 PIECE** 366 cal., 12g fat (5g sat. fat), 135mg chol., 1086mg sod., 38g carb. (31g sugars, 0 fiber), 26g pro.

## AIR-FRYER COWBOY CASSEROLE

When it starts to get cold, I love to make this quick and creamy Tater Tot bake. It's a delightful homey dinner that's easy to put together. I make it ahead of time and keep it in the refrigerator. Then I just pop it into the air fryer when I get home.
*—Donna Donhauser, Remsen, NY*

**Takes:** 30 min. • **Makes:** 2 servings

- ½ lb. lean ground beef (90% lean)
- 1 can (8¾ oz.) whole kernel corn, drained
- ⅔ cup condensed cream of chicken soup, undiluted
- ½ cup shredded cheddar cheese, divided
- ⅓ cup 2% milk
- 2 Tbsp. sour cream
- ¾ tsp. onion powder
- ¼ tsp. pepper
- 2 cups frozen Tater Tots

1. In a large skillet, cook beef over medium heat until no longer pink, breaking it into crumbles. Stir in corn, soup, ¼ cup cheddar cheese, milk, sour cream, onion powder and pepper.
2. Preheat air fryer to 350°. Place 1 cup Tater Tots in a greased 3-cup baking dish that fits into your air fryer. Layer with beef mixture and remaining 1 cup Tater Tots; sprinkle with remaining ¼ cup cheese. Cook, uncovered, until bubbly, 15-20 minutes.

**NOTE** Cook times vary dramatically among brands of air fryers. Refer to your air fryer manual for general cook times and adjust if necessary

**1 SERVING** 714 cal., 38g fat (15g sat. fat), 120mg chol., 1675mg sod., 56g carb. (9g sugars, 6g fiber), 37g pro.

## ONE-SKILLET LASAGNA

This is hands-down one of the best skillet lasagna recipes our testing panel has ever tasted. And with classic flavors and cheesy layers, it's definitely kid-friendly.
—Taste of Home *Test Kitchen*

**Prep:** 15 min. • **Cook:** 25 min.
**Makes:** 6 servings

- ¾ lb. ground beef
- 2 garlic cloves, minced
- 1 can (14½ oz.) diced tomatoes with basil, oregano and garlic, undrained
- 2 jars (14 oz. each) spaghetti sauce
- ⅔ cup condensed cream of onion soup, undiluted
- 2 large eggs, lightly beaten
- 1¼ cups 1% cottage cheese
- ¾ tsp. Italian seasoning
- 9 no-cook lasagna noodles
- ½ cup shredded Colby-Monterey Jack cheese
- ½ cup shredded part-skim mozzarella cheese

**1.** In a large skillet, cook beef and garlic over medium heat until meat is no longer pink, breaking beef into crumbles; drain. Stir in tomatoes and spaghetti sauce; heat through. Transfer to a large bowl.
**2.** In a small bowl, combine the soup, eggs, cottage cheese and Italian seasoning.
**3.** Return 1 cup meat sauce to the skillet; spread evenly. Layer with 1 cup cottage cheese mixture, 1½ cups meat sauce and half the noodles, breaking to fit. Repeat layers of cottage cheese mixture, meat sauce and noodles. Top with remaining meat sauce. Bring to a boil. Reduce heat; cover and simmer for 15-17 minutes or until noodles are tender.
**4.** Remove from the heat. Sprinkle with cheeses; cover and let stand for 2 minutes or until cheese is melted.
**1 SERVING** 478 cal., 20g fat (8g sat. fat), 128mg chol., 1552mg sod., 43g carb. (15g sugars, 4g fiber), 31g pro.

## BURRITO BAKE

When I was in college, my roommate often made this southwestern casserole. One slice fills you right up.
*—Cindee Ness, Horace, ND*

**Prep:** 25 min. • **Bake:** 30 min.
**Makes:** 6 servings

- 1 lb. ground beef
- 1 can (16 oz.) refried beans
- ¼ cup chopped onion
- 1 envelope taco seasoning
- 1 tube (8 oz.) refrigerated crescent rolls
- 1 to 2 cups shredded cheddar cheese
- 1 to 2 cups shredded part-skim mozzarella cheese
- Optional toppings: Chopped green pepper, shredded lettuce, chopped tomatoes and sliced ripe olives

**1.** Preheat oven to 350°. In a large skillet, cook and crumble beef over medium heat until no longer pink; drain. Add beans, onion and taco seasoning.
**2.** Unroll crescent roll dough. Press onto bottom and up the sides of a greased 13x9-in. baking dish; seal seams and perforations.
**3.** Spread beef mixture over crust; sprinkle with cheeses. Bake, uncovered, until golden brown, about 30 minutes. If desired, sprinkle with toppings.
**1 PIECE** 509 cal., 29g fat (12g sat. fat), 78mg chol., 1403mg sod., 32g carb. (4g sugars, 3g fiber), 29g pro.

## BURRITO BAKE TIPS

**What should I serve with the burrito bake?** Cilantro-lime rice, avocado salad or corn on the cob would all pair nicely with this casserole.

**How can I make this dish more nutritious?** Add more veggies like chopped bell peppers and a whole onion, chopped. Saute the veggies with the ground beef until tender. Use lean ground beef, ground turkey or ground chicken. Pile on lots of fresh veggie toppings.

**Can I make this casserole vegetarian?** Yes. Leave out the meat and use extra beans or a plant-based meat alternative.

## PRESSURE-COOKER BEEF TIPS

These beef tips remind me of a childhood favorite. I cook them with mushrooms and serve them over brown rice, noodles or mashed potatoes.
*—Amy Lents, Grand Forks, ND*

**Prep:** 20 min. • **Cook:** 15 min.
**Makes:** 4 servings

- 3 tsp. olive oil
- 1 beef top sirloin steak (1 lb.), cubed
- ½ tsp. salt
- ¼ tsp. pepper
- ⅓ cup dry red wine or beef broth
- ½ lb. sliced baby portobello mushrooms
- 1 small onion, halved and sliced
- 2 cups beef broth
- 1 Tbsp. Worcestershire sauce
- 3 to 4 Tbsp. cornstarch
- ¼ cup cold water
- Hot cooked mashed potatoes

1. Select saute setting on a 6-qt. electric pressure cooker and adjust for medium heat. Add 2 tsp. oil. Sprinkle beef with salt and pepper. Brown meat in batches, adding remaining 1 tsp. oil as needed. Transfer meat to a bowl.
2. Add wine to cooker, stirring to loosen browned bits. Press cancel. Return beef to cooker; add the mushrooms, onion, broth and Worcestershire sauce. Lock lid; close the pressure-release valve. Adjust to pressure-cook on high for 15 minutes. Quick-release pressure.
3. Select saute setting and adjust for low heat; bring liquid to a boil. In a small bowl, mix cornstarch and water until smooth; gradually stir into beef mixture. Cook and stir until sauce is thickened, 1-2 minutes. Serve with mashed potatoes.

**1 CUP** 235 cal., 8g fat (2g sat. fat), 46mg chol., 837mg sod., 10g carb. (2g sugars, 1g fiber), 27g pro.

**STOVETOP BEEF TIPS** Heat oil in a Dutch oven. Season beef with salt and pepper; add to pan and brown on all sides. Add wine, stirring to loosen browned bits. Stir in mushrooms, onion, broth and Worcestershire sauce. Bring to a boil. Reduce heat; cover and simmer until meat is tender, 1½-2 hours. Combine cornstarch and cold water; add to beef mixture. Proceed as directed.

## EASY CORNED BEEF & CABBAGE

I first tried this fuss-free way to cook traditional corned beef and cabbage for St. Patrick's Day a few years ago. Now it's a regular in my menu planning. This is terrific with Dijon mustard and crusty bread.
*—Karen Waters, Laurel, MD*

**Prep:** 15 min. • **Cook:** 8 hours
**Makes:** 8 servings

- 1 medium onion, cut into wedges
- 4 large red potatoes, quartered
- 1 lb. baby carrots
- 3 cups water
- 3 garlic cloves, minced
- 1 bay leaf
- 2 Tbsp. sugar
- 2 Tbsp. cider vinegar
- ½ tsp. pepper
- 1 corned beef brisket with spice packet (2½ to 3 lbs.), cut in half
- 1 small head cabbage, cut into wedges

1. Place the onion, potatoes and carrots in a 6- to 7-qt. slow cooker. Combine the water, garlic, bay leaf, sugar, vinegar, pepper and contents of spice packet; pour over vegetables. Top with brisket and cabbage.
2. Cover and cook on low for 8-9 hours or until meat and vegetables are tender. Discard bay leaf before serving.

**1 SERVING** 414 cal., 19g fat (6g sat. fat), 97mg chol., 1191mg sod., 38g carb. (11g sugars, 6g fiber), 23g pro.

## QUICK BEEF & NOODLES

My family loves this lighter version of beef Stroganoff. Using roast beef from the deli saves the hours spent cooking a whole roast. I serve this entree with a crisp green salad for a home-style meal.
*—Pamela Shank, Parkersburg, WV*

**Takes:** 25 min. • **Makes:** 2 servings

- 2½ cups uncooked yolk-free noodles
- ⅓ cup sliced fresh mushrooms
- ⅓ cup chopped onion
- 1 Tbsp. olive oil
- 1¼ cups reduced-sodium beef broth
- 6 oz. deli roast beef, cubed
- ⅛ tsp. pepper
- Optional: Sour cream and minced fresh parsley

1. Cook noodles according to the package directions. In a large skillet, saute mushrooms and onion in oil until tender. Add broth, roast beef and pepper. Bring to a boil. Reduce heat; simmer, uncovered, for 10 minutes.
2. Drain noodles; stir into skillet. If desired, top with sour cream and parsley.

**1½ CUPS** 375 cal., 10g fat (2g sat. fat), 50mg chol., 778mg sod., 42g carb. (5g sugars, 3g fiber), 26g pro.

## PRESSURE-COOKER PHILLY CHEESESTEAK SANDWICHES

These sandwiches are melt-in-your-mouth delicious! Everybody loves a good cheesesteak smothered with onions and peppers, then topped with cheese.
*—Kimberly Wallace, Dennison, OH*

**Prep:** 15 min. • **Cook:** 15 min. + releasing
**Makes:** 8 servings

- 1 beef top sirloin steak (3 lbs.), thinly sliced
- 2 large onions, cut into ½-in. strips
- 1 can (10½ oz.) condensed French onion soup, undiluted
- 2 garlic cloves, minced
- 1 pkg. Italian salad dressing mix
- 2 tsp. beef base
- ½ tsp. pepper
- 2 large red or green peppers, cut into ½-in. strips
- ½ cup pickled pepper rings
- 8 hoagie buns or French rolls, split
- 8 slices provolone cheese

1. Combine the first 7 ingredients in a 6-qt. electric pressure cooker. Lock lid; close pressure-release valve. Adjust to pressure-cook on high for 10 minutes. Quick-release pressure. Add peppers and pepper rings. Lock lid; close pressure-release valve. Adjust to pressure-cook on high for an additional 5 minutes. Let pressure release naturally for 10 minutes; quick-release any remaining pressure.
2. Place bun bottoms on ungreased baking sheets, cut sides up. Using tongs, top with beef, vegetables and cheese. Broil 3-4 in. from heat until cheese is melted, 1-2 minutes. Add bun tops; serve with cooking juices.

**NOTE** Look for beef base near the broth and bouillon.

**1 SANDWICH** 547 cal., 18g fat (7g sat. fat), 85mg chol., 1381mg sod., 45g carb. (10g sugars, 3g fiber), 51g pro.

**SLOW-COOKER PHILLY CHEESESTEAK SANDWICHES** Combine the first 7 ingredients in a 4- or 5-qt. slow cooker. Cook, covered, on low for 6 hours. Stir in peppers and pepper rings; cover and cook 1-2 hours longer or until meat is tender. Proceed as directed.

> **"I used the slow-cooker method, and I thought these sandwiches were great. I especially liked the melty cheese on top after broiling them. I would definitely make these again!"**
> —AMSM, TASTEOFHOME.COM

## SLOW-COOKER POT ROAST

I work full time, so this slow-cooked pot roast is my go-to when I want a hearty home-cooked meal. It's a comfort to walk in and smell this simmering roast that I know will be fall-apart tender and so delicious.
*—Gina Jackson, Ogdensburg, NY*

**Prep:** 15 min. • **Cook:** 6 hours
**Makes:** 8 servings

- 1 cup warm water
- 1 Tbsp. beef base
- ½ lb. sliced fresh mushrooms
- 1 large onion, coarsely chopped
- 3 garlic cloves, minced
- 1 boneless beef chuck roast (3 lbs.)
- ½ tsp. pepper
- 1 Tbsp. Worcestershire sauce
- ¼ cup butter, cubed
- ⅓ cup all-purpose flour
- ¼ tsp. salt

1. In a 5- or 6-qt. slow cooker, whisk water and beef base; add mushrooms, onion and garlic. Sprinkle roast with pepper; transfer to slow cooker. Drizzle with Worcestershire sauce. Cook roast, covered, on low 6-8 hours or until meat is tender.
2. Remove roast to a serving platter; tent with foil. Strain cooking juices, reserving vegetables. Skim fat from cooking juices. In a large saucepan, melt butter over medium heat. Stir in flour and salt until smooth; gradually whisk in cooking juices. Bring to a boil, stirring constantly; cook and stir 1-2 minutes or until thickened. Stir in cooked vegetables. Serve with roast.

**NOTE** Look for beef base near the broth and bouillon.

**5 OZ. COOKED MEAT WITH ½ CUP GRAVY** 380 cal., 22g fat (10g sat. fat), 126mg chol., 467mg sod., 8g carb. (2g sugars, 1g fiber), 35g pro.

### POT ROAST TIPS

**What can I add to this pot roast?** Toss in some large chunks of red potatoes, carrots and celery. Cut vegetables large so they won't overcook during the dish's long cook time.

**Is low or high heat better?** Low heat yields the most tender, flavorful roast by slowly breaking down its connective tissues. High heat works fine if you're short on time, though.

# EASY SLOW-COOKED SWISS STEAK

Let your slow cooker simmer up this fuss-free and flavorful Swiss steak. It's perfect for busy days—the longer it cooks, the better it tastes!
*—Sarah Burks, Wathena, KS*

**Prep:** 10 min. • **Cook:** 6 hours
**Makes:** 2 servings

- 1 Tbsp. all-purpose flour
- ¼ tsp. salt
- ⅛ tsp. pepper
- ¾ lb. beef top round steak
- ½ medium onion, cut into ¼-in. slices
- ⅓ cup chopped celery
- 1 can (8 oz.) tomato sauce

1. In a large shallow dish, combine the flour, salt and pepper. Cut beef into 2 portions; add to dish and turn to coat.
2. Place onion in a 3-qt. slow cooker coated with cooking spray. Layer with the beef, celery and tomato sauce. Cover and cook on low 6-8 hours or until meat is tender.

**1 SERVING** 272 cal., 5g fat (2g sat. fat), 96mg chol., 882mg sod., 13g carb. (4g sugars, 2g fiber), 41g pro.

HAM & SWISS
WITH A TWIST,
PAGE 90

# QUICK & EASY PORK

SIMPLE MARINATED GRILLED PORK CHOPS, PAGE 122

## TENDERLOIN WITH HERB SAUCE

Tender pork is treated to a rich, creamy sauce with a slight red pepper kick. This hearty dish is simple to prepare and always a dinnertime winner in my home.
*—Monica Shipley, Tulare, CA*

**Takes:** 25 min. • **Makes:** 6 servings

- 2 lbs. pork tenderloins
- ½ tsp. salt
- 4 tsp. butter
- ⅔ cup half-and-half cream
- 2 Tbsp. minced fresh parsley
- 2 tsp. herbes de Provence
- 2 tsp. reduced-sodium soy sauce
- 1 tsp. beef bouillon granules
- ½ to ¾ tsp. crushed red pepper flakes

**1.** Cut each tenderloin into 12 slices; sprinkle with salt. In a large nonstick skillet, heat butter over medium heat; brown pork in batches, 3-4 minutes per side. Return all pork to pan.
**2.** Mix remaining ingredients; pour over pork. Cook, uncovered, over low heat until sauce is thickened and a thermometer inserted in pork reads 145°, 2-3 minutes, stirring occasionally. Let stand 5 minutes before serving.
**NOTE** Look for herbes de Provence in the spice aisle.
**4 OZ. COOKED PORK** 238 cal., 10g fat (5g sat. fat), 104mg chol., 495mg sod., 2g carb. (1g sugars, 0 fiber), 31g pro.

## TANGY PULLED PORK SANDWICHES

The slow cooker not only makes this an easy meal, it also keeps the pork tender, moist and loaded with flavor. The sandwiches are so comforting, they seem anything but light.
*—Beki Kosydar-Krantz, Mayfield, PA*

**Prep:** 10 min. • **Cook:** 4 hours
**Makes:** 4 servings

- 1 pork tenderloin (1 lb.)
- 1 cup ketchup
- 2 Tbsp. plus 1½ tsp. brown sugar
- 2 Tbsp. plus 1½ tsp. cider vinegar
- 1 Tbsp. plus 1½ tsp. Worcestershire sauce
- 1 Tbsp. spicy brown mustard
- ¼ tsp. pepper
- 4 rolls or buns, split and toasted
- Coleslaw, optional

**1.** Cut the tenderloin in half; place in a 3-qt. slow cooker. Combine the ketchup, brown sugar, vinegar, Worcestershire sauce, mustard and pepper; pour over pork.
**2.** Cover and cook on low for 4-5 hours or until meat is tender. Remove meat; shred with 2 forks. Return to slow cooker; heat through. Serve on toasted rolls or buns, with coleslaw if desired.
**1 SANDWICH** 402 cal., 7g fat (2g sat. fat), 63mg chol., 1181mg sod., 56g carb. (18g sugars, 2g fiber), 29g pro.

"This is so good! My husband substituted chicken broth for the water. He also cut the recipe in half and he used kielbasa. This recipe is very flavorful. I have shared it with two others so far."

—STYCRBL53, TASTEOFHOME.COM

## CABBAGE SAUSAGE SUPPER

Everyone is surprised at how this flavorful combination calls for just a few ingredients. I complete the meal with a no-bake fruit dessert.
*—Ruby Williams, Bogalusa, LA*

**Prep:** 10 min. • **Cook:** 40 min.
**Makes:** 8 servings

- 2 lbs. smoked sausage, halved and cut into ¾-in. slices
- 1 large onion, cut into eighths
- 1 medium head cabbage, chopped
- ½ cup water
- 1 lb. carrots, cut into ½-in. slices
- 5 medium potatoes, peeled and cut into ¾-in. cubes

In a Dutch oven, cook sausage and onion over medium heat until sausage is lightly browned and onion is tender; drain. Add cabbage and water. Cover and cook on low for 10 minutes. Stir in carrots and potatoes. Cover and cook for 25-30 minutes or until vegetables are tender.

**1½ CUPS** 490 cal., 31g fat (13g sat. fat), 76mg chol., 1345mg sod., 35g carb. (11g sugars, 6g fiber), 20g pro.

## SKILLET PORK CHOPS WITH APPLES & ONION

Simple recipes that land on the table fast are a lifesaver. I serve skillet pork chops with veggies and, when there's time, cornbread stuffing.
*—Tracey Karst, Ponderay, ID*

**Takes:** 20 min. • **Makes:** 4 servings

- 4 boneless pork loin chops (6 oz. each)
- 3 medium apples, cut into wedges
- 1 large onion, cut into thin wedges
- ¼ cup water
- ⅓ cup balsamic vinaigrette
- ½ tsp. salt
- ¼ tsp. pepper

1. Place a large nonstick skillet over medium heat; brown pork chops on both sides, about 4 minutes. Remove from pan.
2. In same skillet, combine apples, onion and water. Place pork chops over apple mixture; drizzle chops with vinaigrette. Sprinkle with salt and pepper. Reduce the heat; simmer, covered, until a thermometer inserted into chops reads 145°, 3-5 minutes.

**1 PORK CHOP WITH ¾ CUP APPLE MIXTURE** 360 cal., 15g fat (4g sat. fat), 82mg chol., 545mg sod., 22g carb. (15g sugars, 3g fiber), 33g pro.

## HAM & SWISS WITH A TWIST

To satisfy hearty appetites, try this different take on a grilled ham and cheese. The apples give it a sweet twist. Rye bread is a delicious alternative.
*—Marietta Slater, Justin, TX*

**Takes:** 25 min. • **Makes:** 4 servings

- 1 large onion, sliced
- 4 Tbsp. butter, softened, divided
- 8 slices Texas toast
- 2 Tbsp. spicy brown mustard
- ½ lb. thinly sliced deli ham
- 1 medium apple, sliced
- 4 slices Swiss cheese

1. In a large skillet, cook onion in 1 Tbsp. butter over medium heat until golden brown, 8-10 minutes, stirring frequently.
2. Spread remaining 3 Tbsp. butter over 1 side of each slice of Texas toast. Place slices, buttered side down, on a cast-iron skillet or electric griddle. Spread with mustard; layer with ham, apple, onion and cheese. Top with another slice of toast, buttered side up. Cook over medium heat until golden brown, 3-4 minutes. Carefully turn; cook until cheese is melted, 2 minutes longer.

**1 SANDWICH** 510 cal., 26g fat (14g sat. fat), 88mg chol., 1414mg sod., 44g carb. (9g sugars, 3g fiber), 23g pro.

### HAM & SWISS TIPS

**What apples work best?** Crisp, sweet-tart slices—Braeburn, Fuji or Honeycrisp—add snap and balance.

**How can I make this sandwich my own?** Try using bakery sourdough or rye; use Dijon or fig jam; try thin-sliced pear or Asian pear; add arugula or pickled onions for brightness.

## SLOW-COOKED MESQUITE RIBS

When we're missing the grill during winter, these tangy ribs give us that same smoky barbecue taste we love. They're so simple, and they're fall-off-the-bone delicious too!
*—Sue Evans, Marquette, MI*

**Prep:** 10 min. • **Cook:** 6½ hours
**Makes:** 8 servings

- 1 cup water
- 2 Tbsp. cider vinegar
- 1 Tbsp. soy sauce
- 4 lbs. pork baby back ribs, cut into serving-size portions
- 2 Tbsp. mesquite seasoning
- ½ cup barbecue sauce

1. In a 6-qt. slow cooker, mix water, vinegar and soy sauce. Rub ribs with mesquite seasoning; place in slow cooker.
2. Cook, covered, on low 6-8 hours or until tender. Remove ribs to a platter. Brush with barbecue sauce; return to slow cooker. Cook, covered, on low until ribs are glazed, about 30 minutes.

**1 SERVING** 314 cal., 21g fat (8g sat. fat), 81mg chol., 591mg sod., 7g carb. (6g sugars, 0 fiber), 23g pro.

## SAVORY BEER PORK CHOPS

These tender chops cooked in a savory sauce are perfect for a hectic weeknight because they're so easy to prep. Try them with hot buttery noodles.
*—Jana Christian, Farson, WY*

**Takes:** 20 min. • **Makes:** 4 servings

- 4 boneless pork loin chops (4 oz. each)
- ½ tsp. salt
- ½ tsp. pepper
- 1 Tbsp. canola oil
- 3 Tbsp. ketchup
- 2 Tbsp. brown sugar
- ¾ cup beer or nonalcoholic beer

1. Sprinkle pork chops with salt and pepper. In a large skillet, heat oil over medium heat; brown chops on both sides.
2. Mix ketchup, brown sugar and beer; pour over chops. Bring to a boil. Reduce heat and simmer, uncovered, until a thermometer inserted into pork reads 145°, 4-6 minutes. Let stand 5 minutes before serving.

**FREEZE OPTION** Place pork chops in freezer containers; top with sauce. Cool and freeze. To use, partially thaw in refrigerator overnight. Heat through in a covered saucepan, gently stirring sauce; add water if necessary.

**1 PORK CHOP** 239 cal., 10g fat (3g sat. fat), 55mg chol., 472mg sod., 11g carb. (11g sugars, 0 fiber), 22g pro.

## AU GRATIN SAUSAGE SKILLET

Using frozen vegetables and a package of au gratin potatoes, I can get this satisfying stovetop supper on the table in no time. Even our oldest daughter, who can be a picky eater, loves it—and it is an excellent way of getting her to eat her vegetables.
*—Penny Greene, Lancaster, OH*

**Prep:** 15 min. • **Cook:** 30 min.
**Makes:** 4 servings

- 1 lb. smoked kielbasa or Polish sausage, halved and sliced
- 2 Tbsp. canola oil
- 1 pkg. (4.9 oz.) au gratin potatoes
- 2½ cups water
- 1 pkg. (8 oz.) frozen California-blend vegetables
- 1 to 2 cups shredded cheddar cheese

1. In a large skillet, cook sausage in oil until lightly browned; drain. Add potatoes with contents of sauce mix and water. Cover and cook over medium heat for 18-20 minutes or until the potatoes are almost tender, stirring occasionally.
2. Add vegetables; cover and cook for 8-10 minutes or until potatoes and vegetables are tender. Sprinkle with cheese. Remove from heat; cover and let stand for 2 minutes or until the cheese is melted.

**NOTE** The milk and butter listed on the potato package are not used in this recipe.

**1 SERVING** 660 cal., 47g fat (18g sat. fat), 106mg chol., 2093mg sod., 32g carb. (5g sugars, 3g fiber), 25g pro.

## PORK MEDALLIONS WITH GARLIC-STRAWBERRY SAUCE

These crispy pork medallions are treated to a refreshing strawberry sauce that's ideal for a springtime or summer meal.
—Taste of Home *Test Kitchen*

**Takes:** 25 min. • **Makes:** 4 servings

- 2 cups whole fresh strawberries
- ¼ cup water
- 1 tsp. chicken bouillon granules
- ½ cup all-purpose flour
- 2 large eggs, lightly beaten
- ⅔ cup seasoned bread crumbs
- 1 pork tenderloin (1 lb.)
- ¼ tsp. salt
- ¼ tsp. pepper
- 6 Tbsp. butter, divided
- 1 tsp. minced garlic

1. Place strawberries, water and bouillon in a food processor; process until blended. Place flour, eggs and bread crumbs in separate shallow bowls.
2. Cut pork into ½-in. slices; pound each with a meat mallet to ¼-in. thickness. Sprinkle with salt and pepper. Dip pork in flour to coat both sides; shake off excess. Dip in eggs, then in crumbs, patting to adhere.
3. In a large skillet, heat 2 Tbsp. butter over medium-high heat. Add pork; cook until tender, 2-3 minutes per side. Remove from pan; keep warm.
4. In same pan, saute garlic in remaining 4 Tbsp. butter 1 minute. Stir in the strawberry mixture; heat through. Serve pork with sauce.

**1 SERVING** 422 cal., 25g fat (13g sat. fat), 203mg chol., 811mg sod., 21g carb. (5g sugars, 2g fiber), 29g pro.

**"My husband and I just finished eating this, and we are speechless! We never would have thought that these flavors would taste so good together."**
—CBENNE12, TASTEOFHOME.COM

## SLOW-COOKER CUBANO SANDWICHES

This recipe came about because I didn't have pepperoncini for my usual Italian pork recipe, so I used pickles instead. It reminded me of a Cuban sandwich so much that I added some ham and Swiss cheese to complete the dish. Instead of adding cheese to the slow cooker, you can also top the sandwiches with sliced cheese. Place under the broiler to melt.
*—Kristie Schley, Pasadena, MD*

**Prep:** 15 min. • **Cook:** 6½ hours
**Makes:** 8 servings

- 2 lbs. pork tenderloin
- 7 Tbsp. stone-ground mustard, divided
- 1 tsp. pepper, freshly ground
- 1 lb. fully cooked boneless ham steak, cut into ½-in. cubes
- 1 jar (16 oz.) whole baby dill pickles, undrained, sliced thick
- 2 cups shredded Swiss cheese
- 8 submarine buns, split

**1.** Rub pork with 3 Tbsp. mustard, season with pepper and place in a 5- or 6-qt. slow cooker. Add ham and pickles, including pickle juice. Cover and cook on low for 6 hours or until tender, turning halfway through.
**2.** Shred pork with 2 forks. Sprinkle cheese over meat mixture; cover and cook until cheese melts, about 30 minutes.
**3.** When ready to serve, slice rolls and toast lightly in a toaster oven or broiler. Spread remaining mustard evenly over both sides. Using a slotted spoon, top rolls with the meat mixture. Serve immediately.

**1 SANDWICH** 526 cal., 20g fat (8g sat. fat), 118mg chol., 1941mg sod., 36g carb. (4g sugars, 3g fiber), 48g pro.

## PORK TENDERLOIN WITH PEACH HONEY MUSTARD

My grandmother used to make a beef tenderloin stuffed with peaches and basil when I was young, so I altered that recipe and came up with my own unique version for my husband and me. It is now a household favorite!
*—Mary Beth Harris-Murphree, Tyler, TX*

**Prep:** 15 min. • **Grill:** 20 min.
**Makes:** 2 servings

- ½ medium peach, peeled
- 2 Tbsp. Dijon mustard
- 1 Tbsp. honey
- 1 Tbsp. brown sugar
- 1 tsp. salt
- ½ tsp. pepper
- ⅛ tsp. cayenne pepper
- 1 pork tenderloin (¾ lb.)

**1.** Place the peach, mustard and honey in a blender; cover and process until blended.
**2.** Combine the brown sugar, salt, pepper and cayenne; rub over pork. Place pork on an oiled grill rack.
**3.** Grill pork, covered, over indirect medium-hot heat for 20-25 minutes or until a thermometer reads 160°. Let stand for 5 minutes before slicing. Serve with peach sauce.

**1 SERVING** 281 cal., 6g fat (2g sat. fat), 95mg chol., 1611mg sod., 21g carb. (17g sugars, 1g fiber), 34g pro.

## PRESSURE-COOKER SMOKY WHITE BEANS & HAM

I had never made or even eaten this dish before meeting my husband. Now I make it at least once a week. Delicious!
*—Christine Duffy, Sturgis, KY*

**Prep:** 15 min. • **Cook:** 30 min. + releasing
**Makes:** 10 servings

- 1 lb. dried great northern beans
- 3 smoked ham hocks (about 1½ lbs.)
- 3 cans (14½ oz. each) reduced-sodium chicken or beef broth
- 2 cups water
- 1 large onion, chopped
- 1 Tbsp. onion powder
- 1 Tbsp. garlic powder
- 2 tsp. pepper
- Thinly sliced green onions, optional

1. Rinse and sort beans. Transfer to a 6-qt. electric pressure cooker. Add ham hocks. Stir in broth, water, onion and seasonings. Lock lid; close pressure-release valve. Adjust to pressure-cook on high for 30 minutes. Let pressure release naturally for 10 minutes; quick-release any remaining pressure.
2. When cool enough to handle, remove meat from bones; cut ham into small pieces and return to pressure cooker. Serve with a slotted spoon. Sprinkle with green onions if desired.

**⅔ CUP** 196 cal., 2g fat (0 sat. fat), 8mg chol., 594mg sod., 32g carb. (2g sugars, 10g fiber), 15g pro.

**SLOW-COOKER SMOKY WHITE BEANS & HAM** Rinse and sort beans. Add water to cover by 2 in; let soak overnight. Change out water; boil beans for 15 minutes. Drain and rinse beans, discarding liquid. Transfer to a 6-qt. slow cooker. Add the ham hocks, onion, broth, water and seasonings. Cook, covered, on low until beans are tender, 6-8 hours. Proceed as directed in step 2.

## PASTA WITH CHORIZO & SPINACH

This zippy entree looks and tastes special, but it's a cinch to make. When I get home from work, I like to prepare quick dishes, and this is one of our favorites.
*—Athena Russell, Greenville, SC*

**Takes:** 20 min. • **Makes:** 2 servings

- 1¼ cups uncooked penne pasta
- 4 tsp. olive oil
- ⅓ lb. uncooked chorizo or bulk spicy pork sausage
- 1 small onion, thinly sliced
- 4 oz. sliced fresh mushrooms
- ⅓ cup water-packed artichoke hearts, rinsed, drained and quartered
- ⅓ cup chopped oil-packed sun-dried tomatoes, drained
- 1 garlic clove, minced
- ¼ tsp. dried oregano
- ⅛ tsp. salt
- ⅛ tsp. pepper
- 3 cups chopped fresh spinach
- 2 Tbsp. grated Parmesan cheese

1. Cook pasta according to package directions. Meanwhile, heat oil in a large skillet; crumble chorizo into the pan. Add the onion, mushrooms, artichokes, tomatoes, garlic, oregano, salt and pepper. Cook and stir over medium heat unti meat is fully cooked and vegetables are tender.
2. Add spinach; cook and stir for 1-2 minutes or until wilted. Drain pasta; top with chorizo mixture and sprinkle with cheese.

**1 CUP** 635 cal., 37g fat (11g sat. fat), 71mg chol., 1333mg sod., 47g carb. (5g sugars, 5g fiber), 29g pro.

## GREEK PORK CHOPS

My in-laws taught me a lot about cooking, so any time I come across a great new recipe, I enjoy making it for them. These bright, lemony chops quickly became a favorite.
*—Geri Lipczynski, Oak Lawn, IL*

**Prep:** 15 min. + marinating
**Grill:** 10 min. • **Makes:** 4 servings

- 2 Tbsp. olive oil
- 4 tsp. lemon juice
- 1 Tbsp. Worcestershire sauce
- 2 tsp. dried oregano
- 1 tsp. salt
- 1 tsp. onion powder
- 1 tsp. garlic powder
- 1 tsp. pepper
- ½ tsp. ground mustard
- 4 boneless pork loin chops (¾ in. thick and 4 oz. each)
- lemon wedges, optional

1. In a large bowl, mix the first 9 ingredients. Add pork chops and turn to coat. Cover; refrigerate for 8 hours or overnight.
2. Drain pork, discarding marinade. Grill chops, covered, over medium heat or broil 4 in. from heat until a thermometer reads 145°, 4-5 minutes per side. Let stand for 5 minutes before serving. Serve with lemon if desired.

**FREEZE OPTION** Freeze chops with marinade in a freezer container. To use, thaw in refrigerator overnight. Drain pork, discarding marinade. Grill as directed.

**1 PORK CHOP** 193 cal., 10g fat (3g sat. fat), 55mg chol., 349mg sod., 2g carb. (0 sugars, 1g fiber), 22g pro.

## "SECRET'S IN THE SAUCE" BBQ RIBS

A sweet, rich sauce makes these ribs so tender that the meat literally falls off the bones. And the aroma is wonderful. Yum!
*—Tanya Reid, Winston-Salem, NC*

**Prep:** 10 min. • **Cook:** 6 hours
**Makes:** 5 servings

- 4½ lbs. pork baby back ribs
- 1½ tsp. pepper
- 2½ cups barbecue sauce
- ¾ cup cherry preserves
- 1 Tbsp. Dijon mustard
- 1 garlic clove, minced

Cut ribs into serving-size pieces; sprinkle with pepper. Place in a 5- or 6-qt. slow cooker. Combine remaining ingredients; pour over ribs. Cook, covered, on low until meat is tender, 6-8 hours. Serve with sauce.

**1 SERVING** 921 cal., 58g fat (21g sat. fat), 220mg chol., 1402mg sod., 50g carb. (45g sugars, 2g fiber), 48g pro.

## SOUTHERN FRIED PORK CHOPS

Marinated in buttermilk, dredged in seasoned flour and cooked up in hot oil, these tasty pork chops are comfort food at its best!
—Taste of Home *Test Kitchen*

**Prep:** 30 min. + marinating
**Cook:** 10 min./batch
**Makes:** 4 servings

- 1 cup buttermilk
- 1 Tbsp. hot pepper sauce
- 4 bone-in pork loin chops (8 oz. each)

COATING

- 1½ cups all-purpose flour
- 1½ tsp. salt
- 1 tsp. paprika
- ½ tsp. garlic powder
- ½ tsp. onion powder
- ½ tsp. pepper
- Oil for frying

1. In a large shallow dish, whisk buttermilk and hot pepper sauce. Add pork chops; turn to coat. Cover and refrigerate at least 1 hour or overnight.
2. Drain and discard buttermilk mixture. Combine the coating ingredients in another shallow dish. Add pork chops, 1 at a time, and turn to coat. Place chops on a wire rack over a baking sheet. Refrigerate, uncovered, for 30 minutes.
3. In a Dutch oven or deep skillet, heat ½ in. oil over medium heat to 350°. Fry the pork in batches, uncovered, turning occasionally, 5-6 minutes per side or until the coating is dark golden brown and a thermometer reads 145°. Drain on paper towels.

**1 PORK CHOP** 639 cal., 46g fat (9g sat. fat), 112mg chol., 483mg sod., 15g carb. (2g sugars, 1g fiber), 39g pro.

## CHILI SPAGHETTI WITH HOT DOGS

I've been making this dish for over 35 years, but my husband has yet to tire of it! I think that's a sign of a good recipe.
*—Karen Tausend, Bridgeport, MI*

**Takes:** 30 min. • **Makes:** 6 servings

- 8 oz. uncooked spaghetti
- 1 pkg. (1 lb.) hot dogs, sliced
- ½ cup chopped onion
- ½ cup chopped celery
- 2 Tbsp. canola oil
- 1 can (15 oz.) tomato sauce
- 1 Tbsp. prepared mustard
- 1 tsp. chili powder
- ½ tsp. Worcestershire sauce
- ¼ tsp. salt
- ¼ tsp. pepper
- 1 cup shredded cheddar cheese

1. Cook spaghetti according to package directions. Meanwhile, in a large skillet, saute the hot dogs, onion and celery in oil until the vegetables are tender. Add tomato sauce, mustard, chili powder, Worcestershire sauce, salt and pepper; cook and stir until heated through.
2. Drain spaghetti; toss with hot dog mixture. Serve immediately, sprinkling each serving with cheese. Or cool spaghetti; transfer to freezer containers and freeze for up to 3 months.

**TO USE FROZEN SPAGHETTI** Thaw in the refrigerator overnight. Place in a saucepan and heat through. Sprinkle each serving with cheese.

**1 CUP** 523 cal., 34g fat (14g sat. fat), 62mg chol., 1360mg sod., 36g carb. (4g sugars, 2g fiber), 19g pro.

## AIR-FRYER JAMAICAN JERK PORK CHOPS

These sweet, spicy chops can be thrown together in minutes, but they definitely don't taste that way. Served with a side of jasmine rice, every bite is like a trip to a tropical location.
*—Allison Ulrich, Frisco, TX*

**Takes:** 25 min. • **Makes:** 4 servings

- 1 Tbsp. butter, softened
- ¼ cup peach preserves
- 4 boneless thin-cut pork loin chops (2 to 3 oz. each)
- 3 tsp. Caribbean jerk seasoning
- ½ tsp. salt
- ¼ tsp. pepper
- ½ medium sweet orange pepper
- ½ medium sweet yellow pepper
- ½ medium sweet red pepper
- Hot cooked rice, optional

1. Preheat air fryer to 350°. In a small bowl, mix butter and peach preserves until combined.
2. Sprinkle chops with seasonings. Place on greased tray in air-fryer basket. Cook until no longer pink, 2-3 minutes on each side. Remove and keep warm.
3. Cut peppers into thin strips. Place on greased tray in air-fryer basket. Cook until crisp-tender and lightly browned, 5-6 minutes, stirring occasionally. Return chops to air fryer with peppers; top with butter mixture. Cook until butter is melted, 1-2 minutes. If desired, serve with rice.

**1 SERVING** 368 cal., 14g fat (7g sat. fat), 84mg chol., 1099mg sod., 32g carb. (28g sugars, 2g fiber), 28g pro.

## SKILLET HAM & RICE

Ham, rice and mushrooms make a tasty combination in this homey stovetop dish. It goes from start to finish in just 25 minutes.
*—Susan Zivec, Regina, SK*

**Takes:** 25 min. • **Makes:** 2 servings

- 1 tsp. olive oil
- 1 medium onion, chopped
- 1 cup sliced fresh mushrooms
- 1 cup cubed fully cooked ham
- ⅛ tsp. pepper
- ½ cup reduced-sodium chicken broth
- ¼ cup water
- ¾ cup uncooked instant rice
- 2 green onions, sliced
- ¼ cup shredded Parmesan cheese

1. In a large nonstick skillet, heat oil over medium-high heat; saute onion and mushrooms until tender. Stir in ham, pepper, broth and water; bring to a boil. Stir in rice. Reduce heat; simmer, covered, until rice is tender, about 5 minutes.
2. Fluff with a fork. Top with green onions and cheese.

**1¼ CUPS** 322 cal., 8g fat (3g sat. fat), 49mg chol., 1168mg sod., 38g carb. (4g sugars, 2g fiber), 24g pro.

## SLOW-COOKER PORK CHOPS

Everyone will enjoy these fork-tender pork chops with a creamy, light gravy. Serve with a green vegetable, mashed potatoes and coleslaw or a salad.
*—Sue Bingham, Madisonville, TN*

**Prep:** 15 min. • **Cook:** 2 hours
**Makes:** 4 servings

- ½ cup all-purpose flour, divided
- ½ tsp. ground mustard
- ½ tsp. garlic pepper blend
- ¼ tsp. seasoned salt
- 4 boneless pork loin chops (4 oz. each)
- 2 Tbsp. canola oil
- 1 can (14½ oz.) chicken broth

1. In a shallow bowl, combine ¼ cup flour, mustard, garlic pepper and seasoned salt. Add pork chops, 1 at a time, and dredge to coat. In a large skillet, brown chops in oil on both sides.
2. Transfer to a 5-qt. slow cooker. Pour broth over chops. Cook, covered, on low for 2-3 hours or until meat is tender.
3. Remove pork to a serving plate and keep warm. Whisk remaining ¼ cup flour into cooking juices until smooth; cook, covered, on high until gravy is thickened.

**1 PORK CHOP** 279 cal., 14g fat (3g sat. fat), 57mg chol., 606mg sod., 12g carb. (1g sugars, 0 fiber), 24g pro.

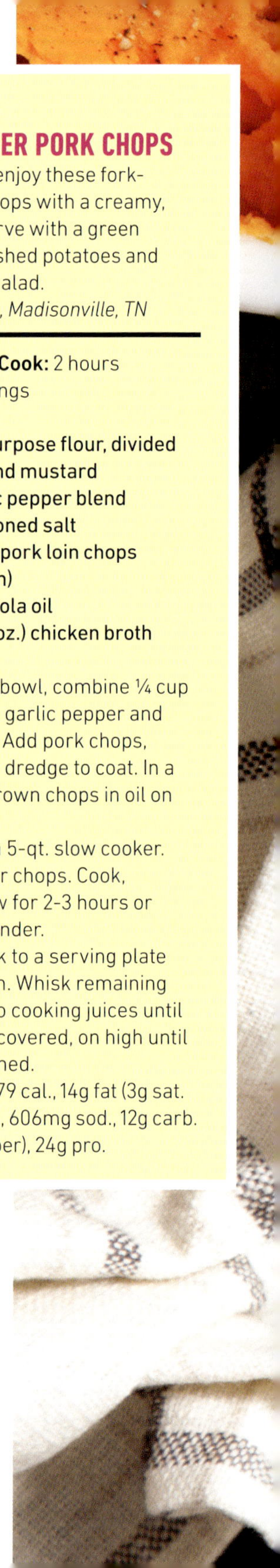

## OVEN-FRIED GREEN TOMATO BLT

For years I have used this same idea to cook eggplant slices, and recently I decided to try it on green tomatoes. It worked! Now my family loves them in BLTs.
*—Jolene Martinelli, Fremont, NH*

**Takes:** 25 min. • **Makes:** 4 servings

- 1 large green tomato (about 8 oz.)
- 1 large egg, beaten
- 1 cup panko bread crumbs
- ¼ tsp. salt
- ¼ cup reduced-fat mayonnaise
- 2 green onions, thinly sliced
- 1 tsp. snipped fresh dill or ¼ tsp. dried dill weed
- 8 slices whole wheat bread, toasted
- 8 cooked center-cut bacon strips
- 4 Bibb or Boston lettuce leaves

1. Preheat broiler. Cut tomato into 8 slices, each about ¼ in. thick. Place egg and bread crumbs in separate shallow bowls; mix salt into bread crumbs. Dip tomato slices in egg, then in bread crumb mixture, patting to help adhere.
2. Place tomato slices on a wire rack set in a 15x10x1-in. baking pan; broil 4-5 in. from heat until golden brown, about 30-45 seconds per side.
3. Mix mayonnaise, green onions and dill. Layer each of 4 slices of bread with 2 bacon strips, 1 lettuce leaf and 2 tomato slices. Spread mayonnaise mixture over remaining bread; place over top layer.

**1 SANDWICH** 313 cal., 12g fat (2g sat. fat), 55mg chol., 744mg sod., 36g carb. (5g sugars, 4g fiber), 16g pro.

## SAUSAGE POTATO SUPPER

One Saturday night, I cooked sausage with potatoes and zucchini—those were the ingredients I had on hand. This spur-of-the-moment supper has been a hit with all six of us ever since.
*—Nancy Russell, Englewood, CO*

**Takes:** 25 min. • **Makes:** 2 servings

- 2 small red potatoes, cubed
- 1 Tbsp. butter
- 1 small zucchini, cut into ¼-in. slices
- ⅛ tsp. garlic salt
- ½ lb. smoked sausage, cut into ½-in. slices
- ⅛ to ¼ tsp. pepper
- Grated Parmesan cheese, optional

**1.** In a small saucepan, combine potatoes and enough water to cover; bring to a boil. Reduce heat; cook, uncovered, until tender, 15-20 minutes.
**2.** In a large skillet, heat butter over medium-high heat; saute zucchini with garlic salt until crisp-tender. Add sausage; cook and stir until browned.
**3.** Drain potatoes and stir into zucchini mixture. Sprinkle with pepper and, if desired, cheese.

**1 SERVING** 448 cal., 37g fat (17g sat. fat), 91mg chol., 1396mg sod., 12g carb. (5g sugars, 1g fiber), 18g pro.

## KIELBASA BOW TIE SKILLET

This meal couldn't make dinnertime any simpler! Not only is it a real crowd-pleaser, it also comes together in just one pan. It freezes and reheats beautifully, too, so you'll want to fix extras for a quick meal later. My daughters are picky eaters, but this dish reminds them of macaroni and cheese. I toss in their favorite veggies and they gobble it up!
*—Lori Daniels, Beverly, WV*

**Takes:** 25 min. • **Makes:** 4 servings

- 8 oz. uncooked bow tie pasta
- 1 lb. smoked kielbasa or smoked Polish sausage, cut into ¼-in. slices
- 1 jar (4½ oz.) sliced mushrooms, drained
- 2 Tbsp. butter
- 2 garlic cloves, minced
- 1 Tbsp. cornstarch
- 1½ cups whole milk
- 1½ cups fresh or frozen snow peas
- 1 cup shredded cheddar cheese

**1.** Cook pasta according to package directions. Meanwhile, in a large skillet, saute sausage and mushrooms in butter. Add garlic; cook 1 minute longer.
**2.** Combine cornstarch and milk until smooth; gradually add to skillet. Bring to a boil; cook and stir for 2 minutes or until thickened. Drain pasta; add to sausage mixture. Stir in peas and cheese; cook until cheese is melted.

**FREEZE OPTION** Cool pasta; transfer to freezer containers. Freeze for up to 3 months. To use, thaw in refrigerator overnight. Place in a Dutch oven; heat through. Sprinkle with additional cheese.

**1½ CUPS** 813 cal., 50g fat (23g sat. fat), 133mg chol., 1624mg sod., 58g carb. (9g sugars, 4g fiber), 35g pro.

## GRILLED PORK & POBLANO PEPPERS

My husband and I entertain a lot in summer, and this has quickly become the most-requested dish at our parties. I usually serve it with Mexican rice and a tossed salad.
*—Donna Gay Harris, Springdale, AR*

**Takes:** 30 min. • **Makes:** 6 servings

- 3 large poblano peppers
- 1½ cups shredded Monterey Jack cheese
- 4½ tsp. chili powder
- 1½ tsp. onion powder
- 1½ tsp. ground cumin
- ½ tsp. garlic powder
- ¼ tsp. salt
- ⅛ tsp. aniseed, ground
- ⅛ tsp. cayenne pepper
- 2 pork tenderloins (about 1 lb. each)

1. Cut each pepper in half and remove the seeds. Stuff peppers with cheese.
2. Combine the seasonings; rub over the pork. Grill pork, covered, over medium-hot heat until a thermometer reads 145°, about 15 minutes. Place peppers over indirect heat; cook until peppers are tender and cheese is melted, 8-10 minutes.

**NOTE** Wear disposable gloves when cutting hot peppers; the oils can burn skin. Avoid touching your face.

**3 OZ. COOKED PORK WITH ½ PEPPER** 304 cal., 14g fat (7g sat. fat), 110mg chol., 389mg sod., 5g carb. (2g sugars, 2g fiber), 38g pro.

## BLT QUINOA BOWLS

I absolutely love a BLT with sliced avocado and an egg. Recently, I've been trying out grain bowls, and I thought the flavors of my favorite sandwich would work really well. My family agreed!
*—Elisabeth Larsen, Pleasant Grove, UT*

**Prep:** 15 min. • **Cook:** 20 min.
**Makes:** 4 servings

- 1 cup quinoa, rinsed
- 4 Tbsp. olive oil, divided
- 2 Tbsp. minced fresh basil
- 2 Tbsp. white wine vinegar, divided
- 1 Tbsp. lemon juice
- 4 large eggs
- 8 oz. cherry tomatoes
- 3 cups fresh arugula
- 1 small ripe avocado, peeled and sliced
- 4 bacon strips, cooked and crumbled

1. Prepare quinoa according to package directions. Combine 3 Tbsp. olive oil, basil, 1 Tbsp. vinegar and lemon juice. Add to cooked quinoa; stir to combine.

2. Place 2-3 in. water in a large skillet with a high side; add remaining 1 Tbsp. vinegar. Bring to a boil; adjust heat to maintain a gentle simmer. Break cold eggs, 1 at a time, into a small cup; holding cup close to surface of water, slip egg into water. Cook, uncovered, until egg whites are completely set and yolks begin to thicken but are not hard, 3-5 minutes. Using a slotted spoon, lift eggs out of water. Keep warm.

3. In a large skillet, heat remaining 1 Tbsp. oil over medium heat. Cook tomatoes until they begin to release their juices, 8-10 minutes. Add arugula; cook and stir just until wilted, 1-2 minutes.

4. To serve, divide the quinoa among 4 bowls. Add tomatoes, arugula, avocado slices and crumbled bacon. Top each with a poached egg.

**1 SERVING** 446 cal., 28g fat (5g sat. fat), 194mg chol., 228mg sod., 33g carb. (2g sugars, 6g fiber), 17g pro.

## GARLIC TOAST PIZZAS

Between working full time, going to school and raising three children, finding time-saving recipes that my family actually enjoys is one of my biggest challenges. These quick little pizzas pack a huge amount of flavor.
*—Amy Grim, Chillicothe, OH*

**Takes:** 15 min. • **Makes:** 8 pieces

- 1 pkg. (11¼ oz.) frozen garlic Texas toast
- ½ cup pizza sauce
- 1 pkg. (3½ oz.) sliced regular or turkey pepperoni
- 2 cups shredded part-skim mozzarella cheese

1. Preheat oven to 425°. Place Texas toast in a 15x10x1-in. baking pan. Bake for 5 minutes.
2. Spread toast with pizza sauce; top with pepperoni and cheese. Bake until cheese is melted, 4-5 minutes longer.

**1 PIECE** 281 cal., 20g fat (8g sat. fat), 58mg chol., 610mg sod., 14g carb. (3g sugars, 1g fiber), 12g pro.

## MAMA'S SPAGHETTI PIE

This savory pie for two has a simple pasta crust and satisfying Italian filling. It freezes well before baking, too.
*—Kathleen Williams, Leesburg, FL*

**Prep:** 20 min. • **Bake:** 20 min.
**Makes:** 2 servings

- 3 oz. uncooked spaghetti or angel hair pasta
- 1 large egg, beaten
- ¼ cup grated Parmesan cheese
- ⅓ lb. bulk pork sausage
- ¼ cup chopped onion
- ½ cup Italian tomato sauce
- ⅓ cup sour cream
- ½ tsp. Italian seasoning
- ½ cup shredded part-skim mozzarella cheese

1. Cook spaghetti according to package directions; drain. In a small bowl, combine the pasta, egg and Parmesan cheese. Press onto bottom and up the side of a 7-in. pie plate or shallow 2-cup round baking dish coated with cooking spray.
2. Crumble sausage into a small skillet; add onion. Cook over medium heat until meat is no longer pink; drain. Stir in the tomato sauce, sour cream and Italian seasoning. Spoon into crust.
3. Bake, uncovered, at 350° for 15-20 minutes or until heated through. Sprinkle with mozzarella; bake 2-3 minutes longer or until cheese is melted. Serve immediately.

**1 PIECE** 511 cal., 19g fat (9g sat. fat), 176mg chol., 1139mg sod., 47g carb. (7g sugars, 2g fiber), 34g pro.

## HOISIN PORK TENDERLOIN

Ramen noodles graduate from college-casual when served with saucy pork tenderloin. Our guests appreciate sitting down to this Asian-style meal.
*—Connie Keller, Lake Ozark, MO*

**Takes:** 30 min. • **Makes:** 4 servings

- ⅓ cup hoisin sauce
- 3 Tbsp. reduced-sodium soy sauce
- 3 Tbsp. sugar
- 3 garlic cloves, minced
- Dash crushed red pepper flakes
- 1 pork tenderloin (1 lb.)
- ¼ cup water
- 2 Tbsp. butter
- 2 pkg. (3 oz. each) ramen noodles or 2 cups hot cooked rice
- Sliced green onions

1. Preheat oven to 475°. Off the heat, mix first 5 ingredients in a small saucepan. Place tenderloin on a greased rack set in a foil-lined 15x10x1-in. pan; brush with ¼ cup hoisin mixture. Roast until a thermometer reads 145°, 15-20 minutes.
2. Stir water into remaining hoisin mixture; bring to a boil. Reduce heat; simmer, uncovered, to allow flavors to blend, about 5 minutes, stirring occasionally. Remove from heat; stir in butter. Keep warm.
3. Remove pork from oven; let stand for 5 minutes before slicing. Cook noodles according to package directions, omitting seasoning packets; drain. Serve with pork; top with sauce and green onions.

**3 OZ. COOKED PORK WITH ½ CUP NOODLES AND 2 TBSP. SAUCE**
458 cal., 17g fat (9g sat. fat), 80mg chol., 1010mg sod., 45g carb. (15g sugars, 1g fiber), 28g pro.

## TACO PORK CHOPS

You'll love these zesty pork chops. A short ingredient list makes them perfect for a weeknight. These tender, saucy chops are just right for the kids.
*—Fay Baswell, Lodi, CA*

**Takes:** 20 min. • **Makes:** 4 servings

- 4 boneless pork loin chops (6 oz. each)
- 1 Tbsp. canola oil
- 1 can (8 oz.) tomato sauce
- 1 cup water, divided
- 1 medium onion, chopped
- 1 envelope taco seasoning
- 2 Tbsp. all-purpose flour

1. In a large skillet, cook chops in oil over medium heat for 2-3 minutes on each side or until lightly browned. In a small bowl, combine the tomato sauce, ¾ cup water, onion and taco seasoning. Pour over pork and bring to a boil. Reduce heat; cover and simmer for 4-5 minutes or until a thermometer reads 145°. Let meat stand 5 minutes before serving.
2. Remove pork to a serving plate and keep warm. Combine flour and remaining ¼ cup water until smooth. Stir into skillet. Bring to a boil; cook and stir for 2 minutes or until sauce is thickened. Serve with pork chops.

**1 SERVING** 327 cal., 13g fat (4g sat. fat), 82mg chol., 1134mg sod., 16g carb. (2g sugars, 1g fiber), 34g pro.

> **"Made this tonight for the roommates and myself, as I had everything on hand. It was awesome! Everybody said this is a keeper. Loved by all."**
> —LCATALANI, TASTEOFHOME.COM

## SMOKED SAUSAGE & VEGGIE SHEET-PAN SUPPER

This recipe is tasty, quick and easily doubled for last-minute dinner guests..
*—Judy Batson, Tampa, FL*

**Takes:** 30 min. • **Makes:** 4 servings

- 1 pkg. (13½ oz.) smoked sausage, cut into ½-in. slices
- 8 fresh Brussels sprouts, thinly sliced
- 1 large sweet onion, halved and sliced
- 1 medium yellow summer squash, halved and sliced
- 1 medium zucchini, halved and sliced
- 1 medium sweet yellow pepper, chopped
- 1 medium green pepper, chopped
- 1 medium tomato, chopped
- ¾ cup sliced fresh mushrooms
- ½ cup Greek vinaigrette

Preheat oven to 400°. Place the first 9 ingredients in a greased 15x10x1-in. baking pan. Drizzle with vinaigrette; toss to coat. Bake, uncovered, 15 minutes. Remove pan from oven; preheat broiler. Broil sausage mixture 3-4 in. from heat until vegetables are lightly browned, 3-4 minutes.

**2 CUPS** 491 cal., 37g fat (13g sat. fat), 64mg chol., 1430mg sod., 22g carb. (13g sugars, 5g fiber), 18g pro.

### DID YOU KNOW?

Dijon, a town in eastern France's famous Burgundy wine-growing region, is the home of Dijon mustard. Mustard is commonly grown as a cover crop among grape vines. The plants attract beneficial insects and give nutrients back to the soil. And the scores of tiny mustard seeds mean the crop replants itself year after year. Dijon mustard contains white wine instead of vinegar.

## PORK TENDERLOIN DIANE

We have pork at least once a week, and this is one dish we especially enjoy. The moist, tender medallions are served up in a savory sauce—a combination that's irresistible. This recipe is also nice for busy days because it's so quick and easy to prepare.
*—Janie Thorpe, Tullahoma, TN*

**Takes:** 20 min. • **Makes:** 4 servings

- 1 pork tenderloin (about 1 lb.)
- 1 Tbsp. lemon-pepper seasoning
- 2 Tbsp. butter
- 2 Tbsp. lemon juice
- 1 tsp. Worcestershire sauce
- 1 tsp. Dijon mustard
- Chopped fresh parsley, optional

1. Cut tenderloin into 8 pieces; place each piece between 2 sheets of waxed paper and flatten to ½-in. thickness. Sprinkle with lemon-pepper seasoning.
2. In a large skillet over medium heat, melt butter; cook pork until a thermometer reads 145°, 3-4 minutes on each side. Remove to a serving platter and keep warm.
3. To the pan drippings, add lemon juice, Worcestershire sauce and mustard; heat through, stirring occasionally. Pour over pork, and sprinkle with parsley if desired.

**3 OZ. COOKED PORK** 214 cal., 14g fat (0 sat. fat), 6mg chol., 491mg sod., 1g carb. (0 sugars, 0 fiber), 18g pro.

## SPAGHETTI WITH BACON

As children, we always requested this dish for our birthday dinners. Our mother got the recipe from her grandmother. Now I pass on our tasty tradition.

*—Ruth Keogh, North St. Paul, MN*

**Prep:** 20 min. • **Bake:** 40 min.
**Makes:** 4 servings

- 8 oz. uncooked spaghetti
- ½ lb. bacon strips, chopped
- 1 medium onion, chopped
- 1 can (14½ oz.) diced tomatoes, undrained
- 1 can (8 oz.) tomato sauce
- Minced fresh parsley, optional

1. Preheat oven to 350°. Cook spaghetti according to package directions for al dente.
2. In a large skillet, cook bacon and onion over medium heat until bacon is crisp, stirring occasionally; drain. Stir in tomatoes and tomato sauce; bring to a boil.
3. Drain spaghetti; transfer to a greased 11x7-in. baking dish. Spread sauce over top. Bake, covered, until bubbly, 40-45 minutes. If desired, sprinkle with parsley.

**1 SERVING** 159 cal., 6g fat (2g sat. fat), 11mg chol., 498mg sod., 18g carb. (4g sugars, 2g fiber), 7g pro.

## BREADED PORK CUTLETS

Meat is a hard sell with my teenage daughter unless I make it look like a restaurant dish. Drizzle ranch dressing or barbecue sauce on top and this dish is a home run.
*—Donna Carney, New Lexington, OH*

**Takes:** 30 min. • **Makes:** 4 servings

- 1 pork tenderloin (1 lb.)
- ⅓ cup all-purpose flour
- ⅓ cup cornbread/muffin mix
- ½ tsp. salt
- ¼ tsp. pepper
- 1 large egg, beaten
- 4 Tbsp. canola oil
- Ranch or barbecue sauce, optional

1. Cut pork crosswise into ½-in. slices. In a shallow bowl, mix flour, cornbread mix, salt and pepper. Place egg in a separate shallow bowl. Dip pork in egg, then in flour mixture, patting to help coating adhere.
2. In a large skillet, heat 2 Tbsp. oil over medium heat. Add half of the pork; cook until a thermometer reads 145°, 3-4 minutes on each side. Drain on paper towels. Wipe skillet clean; repeat with remaining oil and pork. If desired, serve with sauce.

**3 OZ. COOKED PORK** 338 cal., 20g fat (3g sat. fat), 110mg chol., 327mg sod., 12g carb. (2g sugars, 1g fiber), 26g pro.

**COUNTRY CHICKEN BREASTS** Substitute 4 boneless skinless chicken breasts (4 oz. each) for the pork. Cook as directed until a thermometer reads 165°.

### PORK CUTLET TIPS

**Do I need to prep the pork tenderloin before slicing?** Yes—trim any connective tissue that's present. These long, tough strands will not soften during cooking.

**Can I make these in an air fryer?** You bet. Lightly spritz the meat with oil if desired, then cook at 375° until pork reaches 145°.

## PORK CHOPS WITH HONEY-BALSAMIC GLAZE

My husband is something of an expert when it comes to eating pork chops, and he says this recipe is restaurant quality.
*—Nicole Clayton, Prescott, AZ*

**Takes:** 30 min. • **Makes:** 4 servings

- 4 bone-in pork loin chops (1 in. thick and 10 oz. each)
- ½ tsp. crushed red pepper flakes
- ½ tsp. salt
- ½ tsp. pepper
- 2 Tbsp. olive oil

GLAZE

- ½ cup balsamic vinegar
- ½ cup honey
- 3 green onions, chopped
- 2 garlic cloves, minced
- 1 tsp. minced fresh rosemary or ¼ tsp. dried rosemary, crushed
- ⅛ tsp. salt
- ⅛ tsp. pepper
- ¼ cup butter, cubed

1. Sprinkle the pork chops with pepper flakes, salt and pepper. In a large skillet, heat oil over medium heat. Add pork; cook for 5-7 minutes on each side or until meat reaches desired doneness (for medium-rare, a thermometer should read 145°; medium, 160°). Remove and keep warm.

2. In the same skillet, whisk the vinegar, honey, green onions, garlic, rosemary, salt and pepper; bring to a boil. Reduce heat; simmer, uncovered, for 6-8 minutes or until slightly thickened, stirring occasionally. Remove from the heat; whisk in butter until melted. Serve with pork chops.

**1 PORK CHOP WITH 3 TBSP. SAUCE** 715 cal., 41g fat (17g sat. fat), 169mg chol., 557mg sod., 41g carb. (40g sugars, 1g fiber), 46g pro.

## SLOW-COOKER PIZZA CASSEROLE

A comforting casserole with mass appeal is just what you need when cooking for a crowd. For added convenience, it stays warm in a slow cooker.
*—Virginia Krites, Cridersville, OH*

**Prep:** 20 min. • **Cook:** 2 hours
**Makes:** 14 servings

- 1 pkg. (16 oz.) rigatoni or large tube pasta
- 1½ lbs. ground pork or beef
- 1 small onion, chopped
- 4 cups shredded part-skim mozzarella cheese
- 2 cans (15 oz. each) pizza sauce
- 1 can (10¾ oz.) condensed cream of mushroom soup, undiluted
- 1 pkg. (8 oz.) sliced pepperoni
- Chopped fresh basil or arugula, optional

1. Cook pasta according to package directions. Meanwhile, in a skillet, cook pork and onion over medium heat until meat is no longer pink; drain.
2. Drain pasta; place in a 5-qt. slow cooker. Stir in meat mixture, cheese, pizza sauce, soup and pepperoni. Cover and cook on low for 2-3 hours or until heated through. If desired, top with basil before serving.

**1 CUP** 329 cal., 19g fat (8g sat. fat), 57mg chol., 885mg sod., 16g carb. (5g sugars, 2g fiber), 22g pro.

## TUSCAN PORK

Pork tenderloin gets delightful Italian flavor from prosciutto, tomatoes and herbs. The aroma is divine as the rich and creamy sauce cooks.
*—Lorraine Caland, Shuniah, ON*

**Takes:** 30 min. • **Makes:** 2 servings

- ¾ lb. pork tenderloin, cut into 1-in. slices
- ¼ tsp. salt
- ⅛ tsp. pepper
- 1 Tbsp. butter
- 2 thin slices prosciutto or deli ham, chopped
- 2 garlic cloves, minced
- 1½ tsp. minced fresh sage or ½ tsp. dried sage leaves
- 2 Tbsp. balsamic vinegar
- ½ cup heavy whipping cream
- ¾ cup chopped plum tomatoes
- 4 fresh basil leaves, thinly sliced
- 1 tsp. grated Parmesan cheese

1. Sprinkle pork with salt and pepper. In a large skillet over medium heat, cook the pork in butter until meat reaches desired doneness (for medium-rare, a thermometer should read 145°; medium, 160°). Remove and set aside.
2. In the same skillet, saute prosciutto in the drippings until browned. Add garlic and sage; cook 1 minute longer. Add vinegar, stirring to loosen browned bits from pan.
3. Stir in cream; bring to a boil. Reduce heat; cook and stir for 1-2 minutes or until slightly thickened. Add tomatoes and pork; heat through. Sprinkle each serving with basil and cheese.

**1 SERVING** 514 cal., 36g fat (20g sat. fat), 205mg chol., 718mg sod., 8g carb. (4g sugars, 1g fiber), 40g pro.

## LEMON-CAPER PORK MEDALLIONS

Looking for an elegant but easy dinner you can put together in a twinkling for guests or unexpected visitors? These lightly breaded medallions are truly something special!
—Taste of Home *Test Kitchen*

**Takes:** 30 min. • **Makes:** 4 servings

- 1 pork tenderloin (1 lb.), cut into 12 slices
- ½ cup all-purpose flour
- ½ tsp. salt
- ¼ tsp. pepper
- 1 Tbsp. butter
- 1 Tbsp. olive oil
- 1 cup reduced-sodium chicken broth
- ¼ cup white wine or additional reduced-sodium chicken broth
- 1 garlic clove, minced
- 1 Tbsp. capers, drained
- 1 Tbsp. lemon juice
- ½ tsp. dried rosemary, crushed

1. Flatten pork slices to ¼-in. thickness. In a large shallow dish, combine the flour, salt and pepper. Add pork, a few pieces at a time, and turn to coat.
2. In a large nonstick skillet over medium heat, cook pork in butter and oil in batches until juices run clear. Remove and keep warm.
3. Add the broth, wine and garlic to the pan, stirring to loosen browned bits. Bring to a boil; cook until the liquid is reduced by half. Stir in capers, lemon juice and rosemary; heat through. Serve with pork.

**3 MEDALLIONS** 232 cal., 10g fat (4g sat. fat), 71mg chol., 589mg sod., 7g carb. (1g sugars, 0 fiber), 24g pro.

## TEST KITCHEN TIP

Arrange the sausages directly onto the pan, instead of on top of the potatoes, to ensure the potatoes cook evenly.

# POTATO & PEPPER SAUSAGE BAKE

When my family smells this dish baking in the oven, they know they are in for a treat! If you like spice, add a pinch of red pepper flakes or replace the mild Italian sausage with hot Italian sausage.

*—Ashli Claytor, Chesapeake, VA*

**Prep:** 25 min. • **Bake:** 30 min.
**Makes:** 5 servings

- 5 large Yukon Gold potatoes, peeled and cut into 1-in. cubes
- 1 large sweet orange pepper, sliced
- 1 large sweet red pepper, sliced
- 1 shallot, chopped
- 4 garlic cloves, minced
- 1 Tbsp. olive oil
- 2 tsp. paprika
- ¾ tsp. salt
- ½ tsp. dried thyme
- ½ tsp. pepper
- 1 pkg. (19 oz.) Italian sausage links
- Minced fresh thyme, optional

1. Preheat oven to 400°. Place the potatoes, sweet peppers, shallot and garlic in a greased 15x10x1-in. baking pan. Drizzle with oil. Sprinkle with seasonings; toss to coat. Spread evenly over pan, leaving room for sausage. Add sausage to pan.
2. Bake, uncovered, until a thermometer inserted in sausage reads 160° and vegetables are tender, 30-35 minutes. If desired, sprinkle with minced fresh thyme before serving.

**1 SAUSAGE LINK WITH ¾ CUP VEGETABLES** 446 cal., 26g fat (8g sat. fat), 58mg chol., 1021mg sod., 38g carb. (5g sugars, 4g fiber), 16g pro.

## FAVORITE GRILLED PORK CHOPS

I start preparing this entree the night before I plan to grill it. The fabulous marinade officially convinced my family to eat pork chops.
*—Erica Svejda, Janesville, WI*

**Prep:** 5 min. + marinating
**Grill:** 20 min. • **Makes:** 4 servings

- ½ cup Worcestershire sauce
- ¼ cup minced fresh parsley
- ¼ cup balsamic vinegar
- ¼ cup soy sauce
- 2 Tbsp. olive oil
- 1 tsp. minced garlic
- ½ tsp. pepper
- ¼ tsp. cayenne pepper
- 4 boneless pork loin chops (8 oz. each and 1 in. thick)

1. In a large bowl, combine the first 8 ingredients. Add pork chops; turn to coat. Refrigerate for 8 hours or overnight.
2. Drain pork, discarding marinade. Grill pork chops, covered, over medium heat for 10-15 minutes on each side or until a thermometer reads 145°. Let stand for 5 minutes before serving.

**1 PORK CHOP** 328 cal., 14g fat (5g sat. fat), 109mg chol., 358mg sod., 3g carb. (2g sugars, 0 fiber), 44g pro.

## POLISH KRAUT & APPLES

My family loves this hearty meal on cold winter nights. The tender apples, kraut and smoked sausage give it a heartwarming old-fashioned flavor. I like making it because the prep time is very short.
*—Caren Markee, Cary, IL*

**Prep:** 10 min. • **Cook:** 4 hours
**Makes:** 4 servings

- 1 can (14 oz.) sauerkraut, rinsed and well-drained
- 1 lb. smoked Polish sausage or kielbasa, cut up
- 3 medium tart apples, peeled and cut into eighths
- ½ cup packed brown sugar
- ½ tsp. caraway seeds, optional
- ⅛ tsp. pepper
- ¾ cup apple juice

1. Place half the sauerkraut in an ungreased 3-qt. slow cooker. Top with sausage, apples, brown sugar, caraway seeds if desired, and pepper. Top with remaining sauerkraut. Pour apple juice over all.

2. Cover and cook on low until apples are tender, 4-5 hours.

**1 CUP** 546 cal., 31g fat (12g sat. fat), 81mg chol., 1630mg sod., 52g carb. (43g sugars, 4g fiber), 15g pro.

> **"Just like my grandmother used to make! Very happy to find this recipe."**
> —KARENKEEFE, TASTEOFHOME.COM

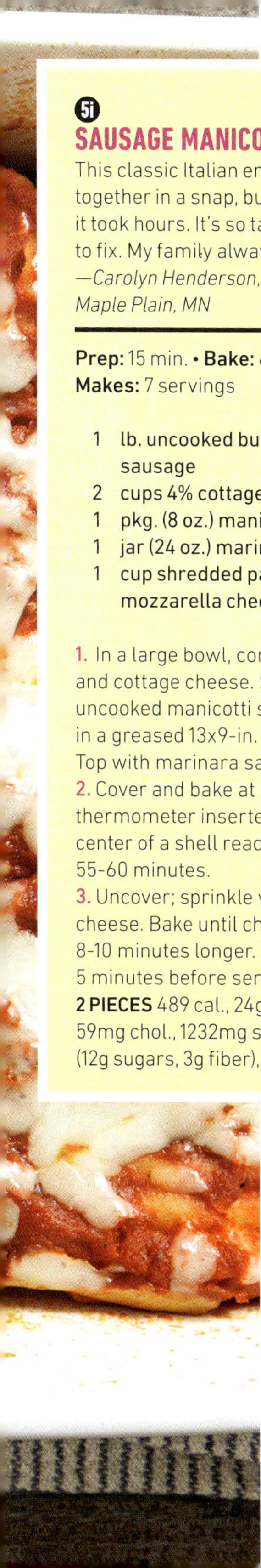

## SAUSAGE MANICOTTI

This classic Italian entree comes together in a snap, but tastes as if it took hours. It's so tasty and easy to fix. My family always enjoys it.
*—Carolyn Henderson, Maple Plain, MN*

**Prep:** 15 min. • **Bake:** 65 min.
**Makes:** 7 servings

- 1 lb. uncooked bulk Italian sausage
- 2 cups 4% cottage cheese
- 1 pkg. (8 oz.) manicotti shells
- 1 jar (24 oz.) marinara sauce
- 1 cup shredded part-skim mozzarella cheese

1. In a large bowl, combine sausage and cottage cheese. Stuff into uncooked manicotti shells. Place in a greased 13x9-in. baking dish. Top with marinara sauce.
2. Cover and bake at 350° until a thermometer inserted into the center of a shell reads 160°, 55-60 minutes.
3. Uncover; sprinkle with mozzarella cheese. Bake until cheese is melted, 8-10 minutes longer. Let stand for 5 minutes before serving.

**2 PIECES** 489 cal., 24g fat (10g sat. fat), 59mg chol., 1232mg sod., 41g carb. (12g sugars, 3g fiber), 27g pro.

## TENDER SWEET & SOUR PORK CHOPS

My best friend gave me the recipe for these delightful pork chops years ago. It's become one of my family's favorites, and I prepare it often.
*—Gina Young, Lamar, CO*

**Takes:** 25 min. • **Makes:** 6 servings

- 6 boneless pork loin chops (4 oz. each)
- 3/4 tsp. pepper
- 1/2 cup water
- 1/3 cup cider vinegar
- 1/4 cup packed brown sugar
- 2 Tbsp. reduced-sodium soy sauce
- 1 Tbsp. Worcestershire sauce
- 1 Tbsp. cornstarch
- 2 Tbsp. cold water

1. Sprinkle pork chops with pepper. In a large skillet coated with cooking spray, cook pork over medium heat until lightly browned, 4-6 minutes on each side. Remove and keep warm.
2. Add the water, vinegar, brown sugar, soy sauce and Worcestershire sauce to skillet; stir to loosen browned bits. Bring to a boil. Combine cornstarch and cold water until smooth; stir into skillet. Bring to a boil; cook and stir until thickened, about 2 minutes.
3. Return chops to the pan. Reduce heat; cover and simmer until a thermometer inserted in pork reads 145°, 4-5 minutes.

**1 PORK CHOP WITH 3 TBSP. SAUCE** 198 cal., 6g fat (2g sat. fat), 55mg chol., 265mg sod., 12g carb. (10g sugars, 0 fiber), 22g pro.

## SIMPLE MARINATED GRILLED PORK CHOPS

This marinade is so simple that I use it on all kinds of meat. For a more robust flavor, let the meat marinate in the refrigerator overnight.
*—Lori Daniels, Beverly, WV*

**Prep:** 10 min. + marinating
**Grill:** 10 min.
**Makes:** 4 servings

- ½ cup packed brown sugar
- ½ cup soy sauce
- 2 garlic cloves, minced
- ¼ tsp. pepper
- 4 bone-in pork loin chops (1 in. thick and 8 oz. each)

1. In a bowl or shallow dish, combine the brown sugar, soy sauce, garlic and pepper. Add pork chops and turn to coat. Cover and refrigerate for 8 hours or overnight.
2. Drain pork chops, discarding marinade. Grill chops on greased grill rack, covered, over medium heat or broil 4-5 in. from the heat for 4-5 minutes on each side or until meat reaches desired doneness (for medium-rare, a thermometer should read 145°; medium, 160°). Let meat stand for 5 minutes before serving.

**1 SERVING** 362 cal., 18g fat (7g sat. fat), 111mg chol., 695mg sod., 9g carb. (9g sugars, 0 fiber), 37g pro.

### PREP AHEAD

To save time, make the marinade up to 1 week ahead and refrigerate. Add the meat no more than 8 hours before grilling—longer and the acidic marinade will break down the muscle fibers, making the pork mushy.

## SPICY MAC & CHEESE

I've been working to perfect a creamy, spicy mac and cheese for years. After adding smoky bacon, jalapeno and pepper jack cheese, this is ultimate! I like to use precooked bacon when I'm pressed for time.
*—Sarah Gilbert, Beaverton, OR*

**Takes:** 30 min. • **Makes:** 6 servings

- 1½ cups uncooked cavatappi pasta or elbow macaroni
- 3 Tbsp. butter
- 3 Tbsp. all-purpose flour
- 1½ cups heavy whipping cream
- ½ cup 2% milk
- 1 tsp. Cajun seasoning
- ¼ tsp. salt
- ¼ tsp. pepper
- 2 cups shredded pepper jack cheese
- 6 bacon strips, cooked and crumbled
- 1 jalapeno pepper, seeded and chopped
- 1 cup crushed kettle-cooked potato chips or panko bread crumbs

1. Cook pasta according to package directions for al dente; drain. Preheat broiler.
2. In a 10-in. cast-iron or other ovenproof skillet, heat butter over medium heat. Stir in flour until blended; cook and stir until lightly browned, 1-2 minutes (do not burn). Gradually whisk in cream, milk, Cajun seasoning, salt and pepper. Bring to a boil, stirring constantly. Reduce heat; cook and stir until thickened, about 5 minutes. Stir in cheese until melted. Add pasta, bacon and jalapeno; cook and stir until heated through. Sprinkle chips over top.
3. Broil 3-4 in. from heat until chips are browned, about 30 seconds.

**NOTE** Wear disposable gloves when cutting hot peppers; the oils can burn skin. Avoid touching your face.

**1 CUP** 673 cal., 50g fat (28g sat. fat), 175mg chol., 705mg sod., 26g carb. (3g sugars, 1g fiber), 32g pro.

## ONE-SKILLET PORK CHOP SUPPER

My husband, Clark, and I reserve this recipe for Sundays after the grandkids have gone home and we're too tired to prepare a big meal. It's comforting and quick.
*—Kathy Thompson, Port Orange, FL*

**Prep:** 10 min. • **Cook:** 30 min.
**Makes:** 4 servings

- 1 Tbsp. butter
- 4 pork loin chops (½ in. thick and 7 oz. each)
- 3 medium red potatoes, cut into small wedges
- 3 medium carrots, cut into ½-in. slices, or 2 cups fresh baby carrots
- 1 medium onion, cut into wedges
- 1 can (10¾ oz.) condensed cream of mushroom soup, undiluted
- ½ cup water
- Optional: Cracked black pepper and chopped fresh parsley

1. In a large cast-iron or other heavy skillet, heat butter over medium heat. Brown pork chops on both sides; remove from pan, reserving drippings.
2. In same pan, saute vegetables in drippings until lightly browned. Whisk together soup and water; stir into vegetables. Bring to a boil. Reduce heat; simmer, covered, just until vegetables are tender, 15-20 minutes.
3. Add chops; cook, covered, until a thermometer inserted in pork reads 145°, 8-10 minutes. Remove from heat; let stand 5 minutes. If desired, sprinkle with pepper and parsley.

**1 SERVING** 390 cal., 15g fat (6g sat. fat), 97mg chol., 700mg sod., 28g carb. (6g sugars, 4g fiber), 33g pro.

## PASTA & BROCCOLI SAUSAGE SIMMER

I created this meal when trying to use up a large head of broccoli. My family requests it at least once a week, which is handy because we always have the ingredients.
*—Lisa Montgomery, Elmira, ON*

**Takes:** 30 min. • **Makes:** 8 servings

- 3 cups uncooked spiral pasta
- 2 lbs. smoked kielbasa or Polish sausage, cut into ¼-in. slices
- 2 medium bunches broccoli, cut into florets
- 1 cup sliced red onion
- 2 cans (14½ oz. each) diced tomatoes, undrained
- 2 Tbsp. minced fresh basil or 2 tsp. dried basil
- 2 Tbsp. minced fresh parsley or 2 tsp. dried parsley flakes
- 2 tsp. sugar

1. Cook pasta according to directions.
2. Meanwhile, in a Dutch oven, saute the sausage, broccoli and onion until broccoli is crisp-tender, 5-6 minutes.
3. Add the tomatoes, basil, parsley and sugar. Cover and simmer for 10 minutes. Drain pasta; stir into the sausage mixture.

**1 SERVING** 544 cal., 32g fat (11g sat. fat), 76mg chol., 1395mg sod., 42g carb. (9g sugars, 8g fiber), 25g pro.

GRILLED HULI HULI CHICKEN, PAGE 155

# QUICK & EASY POULTRY

## WHITE WINE GARLIC CHICKEN

This garlic chicken is terrific over brown rice or your favorite pasta. Don't forget a sprinkle of Parmesan cheese too.
*—Heather Esposito, Rome, NY*

**Takes:** 30 min. • **Makes:** 4 servings

- 4 boneless skinless chicken breast halves (6 oz. each)
- ½ tsp. salt
- ¼ tsp. pepper
- 1 Tbsp. olive oil
- 2 cups sliced baby portobello mushrooms (about 6 oz.)
- 1 medium onion, chopped
- 2 garlic cloves, minced
- ½ cup dry white wine or reduced-sodium chicken broth

1. Pound chicken breasts with a meat mallet to ½-in. thickness; sprinkle with salt and pepper. In a large skillet, heat oil over medium heat; cook chicken until no longer pink, 5-6 minutes per side. Remove from pan; keep warm.
2. Add the mushrooms and onion to pan; cook and stir over medium-high heat until tender and lightly browned, 2-3 minutes. Add garlic; cook and stir 30 seconds. Add wine; bring to a boil, stirring to loosen browned bits from pan. Cook until liquid is slightly reduced, 1-2 minutes; serve over chicken.

**1 CHICKEN BREAST HALF WITH ¼ CUP MUSHROOM MIXTURE** 243 cal., 7g fat (2g sat. fat), 94mg chol., 381mg sod., 5g carb. (2g sugars, 1g fiber), 36g pro.

## ARTICHOKE CHICKEN PESTO PIZZA

Make pizza night an upscale affair with this fun twist on the traditional pie. A prebaked crust and prepared pesto keep things quick and easy.
*—Trisha Kruse, Eagle, ID*

**Takes:** 15 min. • **Makes:** 8 servings

- 1 prebaked 12-in. pizza crust
- ½ cup prepared pesto
- 2 cups cubed cooked chicken breast
- 2 jars (6½ oz. each) marinated artichoke hearts, drained
- 2 cups shredded part-skim mozzarella cheese
- Optional: Grated Parmesan cheese and minced fresh basil

Preheat oven to 425°. Place crust on an ungreased 12-in. pizza pan. Spread with pesto. Arrange chicken and artichokes over top; sprinkle with cheese. Bake until golden brown, 10-12 minutes. If desired, top with Parmesan cheese and basil.

**1 PIECE** 381 cal., 20g fat (6g sat. fat), 45mg chol., 880mg sod., 28g carb. (2g sugars, 4g fiber), 23g pro.

"Fantastic recipe. So easy to put together and yummy. The best part is, I always have the ingredients ready. I buy the ready-made pesto from my market's salad bar."
—FERRYAL, TASTEOFHOME.COM

## ITALIAN SAUSAGE-STUFFED ZUCCHINI

I've always had to be creative when getting my family to eat vegetables, so I decided to make stuffed zucchini using the pizza flavors that everyone loves. It worked! We like to include sausage for a main dish but it could be a meatless side too.
*—Donna Marie Ryan, Topsfield, MA*

**Prep:** 35 min. • **Bake:** 20 min.
**Makes:** 6 servings

- 6 medium zucchini (about 8 oz. each)
- 1 lb. Italian turkey sausage links, casings removed
- 2 medium tomatoes, seeded and chopped
- 1 cup panko bread crumbs
- ⅓ cup grated Parmesan cheese
- ⅓ cup minced fresh parsley
- 2 Tbsp. minced fresh oregano or 2 tsp. dried oregano
- 2 Tbsp. minced fresh basil or 2 tsp. dried basil
- ¼ tsp. pepper
- ¾ cup shredded part-skim mozzarella cheese
- Additional minced fresh parsley, optional

1. Preheat oven to 350°. Cut each zucchini lengthwise in half. Scoop out flesh, leaving a ¼-in. shell; chop flesh. Place zucchini shells in a large microwave-safe dish. In batches, microwave, covered, on high for 2-3 minutes or until crisp-tender.
2. In a large skillet, cook sausage and zucchini flesh over medium heat 6-8 minutes or until sausage is no longer pink, breaking sausage into crumbles; drain. Stir in tomatoes, bread crumbs, Parmesan cheese, herbs and pepper. Spoon into zucchini shells.
3. Place in 2 ungreased 13x9-in. baking dishes. Bake, covered, 15-20 minutes or until zucchini is tender. Sprinkle with mozzarella cheese. Bake, uncovered, 5-8 minutes longer or until cheese is melted. Sprinkle with additional parsley if desired.

**2 STUFFED ZUCCHINI HALVES** 206 cal., 9g fat (3g sat. fat), 39mg chol., 485mg sod., 16g carb. (5g sugars, 3g fiber), 17g pro.

## CHERRY CHICKEN CROISSANTS

I had a similar chicken salad at a restaurant and created my own version. It may seem like an odd combination, but the ingredients work really well together. My children love it, and it only takes a few minutes to cut everything up—so easy!

*—Katrina Gladdish, Grawn, MI*

**Takes:** 10 min. • **Makes:** 6 servings

- 2 cups diced cooked chicken
- 3 celery ribs, chopped
- ½ cup dried cherries
- ½ cup chopped walnuts
- ½ cup halved green grapes
- 8 bacon strips, cooked and crumbled
- ½ cup mayonnaise
- 6 croissants, split

In a large bowl, combine the first 7 ingredients. Serve on croissants.

**1 SANDWICH** 616 cal., 39g fat (12g sat. fat), 92mg chol., 613mg sod., 41g carb. (18g sugars, 3g fiber), 24g pro.

## SHEET-PAN SAUSAGE & POTATO DINNER

Dinner doesn't get much easier. This tasty sheet-pan sausage and potatoes recipe relies on simple ingredients for an all-in-one meal.
*—Laurie Sledge, Brandon, MS*

**Prep:** 20 min. • **Bake:** 30 min.
**Makes:** 4 servings

- 1 lb. potatoes, cut into ½-in. pieces
- 1 pkg. (12 oz.) fully cooked andouille chicken sausage links or flavor of your choice, cut into 1-in. pieces
- 2 cups fresh broccoli florets
- 1 medium red onion, cut into wedges
- 1 medium sweet orange pepper, cut into 1-in. pieces
- 1 Tbsp. olive oil
- ¼ tsp. pepper
- ½ tsp. salt

**1.** Preheat oven to 400°. In a large bowl, combine potatoes, sausage, broccoli, onion and orange pepper. Add oil, pepper and salt; toss to coat.
**2.** Transfer to a 15x10x1-in. baking pan coated with cooking spray. Roast until vegetables are tender, stirring occasionally, 30-35 minutes.

**1½ CUPS** 256 cal., 11g fat (3g sat. fat), 65mg chol., 789mg sod., 24g carb. (5g sugars, 3g fiber), 18g pro.

## COPYCAT FRIED CHICKEN SANDWICH

After trying chicken sandwiches at all the major fast-food chains, I decided to come up with my own version. I know everyone says theirs is better than the original, but mine really is.
*—Ralph Jones, San Diego, CA*

**Prep:** 15 min. + marinating
**Cook:** 20 min./batch • **Makes:** 6 servings

- 3 boneless skinless chicken breast halves (6 oz. each)
- ¾ cup buttermilk
- 2 tsp. hot pepper sauce
- 2 large eggs, beaten
- 2 cups all-purpose flour
- 1 Tbsp. plus 1 tsp. garlic powder
- 1 Tbsp. each onion powder and paprika
- 2 tsp. pepper
- 1 tsp. salt
- ⅓ cup canola oil
- 6 brioche hamburger buns, split
- Optional toppings: Sliced tomatoes, pickle slices, onion slices and Chick-fil-A sauce

1. Cut each chicken breast horizontally in half; place in a large bowl. Add the buttermilk and hot sauce; turn to coat. Refrigerate, covered, for 8 hours or overnight.
2. Preheat air fryer to 400°. Stir eggs into chicken mixture. In a shallow dish, whisk flour, garlic powder, onion powder, paprika, pepper and salt. Remove the chicken from buttermilk mixture. Dredge chicken in flour mixture, firmly patting to help coating adhere. Repeat, dipping chicken again into buttermilk mixture and then dredging in flour mixture.
3. Place chicken on a wire rack over a baking sheet. Refrigerate, uncovered, for 30 minutes. Using a pastry brush, lightly dab both sides of chicken with oil until no dry breading remains.
4. In batches, arrange the chicken in a single layer on a greased tray in air-fryer basket. Cook until a thermometer reads 165° and coating is golden brown and crispy, 7-8 minutes on each side. Remove chicken; keep warm. Toast buns in air fryer until golden brown, 2-3 minutes. Top bun bottoms with chicken. Top as desired; replace bun tops.

**1 SANDWICH** 538 cal., 18g fat (3g sat. fat), 136mg chol., 778mg sod., 63g carb. (8g sugars, 4g fiber), 30g pro.

## GOAT CHEESE-STUFFED CHICKEN WITH APRICOT GLAZE

My original version of this recipe used several tablespoons of butter versus the tablespoon of oil. With a few more tweaks, this special entree for two is now under 350 calories per serving.
—*David Dahlman, Chatsworth, CA*

**Prep:** 20 min. • **Cook:** 20 min.
**Makes:** 2 servings

- 2 boneless skinless chicken breast halves (6 oz. each)
- 1/4 tsp. salt
- 1/4 tsp. pepper
- 2 Tbsp. goat cheese
- 2 Tbsp. part-skim ricotta cheese
- 4 Tbsp. chopped shallots, divided
- 1 tsp. olive oil
- 2/3 cup reduced-sodium chicken broth
- 2 Tbsp. apricot spreadable fruit
- 1 Tbsp. lemon juice
- 1 tsp. spicy brown mustard
- 1 tsp. minced fresh parsley

1. Flatten chicken to 1/4-in. thickness; sprinkle with salt and pepper. Combine the goat cheese, ricotta and 1 Tbsp. shallots; spread over the center of each chicken breast. Roll up and secure with toothpicks.
2. In a small nonstick skillet, brown chicken in oil on all sides. Remove and keep warm.
3. In the same skillet, saute remaining shallots until tender. Stir in the broth, spreadable fruit, lemon juice and mustard. Bring to a boil; cook until liquid is reduced by half.
4. Return chicken to the pan; cook, covered until a thermometer inserted in chicken reads 165°, 6-7 minutes. Discard toothpicks. Serve chicken with cooking liquid. Sprinkle with parsley.

**1 SERVING** 340 cal., 12g fat (5g sat. fat), 110mg chol., 695mg sod., 16g carb. (10g sugars, 0 fiber), 41g pro.

## TURKEY TOSTADAS

Have a delicious fiesta in moments with this dish. Made with tostadas, but just as tasty with tortillas, this simple Mexican classic will be requested by your family again and again!
—Taste of Home *Test Kitchen*

**Takes:** 25 min. • **Makes:** 6 servings

- 1 pkg. (20 oz.) lean ground turkey
- 1/2 cup chopped onion
- 1/2 cup chopped green pepper
- 1 tsp. canola oil
- 3/4 cup water
- 1 envelope taco seasoning
- 1 can (15 1/2 oz.) hominy, rinsed and drained
- 12 tostada shells
- 3 cups shredded lettuce
- 1 cup shredded Mexican cheese blend
- 1 cup chopped tomato
- 1 cup cubed avocado

1. In a large skillet, cook the turkey, onion and green pepper in oil over medium heat for 5 minutes or until meat is no longer pink; drain. Stir in the water, taco seasoning and hominy. Bring to a boil. Reduce heat; simmer, uncovered, for 5 minutes or until heated through.
2. On each tostada shell, layer the lettuce, about 1/3 cup turkey mixture, cheese, tomato and avocado.

**2 TOSTADAS** 432 cal., 23g fat (8g sat. fat), 91mg chol., 1185mg sod., 32g carb. (2g sugars, 5g fiber), 24g pro.

## TURKEY CUTLETS WITH PAN GRAVY

Using cutlets or any boneless meat speeds up cooking time for this quick entree. You can use thin boneless, skinless chicken breast as well.
*—Margaret Wilson, San Bernardino, CA*

**Takes:** 20 min. • **Makes:** 4 servings

- 1 pkg. (20 oz.) turkey breast tenderloins
- 1 tsp. poultry seasoning
- ¼ tsp. seasoned salt
- ¼ tsp. pepper, divided
- 2 Tbsp. canola oil
- 2 Tbsp. butter
- ¼ cup all-purpose flour
- 2 cups chicken broth

1. Cut tenderloins crosswise into 1-in. slices; flatten slices with a meat mallet to ½-in. thickness. Mix the poultry seasoning, seasoned salt and ⅛ tsp. pepper; sprinkle over turkey.
2. In a large skillet, heat oil over medium-high heat. Add turkey in batches; cook until no longer pink, 2-3 minutes per side. Remove from pan; keep warm.
3. In same pan, melt butter over medium heat; stir in flour until smooth. Gradually stir in broth. Bring to a boil; cook and stir until thickened, about 2 minutes. Sprinkle with remaining ⅛ tsp. pepper. Serve with turkey.

**1 SERVING** 292 cal., 15g fat (5g sat. fat), 89mg chol., 772mg sod., 7g carb. (1g sugars, 0 fiber), 31g pro.

## SLOW-COOKED TURKEY STROGANOFF

I have been making this dish for 30-plus years. Our family loves turkey and I make a variety of turkey dishes, but this is our favorite. I love it because I can put it in my slow cooker before I leave for work and come home to a hot, delicious dinner.
*—Cynthia Adams, Tracy, CA*

**Prep:** 20 min. • **Cook:** 6 hours
**Makes:** 6 servings

- 4 turkey thighs (about 4 lbs.)
- 1 large onion, halved and thinly sliced
- 1 can (10¾ oz.) condensed cream of celery soup, undiluted
- ⅓ cup water
- 3 garlic cloves, minced
- 2 tsp. dried tarragon
- ½ tsp. salt
- ½ tsp. pepper
- ½ cup sour cream
- Hot cooked egg noodles

1. Place turkey and onion in a 5-qt. slow cooker. In a large bowl, whisk soup, water, garlic, tarragon, salt and pepper until blended; pour over top. Cook, covered, on low until meat is tender, 6-8 hours.
2. Remove turkey from slow cooker. When cool enough to handle, remove meat from bones; discard bones. Shred meat with 2 forks. Whisk the sour cream into cooking juices; return meat to slow cooker. Serve with noodles.

**1 CUP** 332 cal., 12g fat (5g sat. fat), 195mg chol., 598mg sod., 8g carb. (2g sugars, 2g fiber), 46g pro.

## JUICY AIR-FRYER CORNISH HENS

This easy air-fryer recipe will help you put a gourmet meal on the table with little fuss. It's just perfect for weeknights!
*—Katrina Adams, Mount Olive, AL*

**Prep:** 15 min.
**Cook:** 20 min. + standing
**Makes:** 2 servings

- 4 tsp. salt-free seasoning blend
- 4 tsp. everything seasoning blend
- 2 tsp. lemon-pepper seasoning
- 2 tsp. paprika
- 1 tsp. salt
- ¼ tsp. pepper
- 2 Cornish game hens (20-24 oz. each)
- 2 Tbsp. olive oil

Combine the first 6 ingredients. Tuck wings under hens; tie legs together. Rub oil over hens; sprinkle with seasonings. Place the hens, breast side down, on a greased tray in air-fryer basket. Cook at 375° until a thermometer inserted in thickest part of thigh reads 170°-175°, 18-20 minutes, turning once. (Cover loosely with foil if hens brown too quickly.) Let stand 10 minutes before carving.

**1 HEN** 860 cal., 63g fat (15g sat. fat), 351mg chol., 2313mg sod., 9g carb. (0 sugars, 1g fiber), 60g pro.

### TEST KITCHEN TIP

Cornish hens are young, small chickens, usually 4-5 weeks old when harvested. Their petite size makes them popular for festive occasions, because each bird serves just 1 or 2 people.

## SLOW-COOKER ROAST CHICKEN

Roast chicken is easy to make in a slow cooker. We save the shredded chicken to use throughout the week.
*—Courtney Stultz, Weir, KS*

**Prep:** 20 min. • **Cook:** 4 hours + standing
**Makes:** 6 servings

- 2 medium carrots, cut into 1-in. pieces
- 1 medium onion, cut into 1-in. pieces
- 2 garlic cloves, minced
- 2 tsp. olive oil
- 1 tsp. dried parsley flakes
- 1 tsp. pepper
- ¾ tsp. salt
- ½ tsp. dried oregano
- ½ tsp. rubbed sage
- ½ tsp. chili powder
- 1 broiler/fryer chicken (4 to 5 lbs.)

1. Place carrots and onion in a 6-qt. slow cooker. In a small bowl, mix garlic and oil. In another bowl, mix dry seasonings.
2. Tuck wings under the chicken; tie drumsticks together. With fingers, carefully loosen skin from chicken breast; rub garlic mixture under the skin. Secure skin to underside of breast with toothpicks.
3. Place chicken in slow cooker over carrots and onion, breast side up; sprinkle with seasoning mixture. Cook, covered, on low 4-5 hours or until a thermometer inserted in thigh reads at least 170°.
4. Remove chicken from slow cooker; tent with foil. Discard vegetables. Let chicken stand 15 minutes before carving.

**FREEZE OPTION** Cool chicken pieces and any juices. Freeze in freezer containers. To use, partially thaw in refrigerator overnight. Heat through slowly in a covered skillet until a thermometer inserted in chicken reads 165°, stirring occasionally; add broth or water if necessary.

**5 OZ. COOKED CHICKEN** 408 cal., 24g fat (6g sat. fat), 139mg chol., 422mg sod., 1g carb. (0 sugars, 0 fiber), 44g pro.

## BUFFALO CHICKEN WRAPS TIPS

**Can I use something other than chicken breast?** Yes—use uncooked chicken tenders (no slicing). Or toss heated breaded chicken tenders with hot sauce, or use rotisserie chicken.

**How do I reheat for a Buffalo wrap?** Warm the chicken only—in a microwave, skillet, oven, or air fryer—then add a little fresh sauce and assemble wraps in warmed tortillas.

## SPICY BUFFALO CHICKEN WRAPS

This recipe has a real kick and is one of my husband's favorites. It's ready in a flash, easily doubled, and the closest thing to restaurant Buffalo wings I've ever tasted in a light version.
*—Jennifer Beck, Meridian, ID*

**Takes:** 25 min. • **Makes:** 2 servings

- ½ lb. boneless skinless chicken breast, cubed
- ½ tsp. canola oil
- 2 Tbsp. Louisiana-style hot sauce
- 1 cup shredded lettuce
- 2 flour tortillas (6 in.), warmed
- 2 tsp. reduced-fat ranch salad dressing
- 2 Tbsp. crumbled blue cheese

1. In a large nonstick skillet, cook chicken in oil over medium heat for 6 minutes; drain. Stir in hot sauce. Bring to a boil. Reduce heat; simmer, uncovered, until sauce is thickened and chicken is no longer pink, 3-5 minutes.
2. Place lettuce on tortillas; drizzle with ranch dressing. Top with the chicken mixture and blue cheese; roll up.

**1 WRAP** 273 cal., 11g fat (3g sat. fat), 70mg chol., 453mg sod., 15g carb. (1g sugars, 1g fiber), 28g pro.

## CHICKEN BROCCOLI CASSEROLE

Broccoli is a popular vegetable in our home. This is one dish that always gets rave reviews. Serve it for dinner or even brunch.
*—Colleen Lewis, Cottonwood, AZ*

**Prep:** 10 min. • **Bake:** 25 min.
**Makes:** 6 servings

- 3 cups fresh broccoli florets
- 2 cups cubed cooked chicken or turkey
- 1 can (10¾ oz.) condensed cream of chicken soup, undiluted
- ½ cup mayonnaise
- ½ cup grated Parmesan cheese
- ½ tsp. curry powder
- 1 cup cubed bread
- 2 Tbsp. butter, melted

**1.** Preheat oven to 350°. In a small saucepan, cook broccoli in water until crisp-tender; drain. Place broccoli in a greased 11x7-in. baking dish; set aside.

**2.** Combine the chicken, soup, mayonnaise, cheese and curry powder; spoon over broccoli. Top with bread cubes and butter. Bake, uncovered, until heated through, 25-30 minutes.

**1 SERVING** 347 cal., 26g fat (8g sat. fat), 63mg chol., 691mg sod., 10g carb. (1g sugars, 2g fiber), 18g pro.

## SAUSAGE-STUFFED BUTTERNUT SQUASH

Load butternut squash shells with an Italian turkey sausage and squash mixture for a quick and easy meal. Even better, it's surprisingly low in calories.
*—Katia Slinger, West Jordan, UT*

---

**Takes:** 30 min. • **Makes:** 4 servings

- 1 medium butternut squash (about 3 lbs.)
- 1 lb. Italian turkey sausage links, casings removed
- 1 medium onion, finely chopped
- 4 garlic cloves, minced
- ½ cup shredded Italian cheese blend
- Crushed red pepper flakes, optional

1. Preheat broiler. Cut squash lengthwise in half; discard seeds. Place squash in a large microwave-safe dish, cut side down; add ½ in. water. Microwave, covered, on high 20-25 minutes or until soft. Cool slightly.
2. Meanwhile, in a large nonstick skillet, cook and crumble sausage with onion over medium-high heat until meat is no longer pink, 5-7 minutes. Add garlic; cook and stir 1 minute.
3. Leaving ½-in.-thick shells, scoop flesh from squash and stir it into sausage mixture. Place squash shells on a baking sheet; fill with sausage mixture. Sprinkle with cheese.
4. Broil 4-5 in. from heat until cheese is melted, 1-2 minutes. If desired, sprinkle with pepper flakes. To serve, cut each half into 2 portions.

**1 SERVING** 325 cal., 10g fat (4g sat. fat), 52mg chol., 587mg sod., 44g carb. (10g sugars, 12g fiber), 19g pro.

### HEALTH TIP

Butternut squash is an excellent source of vitamin A in the form of beta-carotene. It's important for normal vision and a healthy immune system, and it helps the heart, lungs and kidneys function properly.

## SHEET-PAN PINEAPPLE CHICKEN FAJITAS

For our fajitas, I combine chicken and pineapple for a different flavor. These fajitas are more on the sweet side, but my family loves them!
*—Nancy Heishman, Las Vegas, NV*

**Prep:** 20 min. • **Cook:** 20 min.
**Makes:** 6 servings

- 2 Tbsp. coconut oil, melted
- 3 tsp. chili powder
- 2 tsp. ground cumin
- 1 tsp. garlic powder
- ¾ tsp. kosher salt
- 1½ lbs. chicken tenderloins, halved lengthwise
- 1 large sweet or red onion, halved and sliced (about 2 cups)
- 1 large sweet red pepper, cut into ½-in. strips
- 1 large green pepper, cut into ½-in. strips
- 1 Tbsp. minced seeded jalapeno pepper
- 2 cans (8 oz. each) unsweetened pineapple tidbits, drained
- 2 Tbsp. honey
- 2 Tbsp. lime juice
- 12 corn tortillas (6 in.), warmed
- Optional: Pico de gallo, sour cream, shredded Mexican cheese blend, sliced avocado and lime wedges

1. Preheat oven to 425°. In a large bowl, mix first 5 ingredients; stir in chicken. Add onion, peppers, pineapple, honey and lime juice; toss to combine. Spread evenly in 2 greased 15x10x1-in. baking pans.
2. Roast 10 minutes, rotating the pans halfway through cooking. Remove pans from oven; preheat broiler.
3. Broil chicken mixture, 1 pan at a time, 3-4 in. from heat until vegetables are lightly browned and chicken is no longer pink, 3-5 minutes. Serve in tortillas, with toppings and lime wedges as desired.

**NOTE** Wear disposable gloves when cutting hot peppers; the oils can burn skin. Avoid touching your face.

**2 FAJITAS** 359 cal., 8g fat (4g sat. fat), 56mg chol., 372mg sod., 45g carb. (19g sugars, 6g fiber), 31g pro.

## SLOW-COOKED TURKEY SLOPPY JOES

This tangy sandwich filling is so easy to prepare in the slow cooker, and it goes over well at gatherings large and small. I often take it to potlucks, and I'm always asked what my secret ingredient is.
*—Marylou LaRue, Freeland, MI*

**Prep:** 15 min. • **Cook:** 4 hours
**Makes:** 8 servings

- 1 lb. lean ground turkey
- 1 small onion, chopped
- ½ cup chopped celery
- ¼ cup chopped green pepper
- 1 can (10¾ oz.) reduced-sodium condensed tomato soup, undiluted
- ½ cup ketchup
- 2 Tbsp. prepared mustard
- 1 Tbsp. brown sugar
- ¼ tsp. pepper
- 8 hamburger buns, split
- Pickle slices, optional

1. In a large skillet coated with cooking spray, cook turkey, onion, celery and green pepper over medium heat until meat is no longer pink, breaking it into crumbles; drain. Stir in soup, ketchup, mustard, brown sugar and pepper.
2. Transfer to a 3-qt. slow cooker. Cover and cook on low to allow flavors to blend, about 4 hours. Serve on buns, with pickles if desired.

**1 SANDWICH** 264 cal., 7g fat (2g sat. fat), 39mg chol., 614mg sod., 34g carb. (13g sugars, 2g fiber), 16g pro.

## COUNTRY ROASTED CHICKEN

This easy home-style chicken gets wonderful flavor from the celery, onion and parsley tucked inside. It's my family's favorite. When my daughter was away, she even called to ask for the recipe so she could make it herself.

*—Judy Page, Edenville, MI*

**Prep:** 15 min.
**Bake:** 65 min. + standing
**Makes:** 4 servings

- 1 broiler/fryer chicken (3 lbs.)
- ½ tsp. dried thyme
- 2 tsp. salt, divided
- 1 large onion, cut into eighths
- 2 celery ribs with leaves, cut into 4-in. pieces
- 4 fresh parsley sprigs
- 8 small red potatoes
- ¼ cup chicken broth
- Chopped parsley, optional

1. Preheat oven to 375°. Sprinkle inside of chicken with thyme and 1 tsp. salt. Stuff chicken with onion, celery and parsley sprigs. Place in a greased Dutch oven.
2. Cover and bake for 30 minutes. Sprinkle remaining 1 tsp. salt over chicken. Add potatoes and broth to pan. Bake, uncovered, 25 minutes longer.
3. Increase oven temperature to 400°. Bake, uncovered, until the potatoes are tender and a thermometer inserted into thickest part of thigh reads 170°-175°, 10-15 minutes. Remove chicken from oven; tent with foil. Let stand 15 minutes before carving. If desired, sprinkle with chopped parsley.

**1 SERVING** 525 cal., 25g fat (7g sat. fat), 157mg chol., 1399mg sod., 19g carb. (3g sugars, 3g fiber), 52g pro.

**"A flavorful, tender, juicy roasted chicken. Beautiful. Made chicken salad with the leftovers."**

—GOODEATS3, TASTEOFHOME.COM

## SLOW-COOKED CHICKEN A LA KING

When I know I'll be having a busy day with little time to prepare a meal, I use my slow cooker to make chicken a la king. It smells so good while it's cooking.
*—Eleanor Mielke, Snohomish, WA*

**Prep:** 10 min. • **Cook:** 7½ hours
**Makes:** 6 servings

- 1 can (10¾ oz.) reduced-fat reduced-sodium condensed cream of chicken soup, undiluted
- 3 Tbsp. all-purpose flour
- ¼ tsp. pepper
- Dash cayenne pepper
- 1 lb. boneless skinless chicken breasts, cubed
- 1 celery rib, chopped
- ½ cup chopped green pepper
- ¼ cup chopped onion
- 1 pkg. (10 oz.) frozen peas, thawed
- 2 Tbsp. diced pimientos, drained
- Hot cooked rice

1. In a 3-qt. slow cooker, combine soup, flour, pepper and cayenne until smooth. Stir in chicken, celery, green pepper and onion.
2. Cover and cook on low for 7-8 hours or until meat is no longer pink. Stir in peas and pimientos. Cook 30 minutes longer or until heated through. Serve with rice.

**1 CUP CHICKEN MIXTURE** 174 cal., 3g fat (1g sat. fat), 44mg chol., 268mg sod., 16g carb. (6g sugars, 3g fiber), 19g pro.

## CRUNCHY ASIAN CHICKEN SALAD

I love this crunchy, citrusy salad. Once I even made my husband drive an hour to the nearest Applebee's restaurant just so I could eat it! That's when I decided to come up with my own version that's a great stand-in for the original. I'm happy and my husband is too!
*—Mandy Bird, Tremonton, UT*

**Takes:** 25 min. • **Makes:** 4 servings

- 4 frozen breaded chicken tenders (about 8 oz.)
- ⅓ cup mayonnaise
- 3 Tbsp. honey
- 2 Tbsp. rice vinegar
- 1½ tsp. Dijon mustard
- ¼ tsp. sesame oil
- 1 pkg. (10 oz.) hearts of romaine salad mix
- 1 pkg. (14 oz.) coleslaw mix
- ¼ cup crispy chow mein noodles
- ⅓ cup sliced almonds, toasted

1. Cook chicken tenders according to package directions. Meanwhile, whisk together mayonnaise, honey, vinegar, mustard and sesame oil.
2. To serve, place romaine and coleslaw mixes in a large bowl; toss with dressing. Divide among 4 plates. Cut chicken into bite-sized pieces; place over salads. Sprinkle with noodles and almonds.

**NOTE** To toast nuts, bake in a shallow pan in a 350°; oven for 5-10 minutes or cook in a skillet over low heat until lightly browned, stirring occasionally.

**1 SERVING** 419 cal., 25g fat (3g sat. fat), 11mg chol., 602mg sod., 42g carb. (20g sugars, 7g fiber), 12g pro.

## CREAMY DIJON CHICKEN

You'll save both time and money with this chicken dish. It makes a nice sauce that works well over brown rice or wide noodles.
*—Irene Boffo, Fountain Hills, AZ*

**Takes:** 25 min. • **Makes:** 4 servings

- ½ cup half-and-half cream
- ¼ cup Dijon mustard
- 1 Tbsp. brown sugar
- 4 boneless skinless chicken breast halves (6 oz. each)
- ¼ tsp. salt
- ¼ tsp. pepper
- 2 tsp. olive oil
- 2 tsp. butter
- 1 small onion, thinly sliced
- Minced fresh parsley

1. Whisk together cream, mustard and brown sugar. Pound chicken breasts with a meat mallet to even thickness; sprinkle with salt and pepper.
2. In a large skillet, heat oil and butter over medium-high heat; brown chicken on both sides. Reduce heat to medium. Add onion and cream mixture; bring to a boil. Reduce heat; simmer, covered, until a thermometer inserted in chicken reads 165°, 10-12 minutes. Sprinkle with parsley.

**1 CHICKEN BREAST HALF WITH 3 TBSP. SAUCE** 295 cal., 11g fat (5g sat. fat), 114mg chol., 621mg sod., 6g carb. (5g sugars, 0 fiber), 36g pro.

## CHICKEN BISCUIT POTPIE

This hearty meal in one takes just 10 minutes to assemble before you pop it into the oven.
*—Dorothy Smith, El Dorado, AR*

**Prep:** 10 min. • **Bake:** 25 min.
**Makes:** 4 servings

- 1⅔ cups frozen mixed vegetables, thawed
- 1½ cups cubed cooked chicken
- 1 can (10¾ oz.) condensed cream of chicken soup, undiluted
- ¼ tsp. dried thyme
- 1 cup biscuit/baking mix
- ½ cup 2% milk
- 1 large egg

1. Preheat oven to 400°. In a large bowl, combine vegetables, chicken, soup and thyme. Pour into an ungreased deep-dish 9-in. pie plate. Combine biscuit mix, milk and egg; spoon over the chicken mixture.
2. Bake until topping is golden brown and a toothpick inserted in center comes out clean, 25-30 minutes.

**1 SERVING** 376 cal., 14g fat (4g sat. fat), 103mg chol., 966mg sod., 38g carb. (5g sugars, 5g fiber), 23g pro.

## TERIYAKI CHICKEN THIGHS

Here's a real slow-cooker sensation: Asian-style chicken and rice. It always goes over big with my family.
*—Gigi Miller, Stoughton, WI*

**Prep:** 15 min. • **Cook:** 4 hours
**Makes:** 8 servings

- 3 lbs. boneless skinless chicken thighs
- ¾ cup sugar
- ¾ cup reduced-sodium soy sauce
- ⅓ cup cider vinegar
- 1 garlic clove, minced
- ¾ tsp. ground ginger
- ¼ tsp. pepper
- 4 tsp. cornstarch
- 4 tsp. cold water
- Hot cooked rice, optional

1. Place chicken in a 4- or 5-qt. slow cooker. In a small bowl, mix sugar, soy sauce, vinegar, garlic, ginger and pepper; pour over chicken. Cook, covered, on low 4-5 hours or until chicken is tender.
2. Remove chicken to a serving platter; keep warm. Transfer cooking juices to a small saucepan; skim fat. Bring cooking juices to a boil. In a small bowl, mix cornstarch and cold water until smooth; stir into cooking juices. Return to a boil; cook and stir 1-2 minutes or until thickened. Serve with chicken and, if desired, rice.

**5 OZ. COOKED CHICKEN WITH ⅓ CUP SAUCE** 342 cal., 12g fat (3g sat. fat), 113mg chol., 958mg sod., 22g carb. (19g sugars, 0 fiber), 33g pro.

## SLOW-COOKER TURKEY BREAST

Try this flavorful, easy-fix, tender entree when you're craving turkey.
*—Maria Juco, Milwaukee, WI*

**Prep:** 10 min. • **Cook:** 5 hours
**Makes:** 14 servings

- 1 bone-in turkey breast (6 to 7 lbs.), skin removed
- 1 Tbsp. olive oil
- 1 tsp. dried minced garlic
- 1 tsp. seasoned salt
- 1 tsp. paprika
- 1 tsp. Italian seasoning
- 1 tsp. pepper
- ½ cup water

1. Brush turkey with oil. Combine the garlic, seasoned salt, paprika, Italian seasoning and pepper; rub over turkey.
2. Transfer to a 6-qt. slow cooker; add the water. Cover and cook on low for 5-6 hours or until tender.

**4 OZ. COOKED TURKEY** 173 cal., 2g fat (0 sat. fat), 100mg chol., 171mg sod., 0 carb. (0 sugars, 0 fiber), 36g pro.

> **"Delicious! I had a 5½-lb. turkey breast that cooked for 5 hours on low and was perfectly done. The only slight change I made was to sub garlic powder for dry minced garlic and use chicken broth instead of water. Excellent! I will use this recipe from now on."**
> —MARINEMOM_TEXASE, TASTEOFHOME.COM

## HAWAIIAN TURKEY BURGERS

My husband and I really love to grill, so hamburgers are often on the menu. This recipe uses ground turkey instead of beef. Topped with pineapple slices, the burgers are moist and juicy.
*—Babette Watterson, Atglen, PA*

**Takes:** 25 min. • **Makes:** 4 burgers

- 1 can (8 oz.) sliced pineapple
- ½ cup dry bread crumbs
- ½ cup sliced green onions
- ½ cup chopped sweet red pepper
- 1 Tbsp. reduced-sodium soy sauce
- ¼ tsp. salt
- 1 lb. lean ground turkey
- 2 Tbsp. reduced-sodium teriyaki sauce
- 4 sesame hamburger buns

1. Drain the pineapple, reserving ¼ cup juice (discard remaining juice or save for another use); set pineapple aside. In a large bowl, combine the bread crumbs, onions, red pepper, soy sauce, salt and reserved pineapple juice. Crumble turkey over the mixture and mix lightly but thoroughly. Shape into 4 patties.
2. On a lightly oiled grill rack, grill patties, covered, over medium heat for 3 minutes on each side. Brush with teriyaki sauce. Grill 4-6 minutes longer on each side or until a thermometer reads 165° and juices run clear.
3. Grill pineapple slices for 2 minutes on each side, basting occasionally with teriyaki sauce. Warm buns on grill; top each with a burger and pineapple slice.

**1 BURGER** 401 cal., 12g fat (3g sat. fat), 78mg chol., 839mg sod., 43g carb. (13g sugars, 3g fiber), 31g pro.

## AIR-FRYER CHICKEN TACO POCKETS

We love these easy taco-flavored sandwiches made with crescent dough. They make a quick and easy lunch or supper with a bowl of soup or a crisp salad. I also like to cut them into smaller servings for parties.
*—Donna Gribbins, Shelbyville, KY*

**Takes:** 25 min. • **Makes:** 8 servings

- 2 tubes (8 oz. each) refrigerated crescent rolls
- ½ cup salsa
- ½ cup sour cream
- 2 Tbsp. taco seasoning
- 1 cup shredded rotisserie chicken
- 1 cup shredded cheddar cheese
- Optional toppings: Shredded lettuce, guacamole, and additional salsa and sour cream

1. Preheat air fryer to 375°. Unroll 1 tube crescent dough and separate into 2 rectangles; press perforations to seal. Repeat with second tube. In a bowl, combine salsa, sour cream and taco seasoning. Spoon chicken onto the left side of each rectangle; top with salsa mixture. Sprinkle with cheese. Fold dough over filling; pinch edges to seal.
2. Working in batches if necessary, place pockets on a tray in air-fryer basket. Cook until golden brown, 13-15 minutes. Cut in half. Serve with optional toppings as desired.

**½ POCKET** 393 cal., 24g fat (7g sat. fat), 47mg chol., 896mg sod., 29g carb. (7g sugars, 0 fiber), 16g pro.

## LEMONY CHICKEN & RICE

I couldn't say who loves this recipe the most, because it gets raves every time I serve it! Occasionally I even get a phone call or an email from a friend requesting the recipe. It's certainly a favorite for my grown children and 15 grandchildren.
*—Maryalice Wood, Langley, BC*

**Prep:** 25 min. + marinating • **Bake:** 55 min.
**Makes:** 2 casseroles (4 servings each)

- 2 cups water
- ½ cup reduced-sodium soy sauce
- ¼ cup lemon juice
- ¼ cup olive oil
- 2 garlic cloves, minced
- 2 tsp. ground ginger
- 2 tsp. pepper
- 16 bone-in chicken thighs, skin removed (about 6 lbs.)
- 2 cups uncooked long grain rice
- 4 Tbsp. grated lemon zest, divided
- 2 medium lemons, sliced

1. In a large shallow dish, combine the first 7 ingredients. Add chicken; turn to coat and cover. Refrigerate 4 hours or overnight.
2. Preheat oven to 325°. Spread 1 cup rice into each of 2 greased 13x9-in. baking dishes. Top dishes with 1 Tbsp. lemon zest each, 8 chicken thighs and half the marinade. Top with sliced lemons.
3. Bake, covered, 40 minutes. Bake, uncovered, 15-20 minutes longer or until a thermometer inserted into chicken reads 170°-175°. Sprinkle with remaining lemon zest.

**2 CHICKEN THIGHS WITH ¾ CUP RICE MIXTURE** 624 cal., 26g fat (6g sat. fat), 173mg chol., 754mg sod., 41g carb. (1g sugars, 1g fiber), 53g pro.

## CRUMB-COATED CHICKEN & BLACKBERRY SALSA

Maple syrup lends a sweet touch to blackberry salsa. Besides chicken, it's also great with fried fish.
*—Tammy Thomas, Morrisville, VT*

**Takes:** 25 min. • **Makes:** 2 servings

- ½ cup fresh blackberries, halved
- 1 jalapeno pepper, seeded and minced
- 2 Tbsp. minced fresh cilantro
- 2 Tbsp. chopped red onion
- 2 Tbsp. maple syrup
- 2 Tbsp. balsamic vinegar
- 2 boneless skinless chicken breast halves (5 oz. each)
- ⅛ tsp. salt
- ⅛ tsp. pepper
- ¼ cup all-purpose flour
- 1 large egg, beaten
- ½ cup panko bread crumbs
- 1 Tbsp. olive oil

1. In a small bowl, combine the first 6 ingredients. Cover and refrigerate until serving.
2. Flatten chicken to ¼-in. thickness; sprinkle with salt and pepper. Place the flour, egg and bread crumbs in separate shallow bowls. Coat chicken with flour, dip in egg, then coat with crumbs.
3. In a large skillet, heat oil over medium heat. Add chicken; cook until no longer pink, 4-6 minutes on each side. Serve with salsa.

**NOTE** Wear disposable gloves when cutting hot peppers; the oils can burn skin. Avoid touching your face.

**1 CHICKEN BREAST HALF WITH ¼ CUP SALSA** 411 cal., 13g fat (3g sat. fat), 175mg chol., 150mg sod., 37g carb. (17g sugars, 3g fiber), 35g pro.

## NECTARINE CHICKEN SALAD

When guests are coming for lunch or dinner in the warm summer months, I like to serve this attractive, colorful salad. The dressing is refreshingly tart. A neighbor shared the recipe years ago and I've passed it on many times.
*—Cathy Ross, Van Nuys, CA*

**Takes:** 15 min. • **Makes:** 4 servings

- ¼ cup lime juice
- 1 Tbsp. sugar
- 1 Tbsp. minced fresh thyme or 1 tsp. dried thyme
- 1 Tbsp. olive oil
- 1 garlic clove, minced
- 6 cups torn mixed salad greens
- 1 lb. boneless skinless chicken breasts, cooked and sliced
- 5 medium ripe nectarines, thinly sliced

1. In a jar with a tight-fitting lid, combine lime juice, sugar, thyme, oil and garlic; shake well.
2. On a serving platter, arrange salad greens, chicken and nectarines. Drizzle with dressing. Serve immediately.

**1½ CUPS** 266 cal., 7g fat (1g sat. fat), 63mg chol., 76mg sod., 27g carb. (21g sugars, 5g fiber), 26g pro.

## MEDITERRANEAN TURKEY PANINI

The word panini refers to sandwiches that are pressed and toasted. I make panini for my fellow teachers and friends. For potlucks, I cut several sandwiches into fourths.
*—Martha Muellenberg, Vermillion, SD*

**Takes:** 25 min. • **Makes:** 4 servings

- 4 ciabatta rolls, split
- 1 jar (24 oz.) marinara or spaghetti sauce, divided
- 1 container (4 oz.) crumbled feta cheese
- 1 jar (7½ oz.) marinated quartered artichoke hearts, drained and chopped
- 2 plum tomatoes, sliced
- 1 lb. sliced deli turkey

1. Spread each ciabatta bottom with 2 Tbsp. marinara sauce. Top with half the cheese; add the artichokes, tomatoes, turkey and remaining cheese. Spread each ciabatta top with 2 Tbsp. marinara sauce; place over turkey.
2. Cook on a panini maker or indoor grill until cheese is melted, 4-5 minutes. Place remaining marinara sauce in a small microwave-safe bowl; cover and microwave on high until heated through. Serve with sandwiches.

**1 SANDWICH WITH ⅓ CUP SAUCE** 701 cal., 18g fat (5g sat. fat), 55mg chol., 2314mg sod., 98g carb. (18g sugars, 8g fiber), 40g pro.

**TEST KITCHEN TIP**
For grilling, we love the moistness of chicken thighs—they're economical too. But you can use any cut of chicken you like for this recipe.

## GRILLED HULI HULI CHICKEN

When I lived in Hawaii, a friend shared this recipe for chicken marinated in a ginger-soy sauce. *Huli* means "turn" in Hawaiian and refers to turning the meat on the grill.
*—Sharon Boling, San Diego, CA*

**Prep:** 15 min. + marinating
**Grill:** 15 min. • **Makes:** 12 servings

- 1 cup packed brown sugar
- ¾ cup ketchup
- ¾ cup reduced-sodium soy sauce
- ⅓ cup sherry or chicken broth
- 2½ tsp. minced fresh gingerroot
- 1½ tsp. minced garlic
- 24 boneless skinless chicken thighs (about 6 lbs.)

1. In a small bowl, combine first 6 ingredients. Reserve 1⅓ cups for basting; cover and refrigerate. Divide the remaining marinade between 2 large shallow dishes. Add 12 chicken thighs to each; turn to coat. Refrigerate, covered, for 8 hours or overnight.
2. Drain chicken, discarding marinade.
3. Grill chicken, covered, on an oiled rack over medium heat for 6-8 minutes on each side or until a thermometer inserted into chicken reads 170°; baste occasionally with reserved marinade during last 5 minutes.

**2 CHICKEN THIGHS** 391 cal., 16g fat (5g sat. fat), 151mg chol., 651mg sod., 15g carb. (14g sugars, 0 fiber), 43g pro.

## SLOW-COOKER BUFFALO CHICKEN LASAGNA

When I make this tasty chicken lasagna at home, I use a whole bottle of Buffalo wing sauce because my family likes it nice and spicy. Increase the pasta sauce and use less wing sauce if you prefer.
*—Heidi Pepin, Sykesville, MD*

**Prep:** 25 min. • **Cook:** 4 hours + standing
**Makes:** 8 servings

- 1½ lbs. ground chicken
- 1 Tbsp. olive oil
- 1 bottle (12 oz.) Buffalo wing sauce
- 1½ cups meatless spaghetti sauce
- 1 carton (15 oz.) ricotta cheese
- 2 cups shredded part-skim mozzarella cheese
- 9 no-cook lasagna noodles
- 2 medium sweet red peppers, chopped
- ½ cup crumbled blue cheese or feta cheese
- Optional: Chopped celery and additional crumbled blue cheese

1. In a Dutch oven, cook chicken in oil over medium heat until no longer pink; drain. Stir in wing sauce and spaghetti sauce. In a small bowl, mix ricotta and mozzarella cheeses.
2. Spread 1 cup sauce onto the bottom of an oval 6-qt. slow cooker. Layer with 3 noodles (breaking noodles to fit), 1 cup sauce, a third of the peppers and a third of the cheese mixture. Repeat layers twice. Top with the remaining sauce; sprinkle with blue cheese.
3. Cover and cook on low for 4-5 hours or until noodles are tender. Let stand 15 minutes before serving. Top with celery and additional blue cheese if desired.

**1 SERVING** 445 cal., 23g fat (11g sat. fat), 104mg chol., 1996mg sod., 28g carb. (9g sugars, 3g fiber), 33g pro.

## MEDITERRANEAN TURKEY SKILLET

I've always heard that it's important to eat a rainbow of colors to get all of the nutrients we need. Thanks to my garden-grown veggies, this dish is in my regular rotation.
*—Nicole Ehlert, Burlington, WI*

**Takes:** 30 min. • **Makes:** 6 servings

- 1 Tbsp. olive oil
- 1 pkg. (20 oz.) lean ground turkey
- 2 medium zucchini, quartered lengthwise and cut into ½-in. slices
- 1 medium onion, chopped
- 2 banana peppers, seeded and chopped
- 3 garlic cloves, minced
- ½ tsp. dried oregano
- 1 can (15 oz.) black beans, rinsed and drained
- 1 can (14½ oz.) diced tomatoes, undrained
- 1 Tbsp. balsamic vinegar
- ½ tsp. salt

In a large skillet, heat oil over medium-high heat. Add turkey, zucchini, onion, peppers, garlic and oregano; cook 10-12 minutes or until the turkey is no longer pink and vegetables are tender, breaking up turkey into crumbles; drain. Stir in remaining ingredients; heat through, stirring occasionally.

**NOTE** Wear disposable gloves when cutting hot peppers; the oils can burn skin. Avoid touching your face.

**1 CUP** 259 cal., 10g fat (2g sat. fat), 65mg chol., 504mg sod., 20g carb. (6g sugars, 6g fiber), 24g pro.

## AIR-FRYER CRISPY CURRY DRUMSTICKS

These air-fryer chicken drumsticks are flavorful, crispy on the outside and juicy on the inside. Sometimes I'll add some red pepper flakes in addition to the curry powder if I want to spice them up.
*—Zena Furgason, Norman, OK*

**Prep:** 35 min. + standing
**Cook:** 15 min./batch **Makes:** 4 servings

- 4 chicken drumsticks
- ¾ tsp. salt, divided
- 2 Tbsp. olive oil
- 2 tsp. curry powder
- ½ tsp. onion salt
- ½ tsp. garlic powder
- Minced fresh cilantro, optional

1. Place the chicken in a large bowl; add ½ tsp. salt and enough water to cover. Let stand 15 minutes at room temperature. Drain and pat dry.
2. Preheat air fryer to 375°. In another bowl, mix oil, curry powder, onion salt, garlic powder and remaining ¼ tsp. salt; add chicken and toss to coat. In batches, place chicken in a single layer on a tray in air-fryer basket. Cook chicken until a thermometer inserted in chicken reads 170°-175°, 15-17 minutes, turning halfway through cooking. If desired, sprinkle with cilantro.

**1 DRUMSTICK** 180 cal., 13g fat (3g sat. fat), 47mg chol., 711mg sod., 1g carb. (0 sugars, 1g fiber), 15g pro.

### GOT LEFTOVERS?

While these drumsticks taste best fresh, you can refrigerate leftovers in an airtight container for 3-4 days. Pop them back into the air fryer to reheat.

## CORNFLAKE "FRIED" CHICKEN

I took a recipe off a box of baking mix and altered it to make the prep easier. The result was this moist oven-fried chicken with a thick golden coating that's a lot more crispy than the original.
*—Angela Capettini, Boynton Beach, FL*

**Prep:** 10 min. • **Bake:** 30 min.
**Makes:** 4 servings

- 2 Tbsp. butter, melted
- 1 cup crushed cornflakes
- 1 cup all-purpose flour
- 1½ tsp. seasoned salt
- ¾ cup egg substitute or 3 large eggs, beaten
- 4 chicken drumsticks, skin removed
- 4 bone-in chicken thighs, skin removed

1. Preheat oven to 425°. Drizzle butter in a 13x9-in. baking dish. In a shallow bowl, combine cornflakes, flour and seasoned salt. Place egg substitute in another shallow bowl. Dip chicken in the egg substitute, then roll in cornflake mixture. Repeat.
2. Arrange chicken in prepared dish, meatier side down. Bake, uncovered, 20 minutes. Turn chicken over; bake 10-15 minutes longer or until a thermometer reads 170°-175°.

**1 DRUMSTICK AND 1 THIGH** 534 cal., 18g fat (7g sat. fat), 143mg chol., 972mg sod., 44g carb. (3g sugars, 1g fiber), 46g pro.

## SUPER QUICK CHICKEN FRIED RICE

After my first child was born, I needed meals that were satisfying and fast. This delicious fried rice is now part of our regular dinner rotation.
*—Alicia Gower, Auburn, NY*

**Takes:** 30 min. • **Makes:** 6 servings

- 1 pkg. (12 oz.) frozen mixed vegetables
- 2 Tbsp. olive oil, divided
- 2 large eggs, lightly beaten
- 4 Tbsp. sesame oil, divided
- 3 pkg. (8.8 oz. each) ready-to-serve garden vegetable rice
- 1 rotisserie chicken, skin removed, shredded
- ¼ tsp. salt
- ¼ tsp. pepper

1. Prepare frozen vegetables according to package directions. Meanwhile, in a large skillet, heat 1 Tbsp. olive oil over medium-high heat. Pour in eggs; cook and stir until eggs are thickened and no liquid egg remains. Remove from pan.
2. In same skillet, heat 2 Tbsp. sesame oil and remaining 1 Tbsp. olive oil over medium-high heat. Add rice; cook and stir 10-12 minutes or until rice begins to brown.
3. Stir in chicken, salt and pepper. Add eggs and vegetables; heat through, breaking eggs into small pieces and stirring to combine. Drizzle with remaining 2 Tbsp. sesame oil.

**1½ CUPS** 548 cal., 25g fat (5g sat. fat), 163mg chol., 934mg sod., 43g carb. (3g sugars, 3g fiber), 38g pro.

### SAVE SOME CASH

Sesame oil adds a nutty flavor and complexity to this dish, but it is expensive. If you don't want to splurge on a bottle, you can instead get a nutty flavor by sprinkling the dish with chopped roasted peanuts or toasted sesame seeds.

## CHICKEN VERONIQUE

I found this recipe in a gardening book. My family just loves it, and it's super easy! We think it's excellent served with rice pilaf on the side.
*—Anita Dudiwka, Akron, OH*

**Prep:** 15 min. • **Cook:** 20 min.
**Makes:** 6 servings

- 6 boneless skinless chicken breast halves (4 oz. each)
- ¼ tsp. salt
- ⅛ tsp. ground nutmeg
- 4 tsp. butter
- ⅔ cup white wine or reduced-sodium chicken broth
- 2 Tbsp. orange marmalade spreadable fruit
- ¾ tsp. dried tarragon
- 2 tsp. all-purpose flour
- ½ cup half-and-half cream
- 1½ cups green grapes, halved

1. Sprinkle chicken with salt and nutmeg. In a large nonstick skillet, cook chicken in butter over medium heat for 3-5 minutes on each side or until lightly browned.
2. In a small bowl, combine the wine, marmalade and tarragon. Add to skillet; bring to a boil. Reduce heat; cover and simmer for 4-6 minutes on each side or until a thermometer reads 170°. Remove chicken and keep warm.
3. Combine flour and cream until smooth. Gradually stir into skillet. Bring to a boil; cook 2 minutes longer or until thickened. Stir in grapes; heat through. Serve with chicken.

**1 SERVING** 226 cal., 7g fat (4g sat. fat), 79mg chol., 191mg sod., 13g carb. (10g sugars, 1g fiber), 24g pro.

## NUTTY OVEN-FRIED CHICKEN

Pecans are plentiful in the South, and so is fried chicken! I love to prepare and serve this easy dish because the chicken comes out moist and crispy.
*—Diane Hixon, Niceville, FL*

**Prep:** 10 min. • **Bake:** 1 hour
**Makes:** 6 servings

- ½ cup evaporated milk
- 1 cup biscuit/baking mix
- ⅓ cup finely chopped pecans
- 2 tsp. paprika
- ½ tsp. salt
- ½ tsp. poultry seasoning
- ½ tsp. rubbed sage
- 1 broiler/fryer chicken (3 to 4 lbs.), cut up
- ⅓ cup butter, melted

1. Preheat oven to 350°. Place milk in a shallow bowl. In another shallow bowl, combine baking mix, pecans and seasonings. Dip chicken pieces in milk, then coat generously with pecan mixture.
2. Place in a lightly greased 13x9-in. baking dish. Drizzle with butter. Bake, uncovered, until chicken is golden brown and crispy and juices run clear, about 1 hour.

**6 OZ. COOKED CHICKEN** 530 cal., 35g fat (13g sat. fat), 138mg chol., 595mg sod., 17g carb. (3g sugars, 1g fiber), 37g pro.

## SLOW-COOKER LUAU CHICKEN

As long as you're cooking bacon for breakfast, save some for the slow cooker. In four short hours, you'll be saying "aloha" to lunch.
*—Cindy Lund, Valley Center, CA*

**Prep:** 15 min. • **Cook:** 4 hours
**Makes:** 6 servings

- 6 bacon strips, divided
- 6 boneless skinless chicken thighs (about 1½ lbs.)
- ¼ tsp. salt
- ⅛ tsp. pepper
- ½ cup chopped red onion
- 1 cup crushed pineapple, drained
- ¾ cup barbecue sauce

1. Cut 3 bacon strips in half; cook until partially cooked but not crisp. Drain on paper towels.
2. Season chicken with salt and pepper; place in a 3-qt. slow cooker. Top each thigh with a half piece of bacon. Top with onion, pineapple and barbecue sauce.
3. Cover and cook on low for 4-5 hours or until chicken is tender. Cook remaining bacon until crisp; drain and crumble. Sprinkle over each serving.

**1 SERVING** 375 cal., 17g fat (5g sat. fat), 135mg chol., 637mg sod., 14g carb. (13g sugars, 1g fiber), 39g pro.

**SLOW-COOKER GINGER-PEACH CHICKEN**
Omit bacon, salt, pepper, onion, pineapple and barbecue sauce. Place chicken in slow cooker. Top with ¾ cup sliced peeled fresh or thawed peaches and ¾ cup golden raisins. Mix ¾ cup peach preserves, ¼ cup chili sauce, 4 tsp. minced crystallized ginger, 2 tsp. minced garlic and 2 tsp. reduced-sodium soy sauce; spoon over the top. Cook as directed. Serve with hot cooked rice if desired.

## CHICKEN GYROS

These yummy Greek specialties are a cinch to prepare at home. Tender chicken strips and a creamy cucumber sauce are tucked into pitas.
—Taste of Home *Test Kitchen*

**Prep:** 20 min. + marinating • **Cook:** 10 min.
**Makes:** 2 servings

- ¼ cup lemon juice
- 2 Tbsp. olive oil
- ¾ tsp. minced garlic, divided
- ½ tsp. ground mustard
- ½ tsp. dried oregano
- ½ lb. boneless skinless chicken breasts, cut into ½-in. strips
- ½ cup chopped peeled cucumber
- ⅓ cup plain yogurt
- ¼ tsp. dill weed
- 2 whole pita breads
- ½ small red onion, thinly sliced

1. In a large shallow dish, combine the lemon juice, oil, ½ tsp. garlic, mustard and oregano. Add chicken and turn to coat; refrigerate for at least 1 hour. In a small bowl, combine the cucumber, yogurt, dill and remaining garlic; cover and refrigerate until serving.
2. Drain the chicken, and discarding marinade. In a large nonstick skillet, cook and stir the chicken for 7-8 minutes or until no longer pink. Spoon onto pita breads. Top with yogurt mixture and onion; fold in half.

**1 GYRO** 367 cal., 9g fat (2g sat. fat), 68mg chol., 397mg sod., 39g carb. (4g sugars, 2g fiber), 30g pro.

## CHICKEN PASTA CAESAR SALAD

My colleagues and I made a pact to eat healthier, and we took turns sharing our favorite dishes. I'm happy to report that, thanks to recipes like this crisp and tangy salad, we all trimmed down.
*—Teresa Jordan, Springville, UT*

**Takes:** 30 min. • **Makes:** 6 servings

- 3 cups uncooked whole wheat spiral pasta (about 8 oz.)
- 6 cups torn romaine
- 3 cups coarsely shredded rotisserie chicken
- 2 medium tomatoes, chopped
- ½ cup shredded Parmesan cheese
- ½ cup creamy Caesar salad dressing
- ⅓ cup slivered almonds, toasted
- Caesar salad croutons, optional

Cook pasta according to package directions. Drain; rinse with cold water and drain again. Toss with romaine, chicken, tomatoes, Parmesan cheese, dressing, almonds and, if desired, croutons; serve immediately.

**NOTE** To toast nuts, bake in a shallow pan in a 350°; oven for 5-10 minutes or cook in a skillet over low heat until lightly browned, stirring occasionally.

**2 CUPS** 422 cal., 22g fat (5g sat. fat), 75mg chol., 416mg sod., 26g carb. (3g sugars, 5g fiber), 30g pro.

## DELICIOUS OVEN BARBECUED CHICKEN

A friend made this moist chicken for us when we had our first child. I pared down the recipe to make it lower in fat and calories. It is now a family favorite, and even the kids ask for it.
*—Marge Wagner, Roselle, Il*

**Prep:** 20 min. • **Bake:** 35 min.
**Makes:** 6 servings

- 6 bone-in chicken breast halves (8 oz. each)
- ⅓ cup chopped onion
- ¾ cup ketchup
- ½ cup water
- ⅓ cup white vinegar
- 3 Tbsp. brown sugar
- 1 Tbsp. Worcestershire sauce
- 1 tsp. ground mustard
- ¼ tsp. salt
- ⅛ tsp. pepper

1. Preheat oven to 350°. In a nonstick skillet coated lightly with oil, brown chicken over medium heat. Transfer to a 13x9-in. baking dish coated with cooking spray.
2. Recoat skillet with oil. Add onion; cook and stir over medium heat until tender. Stir in remaining ingredients; bring to a boil. Reduce heat; simmer, uncovered, 15 minutes. Pour over chicken.
3. Bake, uncovered, until a thermometer inserted in chicken reads 170°, 35-45 minutes.

**1 SERVING** 324 cal., 10g fat (3g sat. fat), 111mg chol., 602mg sod., 16g carb. (15g sugars, 0 fiber), 39g pro.

## SAUSAGE & PEPPER SHEET-PAN SANDWICHES

Sausage with peppers was always on the table when I was growing up. Here's how to do it the easy way: Just grab a sheet pan and the ingredients, then let the oven do the work.
*—Debbie Glasscock, Conway, AR*

**Prep:** 20 min. • **Bake:** 30 min.
**Makes:** 6 servings

- 1 lb. uncooked sweet Italian turkey sausage links, roughly chopped
- 3 medium sweet red peppers, seeded and sliced
- 1 large onion, halved and sliced
- 1 Tbsp. olive oil
- 6 hot dog buns, split
- 6 slices provolone cheese

**1.** Preheat oven to 375°. Place the sausage pieces in a 15x10x1-in. sheet pan, arranging peppers and onion around sausage. Drizzle olive oil over sausage and vegetables; bake 30-35 minutes, stirring mixture after 15 minutes, or until sausage is no longer pink and the vegetables are tender.

**2.** During the last 5 minutes of baking, arrange buns cut side up in a second sheet pan; top each bun bottom with a cheese slice. Bake until buns are golden brown and cheese is melted. Spoon sausage and pepper mixture onto bun bottoms. Replace tops.

**1 SANDWICH** 315 cal., 15g fat (5g sat. fat), 43mg chol., 672mg sod., 28g carb. (7g sugars, 2g fiber), 18g pro.

## PRESSURE-COOKER SAUCY ITALIAN CHICKEN

Serve this chicken with pasta, risotto or polenta to soak up all its saucy goodness.
*—Marisa Loper, Sammamish, WA*

**Prep:** 20 min. • **Cook:** 10 min. + releasing
**Makes:** 4 servings

- 4 boneless skinless chicken breast halves (6 oz. each)
- 1 can (14½ oz.) diced tomatoes, undrained
- 1 jar (12 oz.) marinated quartered artichoke hearts, undrained
- 2 tsp. Italian seasoning
- ¾ tsp. garlic salt
- 1 cup shredded mozzarella cheese
- ¼ cup grated Parmesan cheese

Place chicken in a 6-qt. electric pressure cooker. Top with tomatoes, artichokes, Italian seasoning and garlic salt. Lock lid; close pressure-release valve. Adjust to pressure-cook on high for 10 minutes. Let pressure release naturally for 10 minutes; quick-release any remaining pressure. Sprinkle with cheeses before serving.

**1 CHICKEN BREAST HALF WITH 1 CUP TOMATO MIXTURE** 414 cal., 22g fat (8g sat. fat), 120mg chol., 1303mg sod., 12g carb. (4g sugars, 7g fiber), 43g pro.

**SLOW-COOKER SAUCY ITALIAN CHICKEN**
Place first 5 ingredients in a 3- or 4-qt. slow cooker. Cook, covered, on low until chicken is tender, 4-6 hours. Sprinkle with cheeses. Cover and let stand until melted.

S240
DEXTER

## AIR-FRYER SOUTHERN-STYLE CHICKEN

I call this America's best-loved air-fryer chicken. The secret is in the herby, golden brown breading that makes the chicken super moist and flavorful.

*—Elaina Morgan, Rickman, TN*

**Prep:** 15 min. • **Cook:** 20 min./batch
**Makes:** 6 servings

- 2 cups crushed Ritz crackers (about 50)
- 1 Tbsp. minced fresh parsley
- 1 tsp. garlic salt
- 1 tsp. paprika
- ½ tsp. pepper
- ¼ tsp. ground cumin
- ¼ tsp. rubbed sage
- 1 large egg, beaten
- 1 broiler/fryer chicken (3 to 4 lbs.), cut up
- Cooking spray

1. Preheat air fryer to 375°. In a shallow bowl, mix the first 7 ingredients. Place egg in a separate shallow bowl. Dip chicken in egg, then in cracker mixture, patting to help coating adhere. In batches, place chicken in a single layer on a greased tray in air-fryer basket; spritz with cooking spray.
2. Cook 10 minutes. Turn chicken and spritz with cooking spray. Cook until chicken is golden brown and juices run clear, 10-20 minutes longer.

**5 OZ. COOKED CHICKEN** 410 cal., 23g fat (6g sat. fat), 135mg chol., 460mg sod., 13g carb. (2g sugars, 1g fiber), 36g pro.

## BUFFALO SLOPPY JOES

Lean ground turkey makes this a lighter sloppy joe than the standard ground beef version. A big splash of hot sauce and some optional blue cheese provide that authentic Buffalo-style flavor.

*—Maria Regakis, Saugus, MA*

**Takes:** 30 min. • **Makes:** 8 servings

- 2 lbs. extra-lean ground turkey
- 2 celery ribs, chopped
- 1 medium onion, chopped
- 1 medium carrot, grated
- 3 garlic cloves, minced
- 1 can (8 oz.) tomato sauce
- ½ cup chicken broth
- ¼ cup Louisiana-style hot sauce
- 2 Tbsp. brown sugar
- 2 Tbsp. red wine vinegar
- 1 Tbsp. Worcestershire sauce
- ¼ tsp. pepper
- 8 hamburger buns, split
- Crumbled blue cheese, optional

1. Cook the first 5 ingredients in a Dutch oven over medium heat until turkey is no longer pink, breaking it into crumbles. Stir in the tomato sauce, chicken broth, hot sauce, brown sugar, vinegar, Worcestershire sauce and pepper; heat through.
2. Serve on buns. If desired, sprinkle with blue cheese.

**1 SANDWICH** 279 cal., 3g fat (0 sat. fat), 45mg chol., 475mg sod., 30g carb. (9g sugars, 2g fiber), 33g pro.

> **"A wonderful take on the old sloppy joe! My kids love these!"**
> —SRASMUSSON, TASTEOFHOME.COM

## TURKEY BREAST TENDERLOINS WITH RASPBERRY SAUCE

Sweet and tangy raspberry sauce is a perfect complement to versatile turkey tenderloins. In fact, the sauce is so good, you'll be tempted to eat it with a spoon.

*—Deirdre Cox, Kansas City, MO*

**Takes:** 30 min. • **Makes:** 2 servings

- 2 turkey breast tenderloins (5 oz. each)
- 1/8 tsp. salt
- 1/8 tsp. pepper
- 2 tsp. olive oil
- 1 tsp. cornstarch
- 1/4 cup cranberry-raspberry juice
- 2 Tbsp. Heinz 57 steak sauce
- 2 Tbsp. red raspberry preserves
- 1/2 tsp. lemon juice

1. Sprinkle turkey with salt and pepper. In a large nonstick skillet over medium heat, brown turkey in oil on all sides. Cover and cook until a thermometer reads 165°, 10-12 minutes. Remove and keep warm.
2. Combine cornstarch and juice until smooth; add to the pan. Stir in the steak sauce, preserves and lemon juice. Bring to a boil; cook and stir until thickened, about 1 minute. Slice turkey; serve with sauce.

**1 TENDERLOIN WITH 1/4 CUP SAUCE** 275 cal., 6g fat (1g sat. fat), 69mg chol., 425mg sod., 22g carb. (19g sugars, 0 fiber), 33g pro.

## EASY ASIAN-STYLE CHICKEN SLAW

From the first time I made this chicken dish, I knew it was a winner because the bowl came back to the kitchen scraped clean.
*—Bess Blanco, Vail, AZ*

**Takes:** 15 min. • **Makes:** 8 servings

- 1 pkg. (3 oz.) ramen noodles
- 1 rotisserie chicken, skin removed, shredded
- 1 pkg. (16 oz.) coleslaw mix
- 6 green onions, finely chopped
- 1 cup reduced-fat Asian toasted sesame salad dressing

Discard seasoning packet from noodles or save for another use. Break noodles into small pieces; place in a large bowl. Add chicken, coleslaw mix and green onions. Drizzle with salad dressing; toss to coat.

**1½ CUPS** 267 cal., 10g fat (3g sat. fat), 70mg chol., 405mg sod., 18g carb. (8g sugars, 2g fiber), 26g pro.

### CUSTOMIZE THE FLAVOR

Mix in a little grated fresh ginger for warm pungency, toasted sesame seeds for crunch and to echo the dressing, a splash of soy sauce for savory depth, and chili oil or chili crisp for a bit of heat.

## FAVORITE LASAGNA ROLL-UPS

This crowd-pleasing take on lasagna offers a new way to enjoy a classic dish in individual portions. And it requires only a few ingredients.
*—Susan Sabia, Windsor, CA*

**Prep:** 25 min. • **Bake:** 30 min.
**Makes:** 10 servings

- 10 uncooked lasagna noodles
- 1 pkg. (19½ oz.) Italian turkey sausage links, casings removed
- 1 pkg. (8 oz.) cream cheese, softened
- 1 jar (26 oz.) pasta sauce
- 1¾ cups shredded cheddar cheese, divided
- Minced fresh parsley, optional

1. Preheat oven to 350°. Cook noodles according to package directions. Meanwhile, in a large skillet, cook sausage over medium heat until no longer pink, breaking it into crumbles; drain. Stir in cream cheese and ⅓ cup pasta sauce.
2. Drain noodles; spread ¼ cup meat mixture on each noodle. Sprinkle each with 2 Tbsp. cheese; carefully roll up.
3. Spread ⅔ cup pasta sauce into an ungreased 13x9-in. baking dish. Place roll-ups seam side down over sauce. Top with remaining sauce and cheese. Cover and bake for 20 minutes. Uncover; bake until sauce is bubbly, 10-15 minutes longer. If desired, sprinkle with parsley.

**1 ROLL-UP** 372 cal., 22g fat (11g sat. fat), 81mg chol., 885mg sod., 25g carb. (6g sugars, 2g fiber), 19g pro.

SHRIMP SCAMPI
SPINACH SALAD,
PAGE 197

# QUICK & EASY SEAFOOD

SEARED SALMON WITH STRAWBERRY BASIL RELISH, PAGE 181

## SPECIAL SCALLOP SALAD

What an easy way to fix a special and delicious meal. The balsamic, tarragon and honey blend beautifully.
*—Mary Relyea, Canastota, NY*

**Takes:** 20 min. • **Makes:** 4 servings

- 12 sea scallops (about 1½ lbs.)
- ⅛ tsp. salt
- ⅛ tsp. pepper
- 3 Tbsp. olive oil, divided
- 1 Tbsp. fresh minced chives
- 1 Tbsp. balsamic vinegar
- 2 garlic cloves, minced
- 2 tsp. minced fresh tarragon
- 2 tsp. honey
- 1 tsp. Dijon mustard
- 1 pkg. (5 oz.) spring mix salad greens
- 1 cup shredded carrots
- ½ cup chopped tomato

1. Pat scallops dry with paper towels; sprinkle with salt and pepper. In a large skillet, heat 2 Tbsp. oil over medium-high heat. Add scallops; sear 1-2 minutes on each side or until golden brown and firm. Remove from pan; keep warm.
2. In same pan, combine chives, vinegar, garlic, tarragon, honey, mustard and remaining oil. Bring to a boil; cook and stir until slightly thickened, about 30 seconds.
3. Divide greens, carrots and tomato among 4 plates; top with the scallops. Drizzle with dressing; serve immediately.

**1 SERVING** 247 cal., 11g fat (2g sat. fat), 41mg chol., 821mg sod., 15g carb. (6g sugars, 2g fiber), 22g pro.

## SHRIMP ORZO WITH FETA

Tender, hearty and flavorful, this recipe is one of my favorites! Garlic and a splash of lemon add to the fresh taste and heart-healthy benefits of shrimp.
*—Sarah Hummel, Moon Township, PA*

**Takes:** 25 min. • **Makes:** 4 servings

- 1¼ cups uncooked whole wheat orzo pasta
- 2 Tbsp. olive oil
- 2 garlic cloves, minced
- 2 medium tomatoes, chopped
- 2 Tbsp. lemon juice
- 1¼ lbs. uncooked shrimp (26-30 per lb.), peeled and deveined
- 2 Tbsp. minced fresh cilantro
- ¼ tsp. pepper
- ½ cup crumbled feta cheese

1. Cook orzo according to package directions. Meanwhile, in a large skillet, heat oil over medium heat. Add garlic; cook and stir 1 minute. Add tomatoes and lemon juice. Bring to a boil. Stir in shrimp. Reduce heat; simmer, uncovered, until shrimp turn pink, 4-5 minutes.
2. Drain orzo. Add orzo, cilantro and pepper to shrimp mixture; heat through. Sprinkle with feta cheese.

**1 CUP** 406 cal., 12g fat (3g sat. fat), 180mg chol., 307mg sod., 40g carb. (2g sugars, 9g fiber), 33g pro.

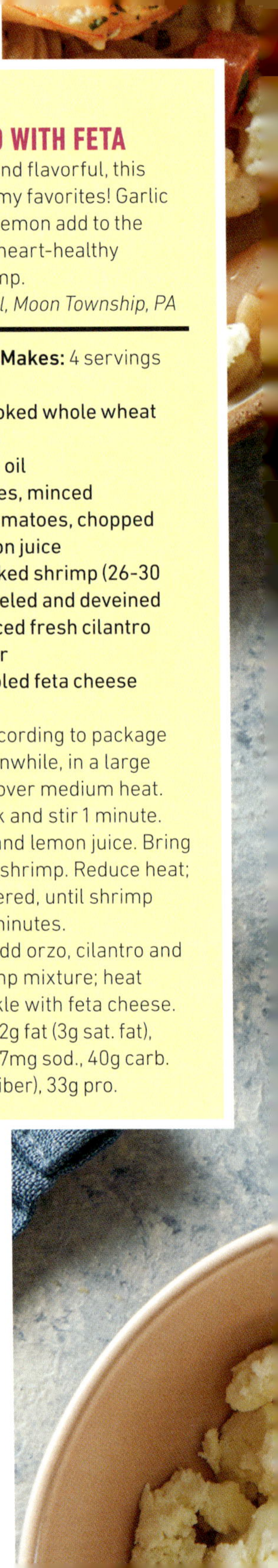

"The orzo and feta are such a nice complement to the shrimp. I like to grill the shrimp in the summertime. It adds a nice smoky element to this dish!"
—TOH_ELLIE, TASTEOFHOME.COM

## TUNA ZUCCHINI CAKES

Here's a great combination of seafood and garden vegetables. Friends like that it's so colorful and pretty, and it's delicious to eat!
*—Billie Blanton, Kingsport, TN*

**Takes:** 25 min. • **Makes:** 3 servings

- 1 Tbsp. butter
- ½ cup finely chopped onion
- 1 pouch (6.4 oz.) light tuna in water
- 1 cup seasoned bread crumbs, divided
- 1 cup shredded zucchini
- 2 large eggs, lightly beaten
- ⅓ cup minced fresh parsley
- 1 tsp. lemon juice
- ½ tsp. salt
- ⅛ tsp. pepper
- 2 Tbsp. canola oil

1. In a large saucepan, heat butter over medium-high heat. Add onion; cook and stir until tender. Remove from heat.
2. Add the tuna, ½ cup bread crumbs, zucchini, eggs, parsley, lemon juice, salt and pepper to onion mixture; mix lightly but thoroughly. Shape into six ½-in.-thick patties; coat with remaining bread crumbs.
3. In a large skillet, heat oil over medium heat. Add patties; cook 3 minutes on each side or until golden brown and heated through.

**2 FISH CAKES** 400 cal., 19g fat (5g sat. fat), 170mg chol., 1261mg sod., 31g carb. (4g sugars, 3g fiber), 26g pro.

## HOMEMADE FISH STICKS

I am a nutritionist and needed a healthy fish fix. Moist inside and crunchy outside, these are amazing with oven fries or roasted veggies and low-fat homemade tartar sauce.
*—Jennifer Rowland, Elizabethtown, KY*

**Takes:** 25 min. • **Makes:** 2 servings

- ½ cup dry bread crumbs
- ½ tsp. salt
- ½ tsp. paprika
- ½ tsp. lemon-pepper seasoning
- ½ cup all-purpose flour
- 1 large egg, beaten
- ¾ lb. cod fillets, cut into 1-in. strips
- Butter-flavored cooking spray

1. Preheat oven to 400°. In a shallow bowl, mix bread crumbs and seasonings. Place flour and egg in separate shallow bowls. Dip fish in flour to coat both sides; shake off excess. Dip in egg, then in crumb mixture, patting to help coating adhere.
2. Place on a baking sheet coated with cooking spray; spritz fish with butter-flavored cooking spray. Bake until fish just begins to flake easily with a fork, 10-12 minutes, turning once.

**1 SERVING** 278 cal., 4g fat (1g sat. fat), 129mg chol., 718mg sod., 25g carb. (2g sugars, 1g fiber), 33g pro.

## FETA SHRIMP SKILLET

My husband and I tried a dish similar to this one on our honeymoon in Greece. I re-created the flavors in this recipe when we got home. When I make it now, it brings back such wonderful memories.
*—Sonali Ruder, New York, NY*

**Takes:** 30 min. • **Makes:** 4 servings

- 1 Tbsp. olive oil
- 1 medium onion, finely chopped
- 3 garlic cloves, minced
- 1 tsp. dried oregano
- ½ tsp. pepper
- ¼ tsp. salt
- 2 cans (14½ oz. each) diced tomatoes, undrained
- ¼ cup white wine, optional
- 1 lb. uncooked shrimp (16-20 per lb.), peeled and deveined
- 2 Tbsp. minced fresh parsley
- ¾ cup crumbled feta cheese

1. In a large nonstick skillet, heat oil over medium-high heat. Add onion; cook and stir 4-6 minutes or until tender. Add garlic and seasonings; cook 1 minute longer. Stir in the tomatoes and, if desired, wine. Bring to a boil. Reduce heat; simmer, uncovered, 5-7 minutes or until sauce is slightly thickened.
2. Add shrimp and parsley; cook 5-6 minutes or until shrimp turn pink, stirring occasionally. Remove from heat; sprinkle with cheese. Let stand, covered, until cheese is softened.

**1¼ CUPS** 240 cal., 8g fat (3g sat. fat), 149mg chol., 748mg sod., 16g carb. (9g sugars, 5g fiber), 25g pro.

## PARMESAN BAKED COD

This is a goof-proof way to keep oven-baked cod moist and flavorful. My mom shared this recipe with me years ago and I've loved it ever since.
*—Mary Jo Hoppe, Pewaukee, WI*

**Takes:** 25 min. • **Makes:** 4 servings

- 4 cod fillets (4 oz. each)
- ⅔ cup mayonnaise
- 4 green onions, chopped
- ¼ cup grated Parmesan cheese
- 1 tsp. Worcestershire sauce

1. Preheat oven to 400°. Place cod in an 8-in. square baking dish coated with cooking spray. Mix remaining ingredients; spread over fillets.
2. Bake, uncovered, until fish just begins to flake easily with a fork, 15-20 minutes.

**1 FILLET** 247 cal., 15g fat (2g sat. fat), 57mg chol., 500mg sod., 7g carb. (2g sugars, 0 fiber), 20g pro.

## TUNA MUSHROOM BAKE

I usually serve this casserole when I'm short on time and we need something hearty and comforting.

*—Connie Moore, Medway, OH*

**Prep:** 20 min. • **Bake:** 35 min.
**Makes:** 6 servings

- 6½ cups uncooked egg noodles
- 1 can (12 oz.) light water-packed tuna, drained and flaked
- 1 can (4 oz.) mushroom stems and pieces, drained
- 1 can (10¾ oz.) condensed cream of mushroom soup, undiluted
- 1⅓ cups 2% milk
- ½ tsp. salt
- ¼ tsp. pepper
- ½ cup crushed saltines
- 3 Tbsp. butter, melted

1. Cook egg noodles according to package directions; stir in tuna and mushrooms. Combine the soup, milk, salt and pepper; add to noodle mixture and mix well.
2. Pour into a greased 2½-qt. baking dish. Combine saltines and butter; sprinkle over noodles. Bake, uncovered, at 350° for 35-45 minutes or until heated through.

**1 SERVING** 399 cal., 13g fat (6g sat. fat), 87mg chol., 879mg sod., 51g carb., 2g fiber, 19g pro.

### TEST KITCHEN TIP

Feel free to use whatever crackers you have on hand. Buttery Ritz crumbs make another classic topping.

## BROWN SUGAR-GLAZED SALMON

Pop these protein-packed salmon fillets in the oven before whipping up a sweet basting sauce. This tangy entree cooks up in minutes, making it a perfect meal for busy families and unexpected weekend guests.

*—Debra Martin, Belleville, MI*

**Takes:** 25 min. • **Makes:** 4 servings

- 1 salmon fillet (1 lb.)
- ¼ tsp. salt
- ¼ tsp. pepper
- 3 Tbsp. brown sugar
- 4 tsp. Dijon mustard
- 1 Tbsp. reduced-sodium soy sauce
- 1 tsp. rice vinegar

1. Preheat oven to 425°. Cut salmon into 4 portions; place in a foil-lined 15x10x1-in. pan. Sprinkle with salt and pepper. Roast 10 minutes. Remove from oven; preheat broiler.
2. In a small saucepan, mix remaining ingredients; bring just to a boil. Brush over salmon. Broil salmon 6 in. from heat until fish just begins to flake easily with a fork, 1-2 minutes.

**3 OZ. COOKED FISH** 225 cal., 10g fat (2g sat. fat), 57mg chol., 491mg sod., 11g carb. (10g sugars, 0 fiber), 19g pro.

## FRIED RICE TIPS

**What is the secret to good fried rice?** Use day-old rice—cook, cool, and refrigerate overnight. Fresh rice is too moist to allow adequate browning.

**What kind of rice should I use?** Choose medium or long grain (e.g., jasmine) rice so the grains stay separate.

**What gives fried rice its flavor?** It develops toasty, caramelized depth when you use a hot pan and let the rice brown before stirring it. Finish with a little soy sauce or oyster sauce for a savory, meaty accent.

## SHRIMP FRIED RICE

This delectable shrimp dish is filled with color and taste that makes it vanish quickly. Our family of four can't get enough of it. Bacon adds crispness and heartiness. Consider it when you need a different entree or brunch item.
*—Sandra Thompson, White Hall, AR*

**Takes:** 20 min. • **Makes:** 6 servings

- 4 Tbsp. butter, divided
- 4 large eggs, lightly beaten
- 3 cups cold cooked rice
- 1 pkg. (16 oz.) frozen mixed vegetables
- 1 lb. uncooked shrimp (31-40 per lb.), peeled and deveined
- ½ tsp. salt
- ¼ tsp. pepper
- 8 bacon strips, cooked and crumbled, optional

1. In a large skillet, melt 1 Tbsp. butter over medium-high heat. Pour eggs into skillet. As the eggs set, lift edges, letting uncooked portion flow underneath. Remove eggs and keep warm.
2. In the same skillet, melt the remaining 3 Tbsp. butter. Add the rice, vegetables and shrimp; cook and stir for 5 minutes or until shrimp turn pink. Meanwhile, chop the eggs into small pieces. Return eggs to the pan; sprinkle with salt and pepper. Cook until heated through, stirring occasionally. Top with with bacon if desired.

**1 SERVING** 332 cal., 12g fat (6g sat. fat), 236mg chol., 422mg sod., 33g carb. (3g sugars, 4g fiber), 21g pro.

## TILAPIA & LEMON SAUCE

Serve this dish with buttered bread and any tossed salad full of your favorite vegetables. It's easy, quick and unique. And it's a big hit with company too.
*—Susan Taul, Birmingham, AL*

**Takes:** 30 min. • **Makes:** 4 servings

- ¼ cup plus 1 Tbsp. all-purpose flour, divided
- 1 tsp. salt
- 4 tilapia fillets (4 oz. each)
- 2 Tbsp. plus 2 tsp. butter, divided
- ⅓ cup reduced-sodium chicken broth
- 2 Tbsp. white wine or additional reduced-sodium chicken broth
- 1½ tsp. lemon juice
- 1½ tsp. minced fresh parsley
- 2 cups hot cooked rice
- ¼ cup sliced almonds, toasted

1. In a shallow bowl, combine ¼ cup flour and salt. Dip fillets in flour mixture.
2. In a large nonstick skillet, cook fillets in 2 Tbsp. butter over medium-high heat until fish just begins to flake with a fork, 4-5 minutes on each side. Remove and keep warm.
3. In the same skillet, melt remaining 2 tsp. butter. Stir in remaining 1 Tbsp. flour until smooth; gradually whisk in broth, wine and lemon juice. Bring to a boil; cook and stir until thickened, about 2 minutes. Stir in parsley. Serve fish and sauce with rice; garnish with almonds.

**1 FILLET WITH ½ CUP RICE AND 4 TSP. SAUCE** 334 cal., 12g fat (6g sat. fat), 76mg chol., 593mg sod., 30g carb. (1g sugars, 1g fiber), 26g pro.

## PESTO CORN SALAD WITH SHRIMP

This recipe showcases the beautiful bounty of summer with its fresh corn, tomatoes and delicious basil.
*—Deena Bowen, Chico, CA*

**Takes:** 30 min. • **Makes:** 4 servings

- 4 medium ears sweet corn, husked
- ½ cup packed fresh basil leaves
- ¼ cup olive oil
- ½ tsp. salt, divided
- 1½ cups cherry tomatoes, halved
- ⅛ tsp. pepper
- 1 medium ripe avocado, peeled and chopped
- 1 lb. uncooked shrimp (31-40 per lb.), peeled and deveined

1. In a pot of boiling water, cook corn until tender, about 5 minutes. Drain; cool slightly. Meanwhile, in a food processor, pulse basil, oil and ¼ tsp. salt until blended.
2. Cut corn from cobs and place in a bowl. Stir in tomatoes, pepper and remaining ¼ tsp. salt. Add avocado and 2 Tbsp. basil mixture; toss gently to combine.
3. Thread shrimp onto metal or soaked wooden skewers; brush with remaining basil mixture. Grill, covered, over medium heat until shrimp turn pink, 2-4 minutes per side. Remove shrimp from skewers; serve with corn mixture.

**1 SERVING** 371 cal., 22g fat (3g sat. fat), 138mg chol., 450mg sod., 25g carb. (8g sugars, 5g fiber), 23g pro.

## SEARED SALMON WITH STRAWBERRY BASIL RELISH

Take a sweet new approach to salmon by topping it with a summery relish of strawberries, basil, honey and pepper.
*—Stacy Mullens, Gresham, OR*

**Takes:** 20 min. • **Makes:** 6 servings

- 6 salmon fillets (4 oz. each)
- 1 Tbsp. butter, melted
- ¼ tsp. salt
- ⅛ tsp. freshly ground pepper

RELISH

- 1¼ cups finely chopped fresh strawberries
- 1 Tbsp. minced fresh basil
- 1 Tbsp. honey
- Dash freshly ground pepper

1. Brush fillets with melted butter; sprinkle with salt and pepper. Heat a large skillet over medium-high heat. Add fillets, skin side up, in batches if necessary; cook 2-3 minutes on each side or until fish just begins to flake easily with a fork.

2. In a small bowl, toss strawberries with basil, honey and pepper. Serve salmon with relish.

**1 SALMON FILLET WITH 3 TBSP. RELISH**
215 cal., 12g fat (3g sat. fat), 62mg chol., 169mg sod., 6g carb. (5g sugars, 1g fiber), 19g pro.

## PARSLEY-CRUSTED COD

Struggling to increase your family's fish servings? You'll appreciate this easy cod with staple ingredients. The flavors are mild and delicious, so even picky eaters won't complain.
*—Judy Grebetz, Racine, WI*

**Takes:** 30 min. • **Makes:** 4 servings

- ¾ cup dry bread crumbs
- 1 Tbsp. minced fresh parsley
- 2 tsp. grated lemon zest
- 1 garlic clove, minced
- ¼ tsp. kosher salt
- ¼ tsp. pepper
- 2 Tbsp. olive oil
- 4 cod fillets (6 oz. each)

1. In a shallow bowl, combine the first 6 ingredients. Brush oil over 1 side of fillets; gently press into crumb mixture.
2. Place crumb side up in a 13x9-in. baking dish coated with cooking spray. Bake at 400° just until fish begins to flake easily with a fork, 15-20 minutes.

**1 FILLET** 215 cal., 8g fat (1g sat. fat), 65mg chol., 194mg sod., 6g carb. (1g sugars, 0 fiber), 28g pro.

"I added some cornmeal and Parmesan cheese to my bread crumbs. Best fish ever."
—PRINCESSTEF5, TASTEOFHOME.COM

## CRUMB-COATED RED SNAPPER

I reel in compliments with this moist, crispy red snapper recipe. Heart-healthy omega-3 oils are an added bonus with my simple but delicious entree that's done in mere minutes. It's one of the best red snapper recipes I've found.
*—Charlotte Elliott, Neenah, WI*

**Takes:** 30 min. • **Makes:** 4 servings

- ½ cup dry bread crumbs
- 2 Tbsp. grated Parmesan cheese
- 1 tsp. lemon-pepper seasoning
- ¼ tsp. salt
- 4 red snapper fillets (6 oz. each)
- 2 Tbsp. olive oil

1. In a shallow bowl, combine the bread crumbs, cheese, lemon pepper and salt; add fillets, 1 at a time, and turn to coat.
2. In a heavy skillet over medium heat, cook fillets in oil, in batches, until fish just begins to flake easily with a fork, 4-5 minutes on each side.

**1 FILLET** 288 cal., 10g fat (2g sat. fat), 62mg chol., 498mg sod., 10g carb. (0 sugars, 0 fiber), 36g pro.

## CREAMY TOMATO SHRIMP WITH PENNE

People love this creamy pasta and think it's complicated, but ready-made sauces make it so quick to prepare. It feels special enough for festive occasions.
*—Cassandra Gourley, Williams, AZ*

**Takes:** 20 min. • **Makes:** 4 servings

- 2 cups uncooked penne pasta
- 2 Tbsp. olive oil
- 1 lb. uncooked shrimp (16-20 per lb.), peeled and deveined
- 1 tsp. minced garlic
- ½ tsp. crushed red pepper flakes
- 1½ cups pasta sauce
- 1 carton (10 oz.) refrigerated Alfredo sauce
- 2 Tbsp. butter
- ¼ tsp. salt
- ⅛ tsp. pepper
- 2 Tbsp. minced fresh parsley

1. Cook pasta according to package directions. Meanwhile, in a large skillet, heat oil over medium heat. Add shrimp, garlic and pepper flakes; cook and stir until shrimp turn pink, 3-5 minutes. Stir in pasta sauce, Alfredo sauce, butter, salt and pepper; heat through.
2. Drain pasta; serve with shrimp mixture. Sprinkle with parsley.

**1 SERVING** 554 cal., 30g fat (13g sat. fat), 188mg chol., 1097mg sod., 42g carb. (11g sugars, 4g fiber), 30g pro.

## SIMPLE HERBED SCALLOPS

In Kansas, fresh seafood can be hard to come by. Luckily, frozen scallops aren't. This dish offers coastal flavor to those of us in landlocked areas.
*—Sarah Befort, Hays, KS*

**Takes:** 30 min. • **Makes:** 2 servings

- ½ to ¾ lb. sea scallops
- 3 Tbsp. butter, divided
- ¾ tsp. lemon juice
- 1 tsp. minced fresh parsley or ¼ tsp. dried parsley
- 1½ tsp. minced fresh chives or ½ tsp. dried chives
- ¼ tsp. minced fresh tarragon or ⅛ tsp. dried tarragon
- ⅛ tsp. garlic salt
- Dash pepper
- 2 Tbsp. dry bread crumbs

1. Preheat oven to 350°. Place scallops in a greased 1-qt. baking dish. Mix 2 Tbsp. melted butter, lemon juice, herbs, garlic salt and pepper; drizzle over scallops.
2. Mix bread crumbs with remaining melted butter; sprinkle over top. Bake, uncovered, until scallops are firm and opaque, 20-25 minutes.

**1 SERVING** 260 cal., 18g fat (11g sat. fat), 73mg chol., 754mg sod., 9g carb. (1g sugars, 1g fiber), 15g pro.

### DID YOU KNOW?

Farmed scallops are becoming more common. Because scallops are filter-feeders that live on plankton, they don't require much feed. Their low environmental impact makes farmed scallops a green choice.

## TUSCAN SALMON PASTA

White kidney beans and plum tomatoes are tossed with salmon and linguine in this fast-to-fix entree that works for special dinners or every day.
*—Dianne Alvine, Toms River, NJ*

**Takes:** 20 min. • **Makes:** 2 servings

- 4 oz. uncooked linguine
- 1 salmon fillet (10 oz.), cut into 1-in. cubes
- 1 tsp. minced fresh rosemary
- 5 Tbsp. olive oil, divided
- ¾ cup cannellini beans, rinsed and drained
- 2 small plum tomatoes, chopped
- 6 garlic cloves, minced
- Salt and pepper to taste

1. Cook linguine according to package directions. Meanwhile, in a small skillet, saute salmon and rosemary in 2 Tbsp. oil for 5 minutes or until salmon flakes easily with a fork. Add the beans, tomatoes, garlic, salt and pepper; heat through.
2. Drain linguine; and transfer to a large bowl. Add salmon mixture; toss gently. Drizzle with remaining oil.

**2 CUPS** 863 cal., 51g fat (8g sat. fat), 84mg chol., 215mg sod., 61g carb. (4g sugars, 7g fiber), 41g pro.

## AIR-FRYER TILAPIA FILLETS

Cooking tilapia fillets in the air fryer means dinner will be on the table in less than half an hour. It's quick and easy, and it doesn't dry out the delicate fillets.
*—Dana Alexander, Lebanon, MO*

**Takes:** 20 min. • **Makes:** 2 servings

- 2 tilapia fillets (6 oz. each)
- 1 Tbsp. butter, melted
- 1 tsp. Montreal steak seasoning
- ½ tsp. dried parsley flakes
- ¼ tsp. paprika
- ¼ tsp. dried thyme
- ⅛ tsp. onion powder
- ⅛ tsp. salt
- ⅛ tsp. pepper
- Dash garlic powder

1. Preheat air fryer to 400°. Brush fillets with butter. In a small bowl, mix the remaining ingredients; sprinkle over fillets.
2. Place fillets in a single layer on greased tray in air-fryer basket. Cook until fish just begins to flake easily with a fork, 6-8 minutes.

**1 FILLET** 193 cal., 7g fat (4g sat. fat), 98mg chol., 594mg sod., 0 carb. (0 sugars, 0 fiber), 32g pro.

**NOTE** Cook times vary dramatically among brands of air fryers. Refer to your air-fryer manual for general cook times and adjust if necessary.

## HONEY WALLEYE

My state is known as the Land of 10,000 Lakes, so fishing is a favorite recreational activity here. This recipe is a quick way to prepare all the fresh walleye hooked by the anglers in my family.

*—Kitty McCue, St. Louis Park, MN*

**Takes:** 20 min. • **Makes:** 6 servings

- 1 large egg
- 2 tsp. honey
- 2 cups crushed Ritz crackers (about 45 to 50)
- ½ tsp. salt
- 1½ lbs. walleye fillets
- ⅓ to ½ cup canola oil
- Optional: Minced fresh parsley and lemon wedges

1. In a shallow bowl, beat egg; add honey. In a shallow dish, combine crackers and salt. Dip fish in egg mixture, then in cracker mixture; turn until coated.
2. In a cast-iron or other heavy skillet, cook fillets in oil over medium heat until golden and fish flakes easily with a fork, 3-5 minutes on each side. If desired, top with parsley and serve with lemon wedges.

**3 OZ. COOKED FISH** 389 cal., 22g fat (3g sat. fat), 133mg chol., 514mg sod., 23g carb. (5g sugars, 1g fiber), 25g pro.

## QUICK MOROCCAN SHRIMP SKILLET

When my niece was attending West Point, she was sent to Morocco for five months. I threw her a going-away party with Moroccan decorations, garments and cuisine, including this saucy shrimp dish. Whenever I make it now, I think of her and I smile.
—*Barbara Lento, Houston, PA*

**Takes:** 25 min. • **Makes:** 4 servings

- 1 Tbsp. canola oil
- 1 small onion, chopped
- ¼ cup pine nuts
- 1 lb. uncooked shrimp (16-20 per lb.), peeled and deveined
- 1 cup uncooked pearl (Israeli) couscous
- 2 Tbsp. lemon juice
- 3 tsp. Moroccan seasoning (ras el hanout)
- 1 tsp. garlic salt
- 2 cups hot water
- Optional: Minced fresh parsley and lemon wedges

1. In a large skillet, heat oil over medium-high heat; saute the onion and pine nuts until onion is tender, 2-3 minutes. Stir in the shrimp, couscous, lemon juice, seasoning, garlic salt and water; bring just to a boil. Reduce heat; simmer, covered, 4-6 minutes or until shrimp turn pink.
2. Remove from heat; let stand 5 minutes. If desired, top with parsley and serve with lemon wedges.

**1 CUP** 335 cal., 11g fat (1g sat. fat), 138mg chol., 626mg sod., 34g carb. (1g sugars, 1g fiber), 24g pro.

### TEST KITCHEN TIPS

- Letting the mixture stand before serving helps the couscous absorb more liquid. It's still a saucy dish, so serve it in a shallow bowl.
- Slivered almonds can be substituted for pine nuts.
- The flavor of this dish is close to a curry, but with more cinnamon.
- For easier eating, remove the shrimp tails before cooking.

## SALMON PASTA SALAD

This recipe was one of my husband's favorite ways to enjoy salmon. I've had it so long I don't even remember where it came from originally. This salad is a nice light meal for a hot summer day, and it lets the salmon flavor come through.
*—Mary Dennis, Bryan, OH*

**Takes:** 15 min. • **Makes:** 8 servings

- 1 pkg. (8 oz.) spiral pasta, cooked and drained
- 2 cups fully cooked salmon chunks or 1 can (14¾ oz.) pink salmon, drained, bones and skin removed
- 1½ cups quartered cherry tomatoes
- 1 medium cucumber, quartered and sliced
- 1 small red onion, sliced
- ½ cup canola oil
- ⅓ cup fresh lemon or lime juice
- 1½ tsp. dill weed
- 1 garlic clove, minced
- ¾ tsp. salt
- ¼ tsp. pepper

In a large bowl, toss the pasta, salmon, tomatoes, cucumber and onion. For dressing, combine the oil, lemon or lime juice, dill, garlic, salt and pepper; mix well. Pour over pasta. Cover; refrigerate until serving.

**1 SERVING** 332 cal., 18g fat (3g sat. fat), 23mg chol., 514mg sod., 27g carb. (4g sugars, 3g fiber), 16g pro.

## BREADED BAKED TILAPIA

So much flavor—so few ingredients! A quick and easy crumb coating makes this yummy tilapia recipe ideal for busy weeknights. Try the breading on cod for a change of pace.
*—Brandi Castillo, Santa Maria, CA*

**Takes:** 20 min. • **Makes:** 4 servings

- ¾ cup soft bread crumbs
- ⅓ cup grated Parmesan cheese
- 1 tsp. garlic salt
- 1 tsp. dried oregano
- 4 tilapia fillets (5 oz. each)

1. Preheat oven to 425°. In a shallow bowl, combine bread crumbs, cheese, garlic salt and oregano. Coat fillets in crumb mixture. Place on a baking sheet coated with cooking spray.
2. Bake 8-12 minutes or until fish flakes easily with a fork.

**NOTE** To make soft bread crumbs, tear bread into pieces and place in a food processor or blender. Cover and pulse until crumbs form. One slice of bread yields ½-¾ cup crumbs.

**1 FILLET** 143 cal., 2g fat (1g sat. fat), 72mg chol., 356mg sod., 2g carb. (0 sugars, 0 fiber), 28g pro.

> **"I dipped the fish in milk first to help the breading stick, and added a little butter as it cooked to get it crispy. Nice, easy way to prepare fish."**
> —CYNANDTOM, TASTEOFHOME.COM

# SHRIMP SALAD-STUFFED AVOCADOS

This is one of my husband's favorites, even though it's pretty enough to serve at a ladies luncheon. When I needed a quick main-dish salad for my book club, I tripled this recipe and got raves! Try it with imitation crabmeat too.
—*Suzanne VanAlstyne, Petoskey, MI*

**Takes:** 15 min. • **Makes:** 4 servings

- ½ lb. cooked shrimp (31-40 per lb.), peeled and deveined, coarsely chopped
- ½ cup chopped celery
- ¼ cup chopped onion
- 3 Tbsp. mayonnaise
- 4½ tsp. capers, drained
- 1 Tbsp. minced fresh parsley
- 2 tsp. Dijon mustard
- 1½ tsp. lemon juice
- ¾ tsp. dried tarragon
- ¼ tsp. seasoned salt
- ⅛ tsp. pepper
- 2 medium ripe avocados, halved and pitted

In a small bowl, combine the first 11 ingredients. Spoon into avocado halves. If desired, garnish with additional minced parsley. Serve immediately.

**1 SERVING** 252cal., 19g fat (3g sat. fat), 90mg chol., 384mg sod., 8g carb. (1g sugars, 5g fiber), 13g pro.

## CAJUN BAKED CATFISH

This well-seasoned fish gets compliments from family and friends whenever I serve it. It's moist and flaky, and the coating is crispy, crunchy and flecked with paprika.
*—Jim Gales, Milwaukee, WI*

**Takes:** 25 min. • **Makes:** 2 servings

- 2 Tbsp. yellow cornmeal
- 2 tsp. Cajun or blackened seasoning
- ½ tsp. dried thyme
- ½ tsp. dried basil
- ¼ tsp. garlic powder
- ¼ tsp. lemon-pepper seasoning
- 2 catfish or tilapia fillets (6 oz. each)
- ¼ tsp. paprika

1. Preheat oven to 400°. In a shallow bowl, mix the first 6 ingredients.
2. Dip fillets in cornmeal mixture to coat both sides. Place on a baking sheet coated with cooking spray. Sprinkle with paprika.
3. Bake until fish begins to flake easily with a fork, 20-25 minutes.

**1 FILLET** 242 cal., 10g fat (2g sat. fat), 94mg chol., 748mg sod., 8g carb. (0 sugars, 1g fiber), 27g pro.

### BUDGET SPICE BLEND

If you don't have Cajun seasoning on hand, make your own with the spices you have. There are many different blends, but a typical mix will include salt, cayenne pepper, garlic powder, paprika, thyme, pepper and onion powder.

## AIR-FRYER SHRIMP

If you like spicy food, this easy dish is a must-try. The shrimp gets its heat from a helping of paprika while also being seasoned with garlic and onion powder. Finish it with a nice, refreshing squeeze of lemon and a sprinkle of parsley to tie it all together.
—Taste of Home *Test Kitchen*

**Prep:** 10 min. • **Cook:** 10 min./batch
**Makes:** 4 servings

- 2 Tbsp. olive oil
- ¾ tsp. salt
- ¼ tsp. paprika
- ¼ tsp. onion powder
- ¼ tsp. garlic powder
- ¼ tsp. pepper
- 1 lb. uncooked shrimp (26-30 per lb.), peeled and deveined
- Chopped fresh parsley
- Lemon wedges, optional

1. Preheat air fryer to 375°. In a large bowl, whisk the first 6 ingredients. Add shrimp; toss to coat.
2. In batches, arrange shrimp in a single layer on a greased tray in air-fryer basket. Cook 6-8 minutes or until lightly browned and shrimp turn pink. Sprinkle with parsley. If desired, serve with lemon wedges.

**ABOUT 7 SHRIMP** 158 cal., 8g fat (1g sat. fat), 138mg chol., 577mg sod., 1g carb. (0 sugars, 0 fiber), 19g pro.

**NOTE** Cook times vary dramatically among brands of air fryers. Refer to your air-fryer manual for general cook times and adjust if necessary.

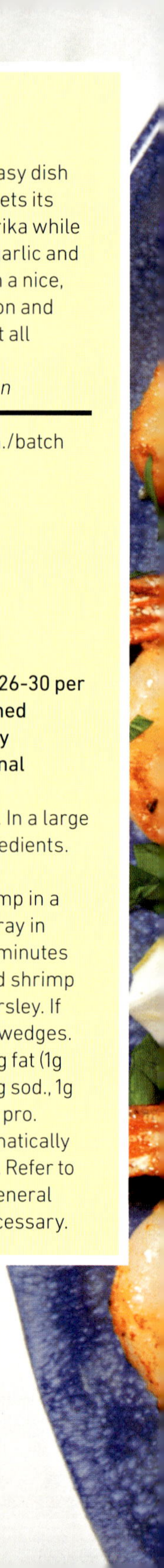

## TUNA MELT SANDWICHES

When our children were young, I often fixed these warm, crunchy sandwiches. They go well with chips and a salad for a quick lunch.
*—Carole Anhalt, Manitowoc, WI*

**Takes:** 30 min. • **Makes:** 6 servings

- ¾ cup chopped celery
- ¾ cup diced cheddar cheese
- 1 can (6 oz.) tuna, drained and flaked
- 1 small onion, chopped
- ¼ cup mayonnaise
- ⅛ tsp. salt
- ¼ cup butter, softened
- 6 hamburger buns, split

1. Preheat oven to 350°. In a bowl, combine first 6 ingredients. Spread butter over cut sides of buns. Spread tuna mixture on bun bottoms; replace tops. Wrap in foil.
2. Bake until cheese is melted, about 15 minutes.

**1 SANDWICH** 363 cal., 23g fat (10g sat. fat), 50mg chol., 629mg sod., 23g carb. (4g sugars, 2g fiber), 15g pro.

### MAKE IT A STOVETOP SAMMIE

Use sliced sandwich bread instead of buns. Butter outsides of sandwiches, then toast in a preheated skillet over medium heat, like a grilled cheese. Cook until golden brown on both sides.

## SOUTHWEST FISH TACOS

These fish tacos are an adaptation of a dish I was served in Bermuda. They're quick because there's so little prep work involved.
*—Jennifer Reid, Farmington, ME*

**Takes:** 20 min. • **Makes:** 4 servings

- 1½ lbs. sole or cod fillets, cut into 1-in. strips
- 1 Tbsp. taco seasoning
- 3 Tbsp. butter, cubed
- 1 pkg. (10 oz.) angel hair coleslaw mix
- ½ cup minced fresh cilantro
- ½ cup mayonnaise
- 1 Tbsp. lime juice
- 1 tsp. sugar
- ¼ tsp. salt
- ¼ tsp. pepper
- 8 corn tortillas or taco shells, warmed
- Lime wedges

1. Sprinkle fish with taco seasoning. In a large skillet, heat butter over medium heat; add fish. Cook until fish just begins to flake easily with a fork, 3-4 minutes on each side.
2. Meanwhile, in a small bowl, combine the coleslaw, cilantro, mayonnaise, lime juice, sugar, salt and pepper.
3. Place fish in tortillas. Top with coleslaw mixture; serve with lime wedges.

**2 TACOS** 510 cal., 37g fat (11g sat. fat), 109mg chol., 1170mg sod., 20g carb. (4g sugars, 3g fiber), 23g pro.

## SPEEDY SALMON PATTIES

When I was a girl growing up on the farm, my mom often fixed these nicely seasoned patties when we were working late in the field. They're also tasty with chopped green peppers added to the mixture.
*—Bonnie Evans, Cameron, NC*

**Takes:** 25 min. • **Makes:** 3 servings

- ⅓ cup finely chopped onion
- 1 large egg, beaten
- 5 saltines, crushed
- ½ tsp. Worcestershire sauce
- ¼ tsp. salt
- ⅛ tsp. pepper
- 1 can (14¾ oz.) salmon, drained, bones and skin removed
- 2 tsp. butter

1. In a large bowl, combine the first 6 ingredients. Crumble salmon over mixture and gently fold in. Shape into 6 patties.
2. In a large skillet over medium heat, fry patties in butter until set and golden brown, 3-4 minutes on each side.

**2 PATTIES** 307 cal., 15g fat (4g sat. fat), 179mg chol., 896mg sod., 6g carb. (1g sugars, 0 fiber), 36g pro.

### SALMON PATTIES TIPS

**How do I keep salmon patties from falling apart?** Finely chop the onion and fully crush the crackers; smaller pieces will bind together better. Refrigerate mixture for up to 30 minutes if desired. Flip gently during cooking.

**Can I freeze salmon patties?** Yes. Freeze uncooked patties on a parchment-lined sheet, then store in a freezer container up to 3 months. Bake from frozen on a greased baking sheet at 400° until a thermometer reads 165°, 12–15 minutes.

## MEDITERRANEAN SHRIMP ORZO SALAD

Loaded with veggies and shrimp, this crowd-pleaser is a tasty change from standard pasta salads.
*—Ginger Johnson, Pottstown, PA*

**Takes:** 30 min. • **Makes:** 8 servings

- 1 pkg. (16 oz.) orzo pasta
- 3/4 lb. peeled and deveined cooked shrimp (31-40 per lb.)
- 1 can (14 oz.) water-packed quartered artichoke hearts, rinsed and drained
- 1 cup finely chopped green pepper
- 1 cup finely chopped sweet red pepper
- 3/4 cup finely chopped red onion
- 1/2 cup pitted Greek olives
- 1/2 cup minced fresh parsley
- 1/3 cup chopped fresh dill
- 3/4 cup Greek vinaigrette

1. Cook orzo according to package directions. Drain; rinse with cold water and drain well.
2. In a large bowl, combine the orzo, shrimp, vegetables, olives and herbs. Add vinaigrette; toss to coat. Refrigerate, covered, until serving.

**1½ CUPS** 397 cal., 12g fat (2g sat. fat), 65mg chol., 574mg sod., 52g carb. (4g sugars, 3g fiber), 18g pro.

### TEST KITCHEN TIP

To make this salad more hearty and satisfying, top it with crumbled feta cheese. Rich, creamy and salty, it rounds out this salad perfectly.

## SHRIMP SCAMPI SPINACH SALAD

My husband and I really enjoy shrimp scampi and fresh spinach salad, so I put the two together. My oldest son loves it, too, and he's only 3!
*—Jamie Porter, Garnett, KS*

**Takes:** 20 min. • **Makes:** 4 servings

- 2 Tbsp. butter
- 1 lb. uncooked shrimp (31-40 per lb.), peeled and deveined
- 3 garlic cloves, minced
- 2 Tbsp. chopped fresh parsley
- 6 oz. fresh baby spinach (about 8 cups)
- 1 cup cherry tomatoes, halved
- Lemon halves
- 1/8 tsp. salt
- 1/8 tsp. coarsely ground pepper
- 1/4 cup sliced almonds, toasted
- Shredded Parmesan cheese, optional

1. In a large skillet, heat butter over medium heat; saute shrimp and garlic 3-4 minutes or until shrimp turn pink. Stir in parsley; remove from heat.
2. To serve, place spinach and tomatoes in a serving dish; top with shrimp mixture. Squeeze lemon juice over salad; sprinkle with salt and pepper. Sprinkle with almonds and, if desired, cheese.

**1 SERVING** 201 cal., 10g fat (4g sat. fat), 153mg chol., 291mg sod., 6g carb. (1g sugars, 2g fiber), 21g pro.

**NOTE** To toast nuts, cook in a skillet over low heat until lightly browned, stirring occasionally.

## BROILED COD

This is the easiest and tastiest fish you'll serve. Even finicky eaters who think they don't like fish will love the beautiful and flaky results.
*—Kim Russell, North Wales, PA*

**Takes:** 30 min. • **Makes:** 2 servings

- 1/4 cup fat-free Italian salad dressing
- 1/2 tsp. sugar
- 1/8 tsp. salt
- 1/8 tsp. garlic powder
- 1/8 tsp. curry powder
- 1/8 tsp. paprika
- 1/8 tsp. pepper
- 2 cod fillets (6 oz. each)
- 2 tsp. butter

1. Preheat broiler. In a shallow bowl, mix first 7 ingredients; add cod, turning to coat. Let stand 10-15 minutes.
2. Place fillets on a greased rack of a broiler pan; discard remaining marinade. Broil 3-4 in. from heat 10-12 minutes or until fish just begins to flake easily with a fork. Top with butter.

**1 FILLET** 168 cal., 5g fat (3g sat. fat), 75mg chol., 365mg sod., 2g carb. (2g sugars, 0 fiber), 27g pro.

## SHRIMP & NOODLE BOWLS

It'll look as if you got takeout, but this dish comes from your kitchen. Convenience items cut down the prep time.
*—Mary Bergfeld, Eugene, OR*

**Takes:** 25 min. • **Makes:** 6 servings

- 8 oz. uncooked angel hair pasta
- 1 lb. cooked shrimp (41-50 per lb.)
- 2 cups broccoli coleslaw mix
- 6 green onions, thinly sliced, optional
- ½ cup minced fresh cilantro
- ⅔ cup reduced-fat sesame ginger salad dressing

Cook pasta according to package directions; drain and rinse in cold water. Transfer to a large bowl. Add the shrimp, coleslaw mix, green onions and cilantro. Drizzle with dressing; toss to coat. Cover and refrigerate until serving.
**1⅓ CUPS** 260 cal., 3g fat (0 sat. fat), 147mg chol., 523mg sod., 36g carb. (6g sugars, 2g fiber), 22g pro.

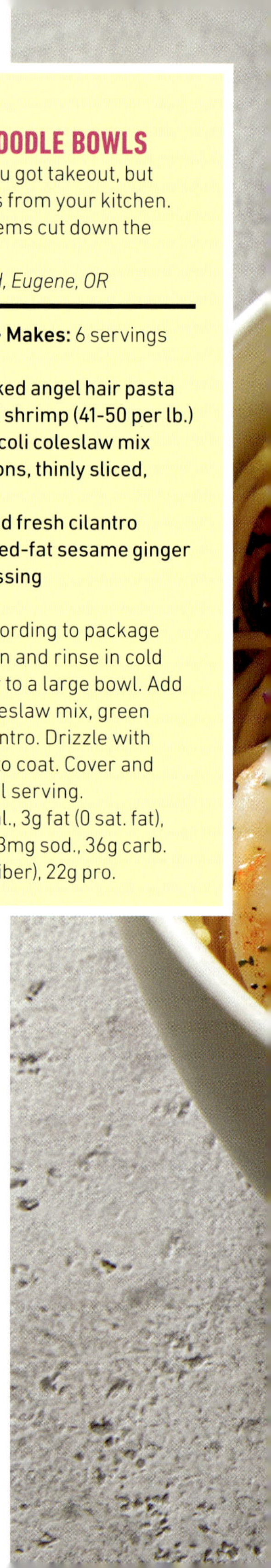

## TILAPIA WITH JASMINE RICE

This tender, full-flavored tilapia with fragrant jasmine rice is absolutely to die for. Your family will love this healthy and delicious dish!
*—Shirl Parsons, Cape Carteret, NC*

**Takes:** 25 min. • **Makes:** 2 servings

- ¾ cup water
- ½ cup uncooked jasmine rice
- 1½ tsp. butter
- ¼ tsp. ground cumin
- ¼ tsp. seafood seasoning
- ¼ tsp. pepper
- ⅛ tsp. salt
- 2 tilapia fillets (6 oz. each)
- ¼ cup Italian salad dressing

1. In a small saucepan, combine water, rice and butter; bring to a boil. Reduce heat; simmer, covered, 15-20 minutes or until liquid is absorbed and rice is tender.
2. Meanwhile, mix seasonings; sprinkle over tilapia. In a large skillet, heat salad dressing over medium heat until hot. Add fillets; cook until fish just begins to flake easily with a fork, 3-4 minutes per side. Serve with rice.

**1 FILLET WITH ¾ CUP RICE** 412 cal., 9g fat (3g sat. fat), 90mg chol., 615mg sod., 42g carb. (2g sugars, 1g fiber), 36g pro.

**HEALTH TIP**

Lighten up this burger by using light mayonnaise and brushing the patties with 1 Tbsp. butter. Then use your broiler instead of pan-frying. You'll save 75 calories and 10 grams of fat per serving.

## TUNA BURGERS

My family members were so accustomed to typical beef burgers that they were hesitant to try these when I first made them. But any skepticism disappeared after just one bite.
*—Kim Stoller, Smithville, OH*

**Takes:** 20 min. • **Makes:** 4 servings

- 1 large egg, lightly beaten
- ½ cup dry bread crumbs
- ½ cup finely chopped celery
- ⅓ cup mayonnaise
- ¼ cup finely chopped onion
- 2 Tbsp. chili sauce
- 1 pouch (6.4 oz.) light tuna in water
- 2 Tbsp. butter
- 4 hamburger buns, split and toasted
- Optional: Lettuce leaves and sliced tomato

1. Mix the first 6 ingredients; gently fold in tuna. Shape into 4 patties.
2. In a large cast-iron or other heavy skillet, heat butter over medium heat. Cook patties until lightly browned, 4-5 minutes on each side. Serve on buns. If desired, top with lettuce and tomato.

**1 BURGER** 417 cal., 23g fat (7g sat. fat), 79mg chol., 710mg sod., 35g carb. (6g sugars, 2g fiber), 17g pro.

## SHRIMP & MACARONI CASSEROLE

I think adding shrimp to this deliciously cheesy casserole is a unique twist to standard macaroni. And you don't have to make a giant batch; this one is perfect for two or three servings.
*—Michael Cohen, Los Angeles, CA*

**Prep:** 20 min. • **Bake:** 20 min.
**Makes:** 2 servings

- 1 cup uncooked elbow macaroni
- 1 large egg, beaten
- ¼ cup half-and-half cream
- 2 Tbsp. butter, melted
- ½ cup grated Parmesan cheese
- ¾ cup shredded part-skim mozzarella cheese, divided
- 1 garlic clove, minced
- ¼ tsp. salt
- ⅛ tsp. pepper
- ¼ lb. uncooked shrimp, peeled, deveined and chopped
- ¾ cup chopped fresh spinach

1. Cook macaroni according to package directions. Meanwhile, in a small bowl, combine the egg, cream and butter; set aside. Drain the macaroni; transfer to another bowl. Add the Parmesan cheese, ½ cup mozzarella cheese, garlic, salt, pepper and egg mixture to the macaroni; toss to coat. Stir in shrimp and spinach.
2. Transfer to a 1-qt. baking dish coated with cooking spray. Sprinkle with remaining mozzarella cheese. Bake, uncovered, at 350° for 20-25 minutes or until shrimp turn pink and cheese is melted.

**1½ CUPS** 371 cal., 21g fat (12g sat. fat), 175mg chol., 671mg sod., 21g carb. (3g sugars, 1g fiber), 25g pro.

## SHRIMP QUESADILLAS

Switch up your normal quesadilla toppings with this recipe. Serve with salsa on the side and a frosty smoothie, if you'd like.
*—Tiffany Bryson, San Antonio, TX*

**Takes:** 30 min. • **Makes:** 2 servings

- 4 tsp. canola oil, divided
- ¼ cup chopped onion
- 1 Tbsp. finely chopped jalapeno pepper
- ½ lb. uncooked shrimp (31-40 per lb.), peeled, deveined and chopped
- ¼ tsp. ground cumin
- ⅛ tsp. pepper
- ¼ cup chopped tomato
- 4 flour tortillas (6 in.)
- ½ cup shredded Mexican cheese blend

1. Heat 2 tsp. oil in a large nonstick skillet over medium heat; add the onion and jalapeno. Cook and stir 3-5 minutes or until tender. Add shrimp, cumin and pepper; cook and stir until shrimp turn pink, 2-3 minutes. Transfer to a small bowl; stir in tomato.
2. Add 1 tsp. oil to the same skillet; add 1 tortilla. Top with half the cheese, half the shrimp mixture and 1 tortilla. Cook over medium heat until lightly browned, 2-3 minutes on each side; remove. Repeat with remaining 1 tsp. oil, tortillas, cheese and shrimp mixture. Cut into wedges.

**NOTE** Wear disposable gloves when cutting hot peppers; the oils can burn skin. Avoid touching your face.

**1 QUESADILLA** 523 cal., 27g fat (8g sat. fat), 163mg chol., 707mg sod., 38g carb. (3g sugars, 4g fiber), 30g pro.

## MINI SCALLOP CASSEROLES

Tiny and tender bay scallops take center stage in these miniature dishes. They're reminiscent of potpies, very creamy and packed with flavorful veggies in every bite.
*—Vivian Manary, Nepean, ON*

**Prep:** 30 min. • **Bake:** 20 min.
**Makes:** 4 servings

- 3 celery ribs, chopped
- 1 cup sliced fresh mushrooms
- 1 medium green pepper, chopped
- 1 small onion, chopped
- 2 Tbsp. butter
- ⅓ cup all-purpose flour
- ¼ tsp. salt
- ¼ tsp. pepper
- 2 cups fat-free milk
- 1 lb. bay scallops

TOPPING

- 1 cup soft bread crumbs
- 1 Tbsp. butter, melted
- ¼ cup shredded cheddar cheese

1. In a large skillet, saute celery, mushrooms, green pepper and onion in butter until tender. Stir in flour, salt and pepper until blended; gradually add milk. Bring to a boil; cook and stir 2 minutes or until thickened.
2. Reduce heat; add scallops. Cook, stirring occasionally, 3-4 minutes or until scallops are firm and opaque.
3. Preheat oven to 350°. Divide mixture among four 10-oz. ramekins or custard cups. In a small bowl, combine bread crumbs and butter; sprinkle over scallop mixture.
4. Bake, uncovered, 15-20 minutes or until bubbly. Sprinkle with the cheese; bake 5 minutes longer or until cheese is melted.

**1 SERVING** 332 cal., 12g fat (7g sat. fat), 70mg chol., 588mg sod., 27g carb. (9g sugars, 2g fiber), 28g pro.

## SHRIMP POMODORO

My husband and I have hectic schedules, so I'm always looking for fast meals that have special-occasion appeal. Shrimp with garlic, tomatoes and pasta is a winner.

*—Catherine Jensen, Blytheville, AR*

**Takes:** 20 min. • **Makes:** 4 servings

- 8 oz. uncooked thin spaghetti
- 1 Tbsp. olive oil
- ¾ lb. uncooked shrimp (26-30 per lb.), peeled and deveined
- 2 cloves garlic, minced
- ¼ to ½ tsp. crushed red pepper flakes
- 1 can (14½ oz.) petite diced tomatoes, undrained
- 10 fresh basil leaves, torn
- ½ tsp. salt
- ⅛ tsp. pepper
- ¼ cup grated Parmesan cheese

1. Cook spaghetti according to package directions.
2. In a large skillet, heat oil over medium-high heat. Add shrimp; cook until shrimp begin to turn pink, 1-2 minutes. Add garlic and pepper flakes; cook 1 minute longer.
3. Add the tomatoes; bring to a boil. Reduce heat; simmer, uncovered, until shrimp turn pink, 2-3 minutes, stirring occasionally. Remove from heat; stir in basil, salt and pepper. Serve with spaghetti and cheese.

**¾ CUP SHRIMP MIXTURE WITH 1 CUP COOKED SPAGHETTI** 357 cal., 7g fat (2g sat. fat), 108mg chol., 653mg sod., 49g carb. (5g sugars, 4g fiber), 24g pro.

## LOBSTER ROLLS

Mayonnaise infused with dill and lemon lends refreshing flavor to these super sandwiches. Try pan-toasting the buns in butter for something special.
—Taste of Home *Test Kitchen*

**Takes:** 30 min.
**Makes:** 8 servings

- 1 cup chopped celery
- ⅓ cup mayonnaise
- 2 Tbsp. lemon juice
- ½ tsp. dill weed
- 5 cups cubed cooked lobster meat (about 4 small lobsters)
- 8 hoagie rolls, split and toasted

In a large bowl, combine the celery, mayonnaise, lemon juice and dill weed. Gently stir in lobster. Serve on rolls.

**1 SANDWICH** 354 cal., 12g fat (2g sat. fat), 133mg chol., 887mg sod., 36g carb. (5g sugars, 1g fiber), 25g pro.

## HERBED TUNA SANDWICHES

A delightful combination of herbs and reduced-fat cheese makes this simple tuna sandwich a standout.
*—Marie Connor, Virginia Beach, VA*

**Takes:** 20 min. • **Makes:** 4 servings

- 1 can (12 oz.) light tuna in water, drained and flaked
- 2 hard-boiled large eggs, chopped
- ⅓ cup reduced-fat mayonnaise
- ¼ cup minced chives
- 2 tsp. minced fresh parsley
- ½ tsp. dried basil
- ¼ tsp. onion powder
- 8 slices whole wheat bread, toasted
- ½ cup shredded reduced-fat cheddar cheese

1. Preheat broiler. Combine the first 7 ingredients. Place 4 pieces of toast on an ungreased baking sheet; top with tuna mixture and sprinkle with cheese.
2. Broil 3-4 in. from the heat until the cheese is melted, 1-2 minutes. Top with remaining toast.

**1 SANDWICH** 367 cal., 15g fat (4g sat. fat), 141mg chol., 718mg sod., 27g carb. (4g sugars, 4g fiber), 31g pro.

## FETA SALMON SALAD

My son David always ordered the salmon sandwich at a local pub. In trying to replicate it, he came up with this salad. It's the only recipe he's ever made, and our entire family thinks it's superb.
*—Susan Griffiths, Mount Pleasant, SC*

**Takes:** 25 min. • **Makes:** 4 servings

- ¼ tsp. salt
- ¼ tsp. garlic powder
- ¼ tsp. ground ginger
- ¼ tsp. dried parsley flakes
- ¼ tsp. pepper
- 4 salmon fillets (6 oz. each)
- 1 pkg. (5 oz.) spring mix salad greens
- 1 large cucumber, chopped
- 1 large tomato, chopped
- ½ cup crumbled feta cheese
- ¼ cup red wine vinaigrette

1. In a small bowl, mix the first 5 ingredients; sprinkle over salmon.
2. Place salmon on oiled grill rack, skin side down. Grill, covered, over medium heat or broil 4 in. from heat until fish just begins to flake easily with a fork, 10-12 minutes.
3. In a large bowl, toss salad greens with cucumber, tomato and cheese; divide among 4 plates. Top with salmon; drizzle with vinaigrette.

**1 SERVING** 352 cal., 18g fat (5g sat. fat), 93mg chol., 531mg sod., 13g carb. (5g sugars, 2g fiber), 33g pro.

## SALMON SALAD TIPS

**How else can I season the salmon?** Use dill and lemon zest, or Italian, Creole or Moroccan seasonings. Or marinate the fish briefly in some of the red wine vinaigrette—but not longer than 30 minutes, or it will turn mushy.

**What add-ins boost the Mediterranean vibe?** Toss in olives, chickpeas or lentils, roasted peppers, baby spinach, chopped dried figs or apricots and toasted pistachios. Consider a lemon vinaigrette or honey-yogurt dressing.

BEAN BURRITOS, PAGE 228

# QUICK & EASY MEATLESS

VEGAN BUTTER CAULIFLOWER, PAGE 215

## EDAMAME SALAD WITH SESAME GINGER DRESSING

This bright baby kale salad is packed with a little bit of everything: hearty greens, a nutty crunch, a zip of citrusy goodness and a big protein punch. It's pure bliss in a bowl.

*—Darla Andrews, Boerne, TX*

**Takes:** 15 min. • **Makes:** 6 servings

- 6 cups baby kale salad blend (about 5 oz.)
- 1 can (15 oz.) garbanzo beans or chickpeas, rinsed and drained
- 2 cups frozen shelled edamame (about 10 oz.), thawed
- 3 clementines, peeled and segmented
- 1 cup fresh bean sprouts
- ½ cup salted peanuts
- 2 green onions, diagonally sliced
- ½ cup sesame ginger salad dressing

Divide salad blend among 6 bowls. Top with all remaining ingredients except salad dressing. Serve with dressing.

**1 SERVING** 317 cal., 17g fat (2g sat. fat), 0 chol., 355mg sod., 32g carb. (14g sugars, 8g fiber), 13g pro.

### HEALTH TIP

Vitamin C–rich clementines help your body absorb iron from plant sources like the kale and edamame in this salad.

## CHICKPEA TACOS

Jazz up your vegetarian taco nights with this chickpea version. The legumes are coated in a spicy seasoning blend and then baked for a crunchy, flavorful bite that's easy to build onto.

*—Margaret Knoebel, Milwaukee, WI*

**Prep:** 20 min. • **Bake:** 20 min.
**Makes:** 4 servings

- 2 Tbsp. canola oil
- 1 tsp. chili powder
- ½ tsp. ground cumin
- ½ tsp. smoked paprika
- ½ tsp. garlic powder
- ½ tsp. salt
- ⅛ tsp. cayenne pepper
- 2 cans (15 lbs. each) garbanzo beans or chickpeas, rinsed and drained
- 8 corn tortillas (6 in.), warmed
- 1 medium ripe avocado, peeled and mashed
- ¼ cup fresh cilantro leaves
- Lime wedges
- Pico de gallo, optional

1. Preheat oven to 425°. Combine first 7 ingredients. Add chickpeas; toss to coat. Transfer to a foil-lined 15x10x1-in. baking pan. Bake, stirring occasionally, until outsides of the chickpeas are crisp and insides are tender, 18-20 minutes.
2. Spread mashed avocado onto center of each tortilla. Top with ¼ cup roasted chickpeas, fresh cilantro and lime wedges. If desired, serve with pico de gallo.

**2 TACOS** 425 cal., 18g fat (1g sat. fat), 0 chol., 615mg sod., 58g carb. (6g sugars, 14g fiber), 12g pro.

## BLACK BEAN & SWEET POTATO RICE BOWLS

I have three hungry boys in my house, so dinners need to be quick and filling, and it helps to get in some veggies too. This one is a favorite because it's hearty and fun to tweak with different ingredients.
*—Kim Van Dunk, Caldwell, NJ*

**Takes:** 30 min. • **Makes:** 4 servings

- ¾ cup uncooked long grain rice
- ¼ tsp. garlic salt
- 1½ cups water
- 3 Tbsp. olive oil, divided
- 1 large sweet potato, peeled and diced
- 1 medium red onion, finely chopped
- 4 cups chopped fresh kale (tough stems removed)
- 1 can (15 oz.) black beans, rinsed and drained
- 2 Tbsp. sweet chili sauce
- Optional: Lime wedges and additional sweet chili sauce

1. Place rice, garlic salt and the water in a large saucepan; bring to a boil. Reduce heat; simmer, covered, until water is absorbed and rice is tender, 15-20 minutes. Remove from heat; let stand 5 minutes.
2. Meanwhile, in a large skillet, heat 2 Tbsp. oil over medium-high heat; saute sweet potato 8 minutes. Add onion; cook and stir until sweet potato is tender, 4-6 minutes. Add kale; cook and stir until tender, 3-5 minutes. Stir in beans; heat through.
3. Gently stir 2 Tbsp. chili sauce and remaining 1 Tbsp. oil into rice; add to sweet potato mixture. If desired, serve with lime wedges and additional chili sauce.

**2 CUPS** 435 cal., 11g fat (2g sat. fat), 0 chol., 405mg sod., 74g carb. (15g sugars, 8g fiber), 10g pro.

## SPINACH PIZZA QUESADILLAS

This simple five-ingredient dinner is special to me because my daughter and I created it together. You can make variations with other veggies you might have at home. It's a smart way to get kids to eat healthier.
*—Tanna Mancini, Gulfport, FL*

**Takes:** 20 min. • **Makes:** 6 servings

- 6 whole wheat tortillas (8 in.)
- 3 cups shredded part-skim mozzarella cheese
- 3 cups chopped fresh spinach
- 1 can (8 oz.) pizza sauce

1. Preheat oven to 400°. On half of each tortilla, layer ½ cup cheese, ½ cup spinach and about 2 Tbsp. sauce. Fold each tortilla in half over filling. Place on baking sheets coated with cooking spray.
2. Bake until cheese is melted, 10-12 minutes. If desired, serve with additional pizza sauce.

**1 QUESADILLA** 301 cal., 13g fat (7g sat. fat), 36mg chol., 650mg sod., 29g carb. (3g sugars, 4g fiber), 19g pro.

## MEDITERRANEAN CHICKPEAS

Add this to your meatless Monday lineup. It's fantastic with feta cheese on top.

*—Elaine Ober, Brookline, MA*

**Takes:** 25 min. • **Makes:** 4 servings

- 1 cup water
- ¾ cup uncooked whole wheat couscous
- 1 Tbsp. olive oil
- 1 medium onion, chopped
- 2 garlic cloves, minced
- 1 can (15 oz.) chickpeas or garbanzo beans, rinsed and drained
- 1 can (14½ oz.) no-salt-added stewed tomatoes, cut up
- 1 can (14 oz.) water-packed artichoke hearts, rinsed, drained and chopped
- ½ cup pitted Greek olives, coarsely chopped
- 1 Tbsp. lemon juice
- ½ tsp. dried oregano
- Dash pepper
- Dash cayenne pepper

1. In a small saucepan, bring water to a boil. Stir in couscous. Remove from heat; let stand, covered, 5-10 minutes or until water is absorbed. Fluff with a fork.
2. Meanwhile, in a large nonstick skillet, heat oil over medium-high heat. Add onion; cook and stir until tender. Add garlic; cook 1 minute longer. Sir in remaining ingredients; heat through, stirring occasionally. Serve with couscous.

**1 CUP CHICKPEA MIXTURE WITH ⅔ CUP COUSCOUS** 340 cal., 10g fat (1g sat. fat), 0 chol., 677mg sod., 51g carb. (9g sugars, 9g fiber), 11g pro.

## VEGAN BUTTER CAULIFLOWER

I created this Indian butter cauliflower recipe for all the picky eaters in my family who love ethnic food. Everyone adores this vegan-friendly dish.
*—Mihaela Metaxa-Albu, London, NY*

**Prep:** 25 min. • **Cook:** 20 min.
**Makes:** 4 servings

- 1 large head cauliflower, cut into florets
- 2 Tbsp. coconut oil, melted
- 1 Tbsp. minced fresh gingerroot
- 2 garlic cloves, minced
- 1 tsp. garam masala
- ¼ tsp. salt
- ¼ tsp. pepper

SAUCE

- 1 Tbsp. olive oil
- ½ cup chopped onion
- 1 Tbsp. minced fresh gingerroot
- 2 garlic cloves, minced
- 2 tsp. garam masala
- 2 tsp. curry powder
- 1 tsp. cayenne pepper, optional
- 1 can (15 oz.) crushed tomatoes
- 1 can (13.66 oz.) coconut milk
- ¼ tsp. salt
- ¼ tsp. pepper
- ¼ cup chopped fresh cilantro
- Optional: Hot cooked rice, naan flatbreads and lime wedges

1. Preheat broiler. In a large bowl, combine first 7 ingredients; toss to coat. Transfer to a rimmed baking sheet. Broil 3-4 in. from heat until brown and crisp-tender, 12-15 minutes, turning once.

2. Meanwhile, in a large skillet, heat olive oil over medium-high heat. Add onion; cook and stir until tender, 4-5 minutes. Add ginger, garlic, garam masala, curry powder and, if desired, cayenne pepper; cook 1 minute longer. Stir in tomatoes, coconut milk, salt and pepper. Bring to a boil; reduce heat. Simmer, uncovered, until thickened, 10-12 minutes, stirring occasionally. Stir in cauliflower; sprinkle with cilantro. If desired, serve with rice, naan and lime.

**1½ CUPS** 349 cal., 27g fat (22g sat. fat), 0 chol., 584mg sod., 24g carb. (11g sugars, 7g fiber), 8g pro.

## CAPRESE EGGPLANT HERO

Here's a wonderful way to showcase fresh produce, including tomatoes, eggplant and basil. During the summer when tomatoes are at the most delicious, I love to create new recipes to eat as many tomatoes as possible! This recipe is so tasty that my family enjoys eating it in every season. You don't need to peel the eggplant. The peel adds some texture and nutrients, and it helps the slices hold their shape a little better. Change it up and add sliced mushrooms in addition to (or instead of) the spinach.
*—Stacy Corday, Waxhaw, NC*

**Prep:** 20 min+ standing • **Grill:** 10 min.
**Makes:** 6 servings

- 1 large eggplant
- 1 tsp. kosher salt, divided
- ¼ cup olive oil, divided
- 3 Tbsp. honey
- 1 tsp. coarsely ground pepper
- ¼ cup balsamic glaze, divided
- 1 loaf (1 lb.) unsliced Italian bread
- 2 large tomatoes, cut into ¼-in. slices
- 1 lb. fresh mozzarella cheese, thinly sliced
- 2 cups fresh arugula
- ½ cup fresh basil leaves, julienned

1. Peel and slice eggplant lengthwise into ¼-in.-thick slices. Place in a colander over a plate; sprinkle with ½ tsp. salt and toss. Let stand 30 minutes.
2. Brush eggplant slices with 2 Tbsp. oil. Drizzle with honey; sprinkle with remaining ½ tsp. salt and the pepper. Grill eggplant, covered, over medium heat until tender, 3-4 minutes per side. Drizzle with 2 Tbsp. balsamic glaze.
3. Cut bread loaf in half horizontally. Drizzle cut sides with remaining 2 Tbsp. olive oil and 2 Tbsp. balsamic glaze. Layer eggplant, tomato and mozzarella slices on bread bottom; top with arugula and basil. Replace top. Slice crosswise into 6 pieces.

**1 PIECE** 600 cal., 28g fat (12g sat. fat), 59mg chol., 856mg sod., 64g carb. (22g sugars, 6g fiber), 22g pro.

## SAGE & BROWNED BUTTER RAVIOLI

After enjoying a similar dish in Italy, we came home and planted sage in our garden to recreate it. It's a quick and easy dinner that reminds us of our trip.
*—Rhonda Hamilton, Portsmouth, OH*

**Takes:** 30 min. • **Makes:** 4 servings

- 1 pkg. (20 oz.) refrigerated cheese ravioli or 2 pkg. (9 oz. each) refrigerated mushroom agnolotti
- ½ cup butter, cubed
- ½ cup coarsely chopped fresh sage
- ½ tsp. salt
- 2 Tbsp. lemon juice
- ¼ cup shredded Parmesan cheese

1. Cook ravioli according to package directions. In a large heavy saucepan, melt butter over medium heat. Heat 5-7 minutes or until golden brown, stirring constantly. Immediately stir in sage and salt; remove from heat.
2. Drain ravioli, reserving 2 Tbsp. pasta water. Add ravioli, reserved pasta water and the lemon juice to butter mixture; gently toss to coat. Serve with cheese.

**1 CUP** 621 cal., 34g fat (21g sat. fat), 120mg chol., 1103mg sod., 58g carb. (2g sugars, 3g fiber), 23g pro.

### BROWNED BUTTER TIPS

**What does browned butter taste like?** It has a nutty, slightly sweet flavor—a bit like caramel.

**Can you brown it too much?** Yes. If your butter becomes too dark, it will take on a bitter, burned flavor.

## SPEEDY HUMMUS PIZZA

What started as an appetizer is now one of my favorite Mediterranean meals. I make sure I always have the ingredients, so I can whip it up anytime. I like to use fresh tomatoes instead of sun-dried ones when they're in season, and sometimes I throw in chopped artichoke hearts too.
*—Nikki Haddad, Germantown, MD*

**Takes:** 20 min. • **Makes:** 4 servings

- 1 prebaked 12-in. pizza crust
- 1 cup hummus
- ¾ tsp. dried oregano
- ¼ tsp. crushed red pepper flakes
- ½ cup crumbled feta cheese
- ½ cup oil-packed sun-dried tomatoes, chopped
- ½ cup pitted Greek olives, chopped
- 1 Tbsp. olive oil

1. Preheat oven to 450°. Place crust on an ungreased baking sheet or a 12-in. pizza pan.
2. In a small bowl, mix hummus, oregano and pepper flakes; spread over crust. Sprinkle with cheese, tomatoes and olives. Bake 8-10 minutes or until heated through. Drizzle with oil.

**2 SLICES** 334 cal., 15g fat (3g sat. fat), 5mg chol., 796mg sod., 38g carb. (1g sugars, 5g fiber), 12g pro.

## TROPICAL SQUASH & BLACK BEAN BURRITOS

The pineapple salsa in these hearty wraps gives you a taste of the tropics on a chilly day. Stuffed with black beans, butternut squash and spinach, they're a nutritious, delicious and fun dinner for any night.
*—Deanna Wolfe, Madison, SD*

**Takes:** 30 min. • **Makes:** 6 servings

- 1 small butternut squash (about 2½ lbs.)
- 1 jar (16 oz.) pineapple salsa
- 1 can (15 oz.) black beans, rinsed and drained
- ½ tsp. salt
- ½ tsp. ground cumin
- ¼ tsp. ground chipotle pepper
- 6 whole wheat tortillas (8 in.), warmed
- 2 cups fresh baby spinach

1. Halve squash lengthwise; remove seeds. Place in a microwave-safe dish, cut side down. Microwave, covered, on high until soft, 15-20 minutes; cool slightly.
2. Meanwhile, in a saucepan, combine salsa and beans; heat through over medium heat, stirring occasionally.
3. Scoop out squash pulp; place in a bowl. Mash until smooth; stir in seasonings. Spoon squash and salsa mixtures onto center of tortillas; top with spinach and roll up.

**1 BURRITO** 290 cal., 1g fat (0 sat. fat), 0 chol., 692mg sod., 62g carb. (13g sugars, 15g fiber), 10g pro.

> **"So tasty. The pineapple salsa is just perfect on this with the healthy whole wheat tortillas. This is a keeper."**
> —BONITO15, TASTEOFHOME.COM

## TORTELLINI WITH TOMATO SPINACH CREAM SAUCE

I enjoy all things pasta, and tortellini is my favorite. The flavor of this dish is amazing. Even my husband, who hates pasta of any kind, loves it! It's also a wonderful recipe for those who don't like spinach.
*—Jenny Dubinsky, Inwood, WV*

---

**Takes:** 30 min. • **Makes:** 6 servings

- 1 Tbsp. olive oil
- 1 small onion, chopped
- 3 garlic cloves, minced
- 1 can (14½ oz.) petite diced tomatoes, undrained
- 5 oz. frozen chopped spinach, thawed and squeezed dry (about ½ cup)
- 1 tsp. dried basil
- ¾ tsp. salt
- ½ tsp. pepper
- 1 cup heavy whipping cream
- 1 pkg. (19 oz.) frozen cheese tortellini
- ½ cup grated Parmesan cheese

1. In a large skillet, heat oil over medium-high heat. Add onion; cook and stir until tender, 2-3 minutes. Add garlic; cook 1 minute longer. Add tomatoes, spinach and seasonings. Cook and stir over medium heat until liquid is absorbed, about 3 minutes.
2. Stir in cream; bring to a boil. Reduce heat; simmer, uncovered, until thickened, about 10 minutes. Meanwhile, cook tortellini according to package directions; drain. Stir into sauce. Sprinkle with cheese.

**1 CUP** 404 cal., 22g fat (13g sat. fat), 80mg chol., 810mg sod., 38g carb. (6g sugars, 4g fiber), 13g pro.

## SPINACH FETA TURNOVERS

These easy turnovers are a favorite with my wife, who says they are delicious and melt in your mouth.
*—David Baruch, Weston, FL*

**Takes:** 30 min. • **Makes:** 4 servings

- 2 large eggs
- 1 pkg. (10 oz.) frozen leaf spinach, thawed, squeezed dry and chopped
- ¾ cup crumbled feta cheese
- 2 garlic cloves, minced
- ¼ tsp. pepper
- 1 tube (13.8 oz.) refrigerated pizza crust

**1.** In a bowl, whisk eggs; set aside 1 Tbsp. of beaten eggs. Combine the spinach, feta cheese, garlic, pepper and remaining beaten eggs.
**2.** Unroll pizza crust; roll into a 12-in. square. Cut into four 6-in. squares. Top each with about ⅓ cup spinach mixture; fold into a triangle and pinch edges to seal. Cut slits in tops; brush with reserved beaten egg.
**3.** Place turnovers on a greased baking sheet. Bake at 425° until golden brown, 10-12 minutes. If desired, serve with tzatziki sauce.
**1 TURNOVER** 361 cal., 9g fat (4g sat. fat), 104mg chol., 936mg sod., 51g carb. (7g sugars, 4g fiber), 17g pro.

# PEANUT BUTTER RAMEN

Elevate simple ramen noodles with some favorite pantry staples. Peanut butter, soy sauce and chili garlic sauce give these noodles a creamy, sweet and spicy profile.
—Taste of Home *Test Kitchen*

**Takes:** 25 min. • **Makes:** 2 servings

- ¼ cup creamy peanut butter
- 2 Tbsp. reduced-sodium soy sauce
- 2 Tbsp. packed brown sugar
- 1 Tbsp. chili garlic sauce
- 1 tsp. sesame oil
- 1 tsp. rice vinegar
- 2 pkg. (3 oz. each) ramen noodles, seasoning packet discarded
- ¼ cup dry roasted peanuts, chopped
- 2 green onions, chopped

1. In a small bowl, whisk together peanut butter, soy sauce, brown sugar, chili garlic sauce, sesame oil and rice vinegar; set aside.
2. Bring a large saucepan of water to a boil. Add ramen noodles; cook until soft, 2-3 minutes. Reserve ¼ cup cooking liquid; discard remaining liquid. Add peanut butter sauce and reserved cooking liquid to the pan with the ramen; stir to combine until sauce is warm.
3. Serve in bowls; top with chopped peanuts and green onion.

**1 SERVING** 780 cal., 42g fat (13g sat. fat), 0 chol., 1433mg sod., 82g carb. (20g sugars, 4g fiber), 21g pro.

## PROTEIN POWERED

For a protein boost, top your ramen with sliced boiled eggs or scrambled eggs cooked in sesame oil. Or stir raw beaten eggs into the ramen during the last 30 seconds of cooking; cook and stir until eggs are firm.

## MUFFIN-TIN LASAGNAS

This is a super fun way to serve lasagna and a nice way to surprise everyone at the table. Easy and quick, these cups can be made with whatever ingredients your family likes best.

*—Sally Kilkenny, Granger, IA*

**Takes:** 30 min. • **Makes:** 1 dozen

- 1 large egg, lightly beaten
- 1 carton (15 oz.) part-skim ricotta cheese
- 2 cups shredded Italian cheese blend, divided
- 1 Tbsp. olive oil
- 24 wonton wrappers
- 1 jar (24 oz.) garden-style pasta sauce
- Minced fresh parsley, optional

1. Preheat oven to 375°. In a bowl, mix egg, ricotta cheese and 1¼ cups Italian cheese blend.
2. Generously grease 12 muffin cups with oil; line each with a wonton wrapper. Fill each with 1 Tbsp. ricotta mixture and 1½ Tbsp. pasta sauce. Top each with a second wrapper, rotating corners and pressing down centers. Repeat ricotta and sauce layers. Sprinkle with remaining ¾ cup cheese blend.
3. Bake until cheese is melted, 20-25 minutes. If desired, sprinkle with parsley.

**2 MINI LASAGNAS** 414 cal., 19g fat (9g sat. fat), 83mg chol., 970mg sod., 36g carb. (8g sugars, 2g fiber), 22g pro.

## CRISPY TOFU WITH BLACK PEPPER SAUCE

Sometimes tofu can be boring and tasteless, but not in this recipe! The crispy vegetarian bean curd is so loaded with flavor, you'll never shy away from tofu again.

*—Nick Iverson, Denver, CO*

**Takes:** 30 min. • **Makes:** 4 servings

- 2 Tbsp. reduced-sodium soy sauce
- 2 Tbsp. chili garlic sauce
- 1 Tbsp. packed brown sugar
- 1 Tbsp. rice vinegar
- 4 green onions
- 8 oz. extra-firm tofu, drained
- 3 Tbsp. cornstarch
- 6 Tbsp. canola oil, divided
- 8 oz. fresh sugar snap peas (about 2 cups), trimmed and thinly sliced
- 1 tsp. freshly ground pepper
- 3 garlic cloves, minced
- 2 tsp. grated fresh gingerroot

1. Mix the first 4 ingredients. Mince white parts of green onions; thinly slice green parts.
2. Cut tofu into ½-in. cubes; pat dry with paper towels. Toss tofu with cornstarch. In a large skillet, heat 4 Tbsp. oil over medium-high heat. Add tofu; cook until crisp and golden brown, 5-7 minutes, stirring occasionally. Remove from pan; drain on paper towels.
3. In same pan, heat 1 Tbsp. oil over medium-high heat. Add peas; stir-fry until crisp-tender, 2-3 minutes. Remove from pan.
4. In same pan, heat remaining 1 Tbsp. oil over medium-high heat. Add pepper; cook 30 seconds. Add garlic, ginger and white parts of green onions; stir-fry for 30-45 seconds. Stir in soy sauce mixture; cook and stir until slightly thickened. Remove from heat; stir in tofu and peas. Sprinkle with sliced green onions.

**1 CUP** 316 cal., 24g fat (2g sat. fat), 0 chol., 583mg sod., 20g carb. (8g sugars, 2g fiber), 7g pro.

## AVOCADO EGG SALAD TOAST

After purchasing far too many unripe avocados for an event, I had a surplus of ripe ones in my kitchen for a week after! I was making some egg salad sandwiches for lunch on one of those days, and I had the great idea to use avocado to bind it together instead of traditional mayonnaise. Not only was this version unbelievably delicious, but also the healthy fats, vitamins and fiber in the avocado make this a more nutritious option than the traditional mayo-laden version.
*—Shannon Dobos, Calgary, AB*

---

**Takes:** 20 min. • **Makes:** 4 servings

- **1 medium ripe avocado, peeled and cubed**
- **6 hard-boiled large eggs, chopped**
- **1 green onion, finely chopped**
- **1 tsp. lemon juice**
- **¼ tsp. salt**
- **⅛ tsp. pepper**
- **4 large slices sourdough bread, halved and toasted**

In a large bowl, mash avocado to desired consistency. Gently stir in eggs, green onion, lemon juice, salt and pepper. Spread over toast. Serve immediately.

**2 PIECES** 367 cal., 15g fat (4g sat. fat), 280mg chol., 671mg sod., 41g carb. (4g sugars, 4g fiber), 18g pro.

## AIR-FRIED BUTTERNUT SQUASH TACOS

Butternut squash tossed with southwestern spices makes a wonderful base for vegetarian tacos. I'm always looking for easy and healthy dinners for my family, and this dish is delicious!
*—Elisabeth Larsen, Pleasant Grove, UT*

**Prep:** 10 min. • **Cook:** 15 min./batch
**Makes:** 6 servings

- 2 Tbsp. canola oil
- 1 Tbsp. chili powder
- ½ tsp. ground cumin
- ½ tsp. ground coriander
- ½ tsp. salt
- ¼ tsp. cayenne pepper
- 1 medium butternut squash (3 to 4 lbs.), peeled and cut into ½-in. pieces
- 12 corn tortillas (6 in.), warmed
- 1 cup crumbled queso fresco or feta cheese
- 1 medium ripe avocado, peeled and sliced thin
- ¼ cup diced red onion
- Pico de gallo, optional

1. Preheat air fryer to 400°. Combine first 6 ingredients. Add squash pieces; toss to coat. In batches, arrange squash in a single layer on greased tray in air-fryer basket. Cook until tender, 15-20 minutes.

2. Divide squash evenly among tortillas. Top with queso fresco, avocado and red onion. If desired, serve with pico de gallo.

**2 TACOS** 353 cal., 13g fat (3g sat. fat), 13mg chol., 322mg sod., 54g carb. (7g sugars, 13g fiber), 11g pro.

> **"One of the best taco recipes ever! I added seasoned black beans and topped them with avocado and sour cream—amazing!"**
> —TERESA155, TASTEOFHOME.COM

## CHILES RELLENOS QUICHE

Wake up with a smoky kick of roasted green chiles. I keep the ingredients for this recipe on hand so I can whip up a tasty breakfast on demand.
*—Linda Miritello, Mesa, AZ*

**Prep:** 25 min. • **Bake:** 35 min.
**Makes:** 6 servings

- Dough for single-crust pie
- 2 Tbsp. cornmeal
- 1½ cups shredded Monterey Jack cheese
- 1 cup shredded cheddar cheese
- 1 can (4 oz.) chopped green chiles
- 3 large eggs
- ¾ cup sour cream
- 1 Tbsp. minced fresh cilantro
- 2 to 4 drops hot pepper sauce, optional

1. On a lightly floured surface, roll dough to a ⅛-in.-thick circle; transfer to a 9-in. pie plate. Trim crust to ½ in. beyond rim of plate; flute edge. Refrigerate 30 minutes. Preheat oven to 450°.
2. Line unpricked crust with a double thickness of heavy-duty foil. Bake at 450° for 8 minutes. Remove foil; bake 5 minutes longer. Cool on a wire rack. Reduce heat to 350°.
3. Sprinkle cornmeal over bottom of crust. In a small bowl, combine cheeses; set aside ½ cup for topping. Add chiles to remaining 2 cups cheese mixture; sprinkle into crust. In a small bowl, whisk the eggs, sour cream, cilantro and, if desired, hot pepper sauce. Pour into crust; sprinkle with reserved ½ cup cheese mixture.
4. Bake until a knife inserted in the center comes out clean, 35-40 minutes. Let stand 5 minutes before cutting.

**FREEZE OPTION** Cover and freeze unbaked quiche. To use, remove from freezer 30 minutes before baking (do not thaw). Preheat oven to 350°. Place quiche on a baking sheet; cover edge of quiche loosely with foil. Bake as directed, increasing time as necessary for a knife inserted in the center to come out clean.
**DOUGH FOR SINGLE-CRUST PIE** Combine 1¼ cups all-purpose flour and ¼ tsp. salt; cut in ½ cup cold butter until crumbly. Gradually add 3-5 Tbsp. ice water, tossing with a fork until dough holds together when pressed. Shape into a disk; wrap and refrigerate 1 hour.
**1 PIECE** 444 cal., 31g fat (18g sat. fat), 178mg chol., 520mg sod., 23g carb. (3g sugars, 1g fiber), 17g pro.

## ITALIAN GRILLED CHEESE SANDWICHES

I made up this recipe for the students in the foods and nutrition class I teach. The kids like it so much, they often go home and fix it for their families.
*—Beth Hiott, York, SC*

**Takes:** 25 min. • **Makes:** 4 servings

- 8 slices Italian bread
- 4 Tbsp. prepared pesto
- 4 slices provolone cheese
- 4 slices part-skim mozzarella cheese
- 5 tsp. olive oil
- Marinara sauce, warmed, optional

1. Spread 4 bread slices with pesto. Layer with cheeses; top with remaining bread. Brush outsides of sandwiches with oil.
2. Using a large cast-iron skillet or electric griddle, toast sandwiches over medium heat until cheese is melted, 3-4 minutes on each side. If desired, serve with marinara sauce.

**1 SANDWICH** 445 cal., 27g fat (10g sat. fat), 35mg chol., 759mg sod., 32g carb. (1g sugars, 2g fiber), 20g pro.

## ROASTED CURRIED CHICKPEAS & CAULIFLOWER

When there's not much time to cook, try roasting potatoes and cauliflower with chickpeas for a warm-you-up dinner. Add chicken or tofu to the sheet pan if you like.
*—pam correll, Brockport, PA*

---

**Prep:** 15 min. • **Bake:** 30 min.
**Makes:** 4 servings

- 2 lbs. potatoes (about 4 medium), peeled and cut into ½-in. cubes
- 1 small head cauliflower, broken into florets (about 3 cups)
- 1 can (15 oz.) chickpeas or garbanzo beans, rinsed and drained
- 3 Tbsp. olive oil
- 2 tsp. curry powder
- ¾ tsp. salt
- ¼ tsp. pepper
- 3 Tbsp. minced fresh cilantro or parsley

1. Preheat oven to 400°. Place first 7 ingredients in a large bowl; toss to coat. Transfer to a 15x10x1-in. baking pan coated with cooking spray.
2. Roast until vegetables are tender, 30-35 minutes, stirring occasionally. Sprinkle with cilantro.

**1½ CUPS** 339 cal., 13g fat (2g sat. fat), 0 chol., 605mg sod., 51g carb. (6g sugars, 8g fiber), 8g pro.

## MEATLESS CHILI MAC

I came across this recipe in a newspaper years ago. It's been a hit at our house ever since. It's fast and flavorful, and it appeals to all ages.
*—Cindy Ragan, North Huntingdon, PA*

**Prep:** 15 min. • **Cook:** 25 min.
**Makes:** 8 servings

- 1 large onion, chopped
- 1 medium green pepper, chopped
- 1 Tbsp. olive oil
- 1 garlic clove, minced
- 2 cups water
- 1½ cups uncooked elbow macaroni
- 1 can (16 oz.) mild chili beans, undrained
- 1 can (15½ oz.) great northern beans, rinsed and drained
- 1 can (14½ oz.) diced tomatoes, undrained
- 1 can (8 oz.) tomato sauce
- 4 tsp. chili powder
- 1 tsp. ground cumin
- ½ tsp. salt
- ½ cup fat-free sour cream

1. In a Dutch oven, saute onion and green pepper in oil until tender. Add garlic; cook 1 minute longer. Stir in the water, macaroni, beans, tomatoes, tomato sauce, chili powder, cumin and salt.
2. Bring to a boil. Reduce heat; cover and simmer for 15-20 minutes or until macaroni is tender. Top each serving with 1 Tbsp. sour cream.

**1¼ CUPS** 206 cal., 3g fat (1g sat. fat), 1mg chol., 651mg sod., 37g carb. (6g sugars, 9g fiber), 10g pro.

## BEAN BURRITOS

I always have the ingredients for this cheesy burrito recipe on hand. Cooking the rice and shredding the cheese the night before saves precious minutes at dinnertime.
*—Beth Osborne Skinner, Bristol, TN*

**Takes:** 30 min. • **Makes:** 6 servings

- 1 can (16 oz.) vegetarian refried beans
- 1 cup salsa
- 1 cup cooked long grain rice
- 2 cups shredded cheddar cheese, divided
- 12 flour tortillas (6 in.)
- Optional: Shredded lettuce, sliced olives, halved grape tomatoes and sliced avocado

1. Preheat oven to 375°. In a large bowl, combine beans, salsa, rice and 1 cup cheese. Spoon about ⅓ cup mixture off-center on each tortilla. Fold the sides and ends over filling and roll up.
2. Arrange burritos in a greased 13x9-in. baking dish. Sprinkle with remaining 1 cup cheese. Cover and bake 20-25 minutes or until heated through. Add toppings as desired.

**2 BURRITOS** 216 cal., 9g fat (4g sat. fat), 23mg chol., 544mg sod., 24g carb. (1g sugars, 3g fiber), 9g pro.

"These were super easy to make and taste great! Next time, I will try refried black beans for a bit of variety. I will be making these again and again."

—CAFEQUEEN, TASTEOFHOME.COM

## SLOW-COOKER CHICKPEA TAGINE

While traveling through Morocco, my wife and I fell in love with the complex flavors of tagines. Resist the urge to stir as it will break down the vegetables. You can also add shredded cooked chicken in the last 10 minutes, or serve with grilled fish.
*—Raymond Wyatt, West St. Paul, MN*

**Prep:** 20 min. • **Cook:** 4 hours
**Makes:** 6 servings

- 1 small butternut squash (about 2 lbs.), peeled and cut into ½-in. cubes
- 2 medium zucchini, cut into ½-in. pieces
- 1 medium sweet red pepper, coarsely chopped
- 1 medium onion, coarsely chopped
- 1 can (15 oz.) chickpeas or garbanzo beans, rinsed and drained
- 12 dried apricots, halved
- 2 Tbsp. olive oil
- 2 garlic cloves, minced
- 2 tsp. paprika
- 1 tsp. ground ginger
- 1 tsp. ground cumin
- ½ tsp. salt
- ¼ tsp. pepper
- ¼ tsp. ground cinnamon
- 1 can (15 oz.) crushed tomatoes
- 2 to 3 tsp. harissa chili paste
- 2 tsp. honey
- ¼ cup chopped fresh mint leaves
- Optional: Plain Greek yogurt and additional olive oil, honey and mint

1. Place first 6 ingredients in a 5-qt. or 6-qt. slow cooker.
2. In a skillet, heat oil over medium heat. Add garlic, paprika, ginger, cumin, salt, pepper and cinnamon; cook and stir until fragrant, about 1 minute. Add tomatoes, harissa and honey; bring to a boil. Pour tomato mixture over vegetables; stir to combine. Cook, covered, on low until vegetables are tender and sauce has thickened, 4-5 hours. Stir in mint.
3. If desired, top wih yogurt, additional olive oil, honey and mint.

**1½ CUPS254** cal., 6g fat (0 sat. fat), 0 chol., 448mg sod., 46g carb. (18g sugars, 12g fiber), 8g pro.

## VEGETARIAN HUMMUS WRAPS

I created this recipe mainly to help get more veggies into my diet. I'm busy and on the go like many other mothers. These wraps give me energy and taste delicious.
*—Amber Indra, Thousand Oaks, CA*

**Takes:** 10 min. • **Makes:** 2 servings

- 6 Tbsp. hummus
- 2 flour tortillas (8 in.), room temperature
- ½ cup shredded carrots
- 1 cup fresh baby spinach
- 6 slices tomato
- 2 Tbsp. green goddess salad dressing

Spread hummus over each tortilla. Layer with carrots, spinach and tomato; drizzle with dressing. Roll up tightly.

**1 SERVING** 276 cal., 8g fat (1g sat. fat), 0 chol., 630mg sod., 43g carb. (5g sugars, 5g fiber), 9g pro.

## LIGHTEN IT UP

A simple switch to light mayonnaise in this recipe can save about 75 calories and 8 grams of fat per serving.

## CURRIED EGG SALAD

A curry kick gives this egg salad big appeal. We love these sandwiches when the weather gets warm.
*—Joyce McDowell, West Union, OH*

**Takes:** 15 min. • **Makes:** 6 servings

- ½ cup mayonnaise
- ½ tsp. curry powder
- ½ tsp. honey
- Dash ground ginger
- 6 hard-boiled large eggs, coarsely chopped
- 3 green onions, sliced
- 6 slices whole wheat bread
- Optional: Tomato slices and cracked pepper

Mix the first 4 ingredients; stir in eggs and green onions. Spread on bread. If desired, top with tomato and sprinkle with pepper.

**1 OPEN-FACED SANDWICH** 273 cal., 20g fat (4g sat. fat), 188mg chol., 284mg sod., 14g carb. (2g sugars, 2g fiber), 10g pro.

# LAZY LASAGNA FOR 2

Lasagna may seem like it's a lot of work on a busy evening. But one day when I had a craving for it, I devised this simple recipe, and it worked out beautifully.

*—Carol Mead, Los Alamos, NM*

**Takes:** 30 min. • **Makes:** 2 servings

- 1 cup meatless pasta sauce
- ¾ cup shredded part-skim mozzarella cheese
- ½ cup 4% cottage cheese
- 1½ cups cooked wide egg noodles
- 2 Tbsp. grated Parmesan cheese
- Chopped fresh parsley, optional

**1.** Warm the pasta sauce; stir in mozzarella and cottage cheeses. Fold in noodles. Pour into 2 greased 2-cup baking dishes. Sprinkle with Parmesan cheese.

**2.** Bake, uncovered, at 375° until bubbly, about 20 minutes. If desired, top with parsley.

**1 SERVING** 399 cal., 16g fat (8g sat. fat), 68mg chol., 1120mg sod., 37g carb. (12g sugars, 3g fiber), 25g pro.

## THREE-CHEESE QUESADILLAS

You will swear this dish was from a restaurant. If desired, you can also make this recipe with reduced-fat products to lighten it up.
*—Sandy Smith, Saugerties, NY*

**Takes:** 20 min. • **Makes:** 2 servings

- 1 Tbsp. butter
- 4 flour tortillas (8 in.)
- 2 oz. cream cheese, softened
- ¼ cup shredded sharp cheddar cheese
- ¼ cup shredded Monterey Jack cheese
- 2 Tbsp. thinly sliced green onion
- 1 Tbsp. minced fresh cilantro
- 2 tsp. chopped ripe olives
- ¼ cup salsa
- Sour cream, optional

1. Spread butter over 1 side of each tortilla. Spread cream cheese over unbuttered sides of 2 tortillas. Sprinkle with cheeses, onion, cilantro and olives. Top with remaining 2 tortillas, buttered side up.
2. Cook on a griddle over medium heat for 1-2 minutes on each side or until cheese is melted. Cut into wedges. Serve with salsa and sour cream if desired.

**1 QUESADILLA** 560 cal., 30g fat (16g sat. fat), 74mg chol., 928mg sod., 55g carb. (1g sugars, 0 fiber), 18g pro.

> **"Liked this recipe very much just the way it is—especially how the outsides of the tortillas got so crispy!"**
> —BARBARAE, TASTEOFHOME.COM

## SALSA BLACK BEAN BURGERS

Meatless meals will be so tasty when these hearty bean burgers are on the menu. Guacamole and sour cream make them seem decadent.
*—Jill Reichardt, St. Louis, MO*

**Takes:** 20 min. • **Makes:** 4 servings

- 1 can (15 oz.) black beans, rinsed and drained
- ⅔ cup dry bread crumbs
- 1 small tomato, seeded and finely chopped
- 1 jalapeno pepper, seeded and finely chopped
- 1 large egg
- 1 tsp. minced fresh cilantro
- 1 garlic clove, minced
- 1 Tbsp. olive oil
- 4 whole wheat hamburger buns, split
- Optional: Reduced-fat sour cream, guacamole, spicy ranch salad dressing, lettuce, sliced tomato and sliced red onions

1. Place beans in a food processor; cover and process until blended. Transfer to a large bowl. Add the bread crumbs, tomato, jalapeno, egg, cilantro and garlic. Mix until combined. Shape into 4 patties.
2. In a large nonstick skillet, cook patties in oil over medium heat until lightly browned, 4-6 minutes on each side. Serve on buns; add toppings as desired.

**NOTE** Wear disposable gloves when cutting hot peppers; the oils can burn skin. Avoid touching your face.

**1 BURGER** 323 cal., 8g fat (1g sat. fat), 53mg chol., 557mg sod., 51g carb. (6g sugars, 9g fiber), 13g pro.

## FETA GARBANZO BEAN SALAD

This super-quick chickpea salad is a hit with my crowd. If there are any leftovers, which rarely happens, I pile them into pitas for lunches the next day!
*—Judy Doepel, Ballston Lake, NY*

**Takes:** 15 min. • **Makes:** 4 servings

- 1 can (15 oz.) garbanzo beans or chickpeas, rinsed and drained
- 1½ cups coarsely chopped English cucumber (about ½ medium)
- 1 can (2¼ oz.) sliced ripe olives, drained
- 1 medium tomato, seeded and chopped
- ¼ cup thinly sliced red onion
- ¼ cup chopped fresh parsley
- 3 Tbsp. olive oil
- 1 Tbsp. lemon juice
- ¼ tsp. salt
- ⅛ tsp. pepper
- 5 cups torn mixed salad greens
- ½ cup crumbled feta cheese

Place the first 11 ingredients in a large bowl; toss to combine. Sprinkle with cheese.

**2 CUPS** 268 cal., 16g fat (3g sat. fat), 8mg chol., 586mg sod., 24g carb. (4g sugars, 7g fiber), 9g pro.

### SERVING OPTIONS

Salty, crumbly Greek feta cheese is traditionally made with sheep's or goat's milk, but most American brands are made with cow's milk instead. If you're not fond of feta, you could substitute queso blanco, which is milky and mild-tasting. Add fresh oregano or mint if desired.

## GRILLED CHEESE & TOMATO SOUP BAKE

This casserole brings together the flavors of two classic comfort foods, with no dipping required.
*—Megan Kuns, Perrysburg, OH*

**Prep:** 25 min. • **Bake:** 25 min. + standing
**Makes:** 6 servings

- 3 oz. reduced-fat cream cheese
- 1½ tsp. dried basil, divided
- 12 slices Italian, sourdough or rye bread (½ in. thick)
- 6 slices part-skim mozzarella cheese
- 6 Tbsp. butter, softened
- ½ cup tomato paste
- 1 garlic clove, minced
- ¼ tsp. salt
- ¼ tsp. pepper
- 1¾ cups 2% milk
- 2 large eggs
- 1 cup shredded Italian cheese blend or part-skim mozzarella cheese

1. Preheat oven to 350°. In a small bowl, mix cream cheese and 1 tsp. basil until blended; spread onto 6 bread slices. Top with cheese slices and remaining 6 bread slices. Spread outsides of sandwiches with butter. Arrange in a greased 13x9-in. baking dish.
2. In a small saucepan, combine tomato paste, garlic, salt, pepper and remaining ½ tsp. basil; cook and stir over medium heat for 1 minute. Gradually whisk in the milk; bring to a boil. Reduce heat and simmer, uncovered, for 4-5 minutes or until thickened, stirring frequently. Remove from heat.
3. In a large bowl, whisk eggs; gradually whisk in a third of the milk mixture. Stir in remaining milk mixture; pour over the sandwiches. Sprinkle with Italian cheese blend.
4. Bake, uncovered, until golden brown and cheese is melted, 25-30 minutes. Let stand for 10 minutes before serving.

**1 SANDWICH** 485 cal., 29g fat (17g sat. fat), 137mg chol., 918mg sod., 33g carb. (7g sugars, 2g fiber), 23g pro.

### TEST KITCHEN TIP

When this casserole comes out of the oven, it's best to let it sit for the full 10 minutes, if not a little longer. You'll end up with a rich, creamy texture similar to a breakfast strata or a savory bread pudding.

## BLACK BEANS WITH BROWN RICE

Your family will never miss the meat in this hearty, colorful and fresh-tasting main dish. Served over brown rice, these beans make a healthy, stick-to-the-ribs dinner.

*—Sheila Meyer, North Canton, OH*

**Prep:** 15 min. • **Cook:** 20 min.
**Makes:** 5 servings

- 1 small green pepper, chopped
- ½ cup chopped sweet red pepper
- ½ cup chopped sweet yellow pepper
- ½ cup chopped red onion
- 2 Tbsp. canola oil
- 2 cans (15 oz. each) black beans, rinsed and drained
- 1 can (14½ oz.) diced tomatoes, undrained
- 2 Tbsp. cider vinegar
- ½ tsp. garlic salt
- ⅛ tsp. pepper
- ⅛ tsp. cayenne pepper
- 2½ cups hot cooked brown rice

In a large saucepan, saute peppers and onion in oil until tender. Stir in the beans, tomatoes, vinegar, garlic salt, pepper and cayenne. Bring to a boil. Reduce heat; simmer, uncovered, for 12-15 minutes or until desired consistency is reached, stirring occasionally. Serve with rice.

**1 SERVING** 327 cal., 7g fat (1g sat. fat), 0 chol., 614mg sod., 55g carb. (6g sugars, 11g fiber), 12g pro.

## PORTOBELLO MELTS

We're always looking for satisfying vegetarian meals, and this one tops the list. These melts are especially delicious in the summer when we have tons of homegrown tomatoes.

*—Amy Smalley, Morehead, KY*

**Takes:** 20 min. • **Makes:** 2 servings

- 2 large portobello mushrooms (4 oz. each), stems removed
- ¼ cup olive oil
- 2 Tbsp. balsamic vinegar
- ½ tsp. salt
- ½ tsp. dried basil
- 4 tomato slices
- 2 slices mozzarella cheese
- 2 slices Italian bread (1 in. thick)
- Chopped fresh basil

1. Preheat broiler. Place mushrooms in a shallow bowl. Mix oil, vinegar, salt and dried basil; brush onto both sides of mushrooms. Let stand 5 minutes. Reserve remaining marinade.
2. Place mushrooms on a greased rack of a broiler pan, stem side down. Broil mushrooms 4 in. from heat until tender, 3-4 minutes per side. Top stem sides with tomato and cheese. Broil until cheese is melted, about 1 minute.
3. Place bread on a baking sheet; brush with reserved marinade. Broil 4 in. from heat until lightly toasted, 45-60 seconds. Top with mushrooms. Sprinkle with chopped basil.

**1 OPEN-FACED SANDWICH** 460 cal., 35g fat (7g sat. fat), 22mg chol., 934mg sod., 26g carb. (8g sugars, 3g fiber), 12g pro.

## SLOW-COOKER MAC & CHEESE

This classic casserole is a rich and cheesy meatless main dish. I've never met anyone who didn't ask for a second helping.

*—Bernice Glascoe, Roxboro, NC*

**Prep:** 15 min. • **Cook:** 3¾ hours
**Makes:** 10 servings

- 1 pkg. (16 oz.) elbow macaroni
- ½ cup butter, melted
- 4 cups shredded cheddar cheese, divided
- 1 can (12 oz.) evaporated milk
- 1 can (10¾ oz.) condensed cheddar cheese soup, undiluted
- 1 cup 2% milk
- 2 large eggs, beaten
- ⅛ tsp. coarsely ground pepper

1. Cook macaroni according to package directions; drain. Place in a 5-qt. slow cooker; add butter. In a large bowl, mix 3 cups cheese, evaporated milk, soup, milk and eggs. Pour over macaroni mixture; stir to combine. Cook mixture, covered, on low for 3½-4 hours or until a thermometer inserted in center reads at least 160°.
2. Sprinkle with remaining cheese. Cook, covered, on low until cheese is melted, 15-20 minutes longer. Sprinkle with pepper.

**1 SERVING** 502 cal., 28g fat (18g sat. fat), 131mg chol., 638mg sod., 42g carb. (7g sugars, 2g fiber), 21g pro.

### TEST KITCHEN TIPS

- No evaporated milk? No problem! Swap in 12 oz. of half-and-half instead.
- The gooey goodness of mac & cheese makes a perfect base for almost any vegetable. Try adding cooked broccoli, zucchini or spinach.

## GNOCCHI WITH PESTO SAUCE

Perk up gnocchi and vegetables with a flavorful pesto sauce. If you don't have pine nuts for the pesto, substitute any nut you like.
—Taste of Home *Test Kitchen*

---

**Takes:** 25 min. • **Makes:** 4 servings

- 1 pkg. (16 oz.) potato gnocchi
- 2 tsp. olive oil
- 1 cup diced zucchini
- ½ cup chopped sweet yellow pepper
- ¼ cup prepared pesto
- 1 cup chopped tomatoes
- Toasted pine nuts, optional

1. Cook gnocchi according to package directions; drain.
2. Meanwhile, in a large skillet, heat oil over medium-high heat; saute zucchini and pepper until tender.
3. Add pesto and gnocchi, stirring gently to coat. Stir in tomatoes. If desired, top with pine nuts.

**1 CUP** 327 cal., 9g fat (2g sat. fat), 8mg chol., 682mg sod., 52g carb. (10g sugars, 4g fiber), 9g pro.

## FRESH VEGGIE POCKETS

One summer, I worked at a health food store that sold sandwiches. We were close to a college campus, so I made lots of these filled pitas for the students. Packed with fresh veggies and nutty sunflower kernels, they're a fast-to-fix meal when you're on the go.
*—Linda Reeves, Cloverdale, IN*

**Takes:** 15 min. • **Makes:** 4 servings

- 1 carton (8 oz.) spreadable cream cheese
- ¼ cup sunflower kernels
- 1 tsp. seasoned salt or salt-free seasoning blend
- 4 whole wheat pita breads (6 in.), halved
- 1 medium tomato, thinly sliced
- 1 medium cucumber, thinly sliced
- 1 cup sliced fresh mushrooms
- 1 ripe avocado, peeled and sliced

In a large bowl, combine cream cheese, sunflower kernels and seasoned salt; spread about 2 Tbsp. on the inside of each pita half. Layer with tomato, cucumber, mushrooms and avocado.

**2 FILLED PITA HALVES** 434 cal., 23g fat (9g sat. fat), 37mg chol., 571mg sod., 48g carb. (6g sugars, 8g fiber), 14g pro.

### CUSTOMIZE IT

To boost the protein in these pockets, add some hummus from the deli or cooked chickpeas.

PEACH & BURRATA SALAD, PAGE 248

# QUICK & EASY DINNER ADD-ONS

DISCO FRIES, PAGE 257

## AIR-FRYER CARROTS

I love roasting carrots to bring out their sweetness. I think thyme really complements their flavor, but feel free to mix it up with other herbs, like rosemary or tarragon.
*—Marlene Schott, Devine, TX*

**Takes:** 30 min. • **Makes:** 4 servings

- 1 lb. baby carrots
- 2 small onions, quartered
- 3 garlic cloves, peeled
- 1 Tbsp. olive oil
- 1 tsp. white wine vinegar
- 1 tsp. dried thyme
- ¼ tsp. salt
- ⅛ tsp. pepper
- Fresh thyme, optional

Preheat air fryer to 375°. In a large bowl, toss first 8 ingredients. Place carrots on greased tray in air-fryer basket. Cook 18-20 minutes or until carrots are crisp-tender, stirring occasionally. If desired, sprinkle with fresh thyme.

**¾ CUP** 88 cal., 3g fat (0 sat. fat), 0 chol., 230mg sod., 15g carb. (7g sugars, 3g fiber), 2g pro.

> **"Really good! I used regular carrots, cut into 2-in. sticks. My air fryer took a little longer to get them nicely roasted."**
> —TAMMYCOOKSBLOGSBOOKS, TASTEOFHOME.COM

## QUICK GREEN BEANS WITH BACON

Bits of bacon and onion dress up the green beans in this easy-to-prepare side dish. These beans lend a crisp, fresh flavor to any meal, from steaks to chicken.
*—Mari Anne Warren, Milton, WI*

**Takes:** 25 min. • **Makes:** 8 servings

- 8 cups fresh green beans, trimmed
- 4 bacon strips, chopped
- ½ cup chopped onion
- ¼ tsp. salt
- ⅛ tsp. pepper

1. Place beans in a large saucepan and cover with water. Bring to a boil. Cook, uncovered, until beans are crisp-tender, 8-10 minutes; drain. In a large skillet, cook bacon and onion over medium heat until bacon is crisp and onion is tender, stirring occasionally, 3-5 minutes.
2. Add beans to bacon mixture. Sprinkle with salt and pepper; toss to coat.

**1 CUP** 62 cal., 2g fat (1g sat. fat), 6mg chol., 177mg sod., 8g carb. (4g sugars, 3g fiber), 4g pro.

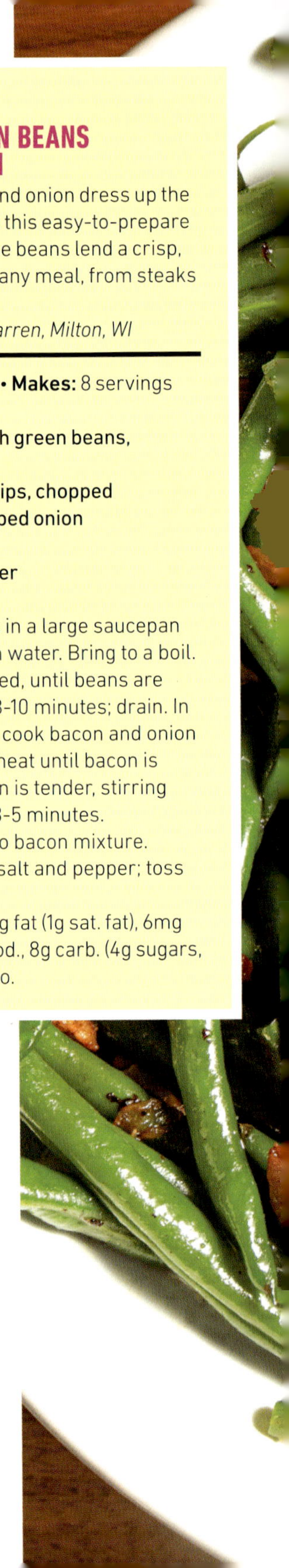

**TEST KITCHEN TIP**
For extra-bacony beans, cook them with the bacon and onions a few minutes longer so they soak up the drippings; serve warm.

## AIR-FRYER CORNBREAD

An air fryer gives cornbread a crisp, golden crust and a tender center, just like the oven but with quicker preheat and cook times. It's ideal for small batches.
—Taste of Home *Test Kitchen*

**Takes:** 30 min. • **Makes:** 8 servings

- 1 cup yellow cornmeal
- 1 cup all-purpose flour
- ¼ cup sugar
- 1 Tbsp. baking powder
- 1¼ tsp. salt
- 1 cup buttermilk
- ⅓ cup canola oil
- 1 large egg, room temperature, beaten

1. Preheat air fryer to 350°. In a small bowl, whisk together cornmeal, flour, sugar, baking powder and salt.
2. In a large bowl, whisk together buttermilk, oil and egg. Add cornmeal mixture; stir until combined. Transfer batter to a greased 8-in. round cake pan.
3. Place cake pan in air fryer basket; bake until top is golden brown and toothpick inserted in the center comes out clean, 18-20 minutes. Cool slightly before slicing into 8 pieces.

**1 PIECE** 257 cal., 11g fat (1g sat. fat), 24mg chol., 618mg sod., 35g carb. (8g sugars, 1g fiber), 5g pro.

### THRIFTY TIP

Instead of buying buttermilk, you can place 1 Tbsp. white vinegar or lemon juice in a liquid measuring cup and add enough milk to measure 1 cup. Stir, then let stand for 5 minutes. Or use 1 cup plain yogurt.

## SPINACH-PARM CASSEROLE

For those who ignore Popeye and won't eat their spinach, I find that spinach with garlicky butter and Parmesan helps change their minds.
*—Judy Batson, Tampa, FL*

**Takes:** 25 min. • **Makes:** 6 servings

- 2 lbs. fresh baby spinach
- 5 Tbsp. butter
- 3 Tbsp. olive oil
- 3 garlic cloves, minced
- 1 Tbsp. Italian seasoning
- ¾ tsp. salt
- 1 cup grated Parmesan cheese

1. Preheat oven to 400°. In a stockpot, bring 5 cups water to a boil. Add spinach; cook, covered, 1 minute or just until wilted. Drain well.
2. In a small skillet, heat butter and oil over medium-low heat. Add garlic, Italian seasoning and salt; cook and stir until garlic is tender, 1-2 minutes.
3. Spread spinach in a greased 1½-qt. or 8-in. square baking dish. Drizzle with butter mixture; sprinkle with cheese. Bake, uncovered, until cheese is lightly browned, 10-15 minutes.

**⅔ CUP** 239 cal., 21g fat (9g sat. fat), 37mg chol., 703mg sod., 7g carb. (1g sugars, 3g fiber), 10g pro.

## SLOW-COOKED APPLE CIDER

There's no last-minute rush when you slowly simmer this punch.
—*Alpha Wilson, Roswell, NM*

**Prep:** 5 min. • **Cook:** 2 hours
**Makes:** 8 servings (2 qt.)

- 2 cinnamon sticks (3 in. each)
- 1 tsp. whole cloves
- 1 tsp. whole allspice
- 2 qt. apple cider
- ½ cup packed brown sugar
- 1 orange, sliced

1. Place cinnamon, cloves and allspice on a double thickness of cheesecloth; bring up corners of cloth and tie with a string to form a bag.
2. Place cider and brown sugar in a 3-qt. slow cooker; stir until sugar dissolves. Add spice bag. Place orange slices on top. Cover and cook on low for 2-3 hours or until heated through. Discard spice bag.

**1 CUP** 177 cal., 0 fat (0 sat. fat), 0 chol., 30mg sod., 44g carb. (40g sugars, 0 fiber), 0 pro.

## GARDEN SHELL SALAD

Fresh basil marries the flavors of this splendid salad, which is lightly dressed and can accompany almost any entree.

*—Kathy Glasgow, Marysville, CA*

**Prep:** 30 min. + chilling
**Makes:** 8 servings

- 8 oz. uncooked small pasta shells
- 2 cups frozen peas
- 1 cup thinly sliced celery
- ½ cup chopped sweet red pepper
- ¼ cup chopped onion
- ⅔ cup fat-free mayonnaise
- 1 Tbsp. white balsamic vinegar
- 1 Tbsp. minced fresh basil or 1 tsp. dried basil
- 1 tsp. Dijon mustard
- ½ tsp. salt
- ¼ tsp. pepper

1. Cook pasta according to package directions, adding the peas during the last 2-3 minutes of cooking time. Drain and rinse in cold water.
2. In a large bowl, combine the pasta, peas, celery, red pepper and onion. In a small bowl, whisk the mayonnaise, vinegar, basil, mustard, salt and pepper. Pour over pasta mixture; toss to coat. Cover and refrigerate for at least 1 hour before serving.

**¾ CUP** 157 cal., 1g fat (0 sat. fat), 2mg chol., 380mg sod., 31g carb. (5g sugars, 3g fiber), 6g pro.

**CRAB SHELL SALAD** Reduce peas to 1 cup. Add 1 package (8 oz.) chopped imitation crabmeat and 1 cup fresh broccoli florets.

## CREAMY POLENTA WITH BALSAMIC GLAZE

This delicious, easy side dish goes incredibly well with braised meat and can elevate any meal.
*—Sarah Vasques, Milford, NH*

**Prep:** 15 min. • **Cook:** 2 hours
**Makes:** 4 servings

- 4 Tbsp. butter, divided
- 1½ cups half-and-half cream, divided
- 1 cup 2% milk
- ¼ tsp. salt
- ⅓ cup cornmeal
- 1 cup balsamic vinegar
- 1 Tbsp. sugar
- ½ cup grated Parmesan cheese

1. In a medium saucepan, melt 2 Tbsp. butter over medium heat. Add 1 cup cream, milk and salt. Bring to a low simmer. Gradually whisk in cornmeal. Cook and stir for 3 minutes.
2. Pour polenta into a 3-qt. slow cooker coated with cooking spray. Cook, covered, on low for 2 hours, stirring every 30 minutes. Meanwhile, in a small saucepan, bring vinegar and sugar to a boil. Reduce heat; simmer, uncovered, until reduced to ⅓ cup.
3. Just before serving, stir cheese and the remaining ½ cup cream and 2 Tbsp. butter into polenta. To serve, drizzle with balsamic glaze.

**½ CUP POLENTA WITH 1 TBSP. GLAZE** 415 cal., 25g fat (16g sat. fat), 89mg chol., 494mg sod., 37g carb. (25g sugars, 1g fiber), 9g pro.

> **"My entire family loved this recipe. Creamy, as it is titled, and the glaze adds a nice touch."**
> —PATRICA320, TASTEOFHOME.COM

## FARMHOUSE APPLE COLESLAW

A friend from church gave me this apple coleslaw recipe that her grandmother handed down to her. All the flavors complement each other well, while the fruit creates a refreshing change of pace from the usual coleslaw.
*—Jan Myers, Atlantic, IA*

**Prep:** 20 min. + chilling
**Makes:** 12 servings

- 4 cups shredded cabbage
- 1 large apple, chopped
- ¾ cup raisins
- ½ cup chopped celery
- ¼ cup chopped onion
- ¼ cup mayonnaise
- 2 Tbsp. lemon juice
- 1 Tbsp. sugar
- 1 Tbsp. olive oil
- ½ tsp. salt
- ⅛ tsp. pepper

In a serving bowl, combine the cabbage, apple, raisins, celery and onion. In a small bowl, combine the remaining ingredients. Pour over cabbage mixture and toss to coat. Cover and refrigerate for at least 30 minutes.

**⅔ CUP** 87 cal., 5g fat (1g sat. fat), 0 chol., 131mg sod., 12g carb. (8g sugars, 1g fiber), 1g pro.

## PEACH & BURRATA SALAD

The star of this salad is the creamy burrata cheese. It sits on a bed of arugula with grilled peaches, rustic croutons, pistachios, basil and homemade raspberry vinaigrette. Peaches have that perfect sweet-tart taste that cuts the richness of the cheese. No grill? Drizzle olive oil in a large skillet over medium-high heat and cook peaches 3-4 minutes per side or until lightly browned.

*—Grace Vallo, Salem, NH*

**Takes:** 25 min. • **Makes:** 6 servings

- 10 fresh raspberries
- ½ cup orange juice
- ⅓ cup extra virgin olive oil
- 3 Tbsp. champagne vinegar
- ½ tsp. grated orange zest

SALAD

- 3 medium peaches, halved
- 4 cups cubed ciabatta bread
- 1 Tbsp. extra virgin olive oil
- ¼ tsp. salt
- 6 cups fresh arugula
- 8 oz. burrata cheese, torn into bite-sized pieces
- ½ cup salted shelled pistachios
- ⅓ cup thinly sliced fresh basil

1. In a small bowl, crush raspberries. Whisk in next 4 ingredients.
2. Grill peaches, covered, over medium heat for 3-4 minutes on each side, or until light grill lines appear. Remove to a cutting board. Cut into slices.
3. Arrange ciabatta in a single layer on an ungreased baking sheet. Drizzle with olive oil and sprinkle with salt; toss to coat. Broil 3-4 in. from the heat until golden brown, 3-5 minutes, stirring once.
4. In a large bowl, toss arugula with half the vinaigrette; arrange on a large serving platter. Top with peaches, burrata, croutons, pistachios and basil. Drizzle with remaining vinaigrette.

**1 CUP** 401 cal., 28g fat (8g sat. fat), 27mg chol., 322mg sod., 27g carb. (12g sugars, 4g fiber), 12g pro.

**TEST KITCHEN TIP**

For a little extra crispiness, toss the cauliflower with panko breadcrumbs before air-frying, or turn up the temperature by about 10 degrees. Also be careful not to overcrowd the air fryer—leave room for the cauliflower to cook and for steam to escape.

## AIR-FRYER BUFFALO CAULIFLOWER

I love Buffalo wings, but sometimes I'm looking for something a little different. Enter the cauliflower! This is fantastic as an appetizer or as a side dish.
*—Emily Tyra, Lake Ann, MI*

**Takes:** 20 min. • **Makes:** 8 servings

- 1 medium head cauliflower (about 2¼ lbs.), cut into florets
- 1 Tbsp. canola oil
- ½ cup Buffalo wing sauce
- Blue cheese salad dressing

1. Preheat air fryer to 400°. Toss cauliflower with oil. Place in a single layer on tray in air-fryer basket. Cook until tender and lightly browned, 15-20 minutes, stirring halfway through.
2. Transfer to a serving bowl; toss with wing sauce. Serve with dressing.

**⅓ CUP** 39 cal., 2g fat (0 sat. fat), 0 chol., 474mg sod., 5g carb. (2g sugars, 2g fiber), 2g pro.

## GLAZED RANCH CARROTS

Ranch dressing mix flavors these tasty veggies in a flash. Using baby carrots means there's no time-consuming peeling or slicing needed.
*—Marion Reed, Omak, WA*

**Takes:** 25 min. • **Makes:** 12 servings

- 2 lbs. fresh baby carrots
- ½ cup butter, cubed
- ½ cup packed brown sugar
- 2 envelopes ranch salad dressing mix
- Minced fresh parsley, optional

1. Place carrots in a saucepan; add 1 in. of water. Bring to a boil. Reduce heat; cover and cook for 8-10 minutes or until crisp-tender. Drain and set aside.
2. In the same pan, combine the butter, brown sugar and salad dressing mix until blended. Add carrots. Cook and stir over medium heat for 5 minutes or until glazed. Sprinkle with parsley if desired.

**¾ CUP** 129 cal., 8g fat (5g sat. fat), 20mg chol., 477mg sod., 15g carb. (13g sugars, 1g fiber), 1g pro.

### EASY WAY TO CUT SODIUM

To decrease the sodium by more than a third (180mg per serving), use just 1 packet of ranch dressing mix.

## AU GRATIN PEAS & POTATOES

While this delicious potato skillet is a wonderful side dish, we find it satisfying enough to be a main course too. The skillet preparation takes less time than baking an au gratin casserole or scalloped potatoes—and it's still good old-fashioned comfort food at its best!
*—Marie Peterson, DeForest, WI*

**Takes:** 30 min. • **Makes:** 8 servings

- 6 bacon strips, diced
- 1 medium onion, chopped
- 4 cups peeled cooked potatoes, sliced
- ½ tsp. salt
- 1 pkg. (10 oz.) frozen peas, cooked and drained
- 2 cups shredded sharp cheddar cheese, divided
- ½ cup mayonnaise
- ½ cup 2% milk

1. In a large skillet, cook bacon until crisp. Remove with a slotted spoon to paper towels. Drain, reserving 1 Tbsp. drippings in pan. Saute onion in drippings until tender.
2. Add potatoes, salt, peas, 1 cup of cheese and bacon. Reduce heat; cover and simmer until heated through, about 10 minutes.
3. Combine mayonnaise and milk until smooth; pour over top. Sprinkle with remaining 1 cup cheese. Remove from the heat; let stand for 5 minutes before serving.

**¾ CUP** 354 cal., 23g fat (8g sat. fat), 43mg chol., 596mg sod., 24g carb. (4g sugars, 3g fiber), 13g pro.

## JUICY WATERMELON SALAD

This fruit salad has such a surprising yet fabulous mix of flavors that friends often ask for the recipe. Combine seedless watermelon varieties in yellow, red and pink for a colorful twist.
*—Heidi Haight, Macomb, MI*

**Prep:** 20 min. + chilling
**Makes:** 10 servings

- 8 cups cubed seedless watermelon (about 1 medium)
- 1 small red onion, cut into rings
- 1 cup coarsely chopped macadamia nuts or sliced almonds, toasted
- 1 cup fresh arugula or baby spinach
- ⅓ cup balsamic vinaigrette
- 3 Tbsp. canola oil
- Watermelon slices, optional
- 1 cup (4 oz.) crumbled blue cheese

In a large bowl, combine watermelon and onion; cover and refrigerate until cold, about 30 minutes. Just before serving, add macadamia nuts and arugula to watermelon mixture. In a small bowl, whisk vinaigrette and oil; drizzle over salad and toss to coat. Serve in bowls or, if desired, on slices of watermelon. Sprinkle with cheese.

**1 CUP** 232 cal., 20g fat (5g sat. fat), 10mg chol., 295mg sod., 15g carb. (12g sugars, 2g fiber), 4g pro.

**"It is surprising to put the cheese and onions with watermelon, but sooo good! I served as a side at a party, was a big hit!"**
—MRSDUMAIS, TASTEOFHOME.COM

## ROQUEFORT PEAR SALAD

Guests at a barbecue we hosted last summer brought this cool, refreshing salad. Now it's a mainstay at most of our cookouts. The mingling of zesty tastes and textures instantly wakes up the taste buds!
*—Sherry Duval, Baltimore, MD*

**Takes:** 20 min. • **Makes:** 10 servings

- 10 cups torn salad greens
- 3 large ripe pears, sliced
- ½ cup thinly sliced green onions
- 4 oz. crumbled Roquefort blue cheese
- ¼ cup slivered almonds, toasted

MUSTARD VINAIGRETTE

- ⅓ cup olive oil
- 3 Tbsp. cider vinegar
- 1½ tsp. sugar
- 1½ tsp. Dijon mustard
- 1 garlic clove, minced
- ½ tsp. salt
- Pepper to taste

In a large bowl, combine the salad greens, pears, onions, cheese and almonds. In a jar with a tight-fitting lid, combine the vinaigrette ingredients; shake well. Pour over salad; toss to coat.

**1¼ CUPS** 171 cal., 12g fat (3g sat. fat), 9mg chol., 303mg sod., 14g carb. (8g sugars, 4g fiber), 4g pro.

## NO-KNEAD HONEY OATMEAL BREAD

We especially enjoy this tasty bread because we like using honey as a natural sweetener. We use the bread for both toast and sandwiches. It's great for special occasions too.
*—Janice Dancer, Williamstown, VT*

**Prep:** 25 min. + rising • **Bake:** 40 min.
**Makes:** 2 loaves (12 pieces each)

- 2 cups water, divided
- 1 cup rolled oats
- ⅓ cup butter, softened
- ⅓ cup honey
- 1 Tbsp. salt
- 2 pkg. (¼ oz. each ) active dry yeast
- 1 large egg, room temperature
- 4 to 5 cups all-purpose flour
- Melted butter, optional

1. In a small saucepan, heat 1 cup water to boiling. Stir in oats, butter, honey and salt. Let stand until mixture cools to 110°-115°, stirring occasionally. Heat remaining 1 cup water to 110°-115°.
2. In a large bowl, dissolve yeast in warm water. Add egg, oat mixture and 2 cups flour. Beat until smooth. Stir in enough remaining flour to form a soft dough (dough will be sticky). Do not knead. Place in a greased bowl, turning once to grease the top. Cover and let rise in a warm place until doubled, about 1 hour.
3. Punch down dough; divide evenly between 2 greased 8x4-in. loaf pans. Smooth tops of loaves. Cover and let rise in a warm place until doubled, 35-40 minutes. Using a sharp knife, make a shallow slash down the center of each loaf.
4. Bake at 375° until golden brown, 40-45 minutes. Remove from pans to wire racks to cool. If desired, brush with melted butter.

**1 PIECE** 132 cal., 3g fat (2g sat. fat), 16mg chol., 325mg sod., 22g carb. (4g sugars, 1g fiber), 3g pro.

## SUNFLOWER NOODLE COLESLAW

Dressed with sunflower oil and kernels, this slaw is always requested at our family get-togethers. Make it once, and it might become your signature dish.
*—Eileen Herman, Brinsmade, ND*

**Takes:** 15 min. • **Makes:** 10 servings

- 1 pkg. (3 oz.) chicken ramen noodles
- 1 pkg. (14 oz.) coleslaw mix
- ½ cup unsalted sunflower kernels
- ¼ cup chopped green pepper
- ⅓ cup sunflower oil
- ¼ cup white vinegar
- 3 Tbsp. sugar
- 1 Tbsp. poppy seeds
- ¾ tsp. pepper

1. Break noodles into small pieces; reserve seasoning packet. In a large bowl, combine the noodles, coleslaw mix, sunflower kernels and green pepper.
2. In a small bowl, whisk the oil, vinegar, sugar, poppy seeds, pepper and contents of seasoning packet. Pour over salad and toss to coat. Chill until serving.

**¾ CUP** 169 cal., 12g fat (2g sat. fat), 0 chol., 170mg sod., 14g carb. (6g sugars, 2g fiber), 3g pro.

"A family favorite. It's easy to make and easy to substitute ingredients to adjust to your family's tastes."

—PAGERD, TASTEOFHOME.COM

## QUICK AMBROSIA FRUIT SALAD

I mix in a little coconut and just enough marshmallows so it tastes like the creamy ambrosia I grew up with. Now everyone in my home loves it too.
*—Trisha Kruse, Eagle, ID*

**Takes:** 10 min. • **Makes:** 6 servings

- 1 can (8¼ oz.) fruit cocktail, drained
- 1 can (8 oz.) unsweetened pineapple chunks, drained
- 1 cup green grapes
- 1 cup seedless red grapes
- 1 cup miniature marshmallows
- 1 medium banana, sliced
- ¾ cup vanilla yogurt
- ½ cup sweetened shredded coconut

In a large bowl, combine all ingredients. Chill until serving.
**¾ CUP** 191 cal., 4g fat (3g sat. fat), 2mg chol., 48mg sod., 40g carb. (34g sugars, 2g fiber), 3g pro.

## HONEY-THYME BUTTERNUT SQUASH

Instead of potatoes, try whipping up mashed butternut squash with honey, butter and thyme. More than a festive Thanksgiving side, this 30-minute dish will be a new fall favorite for your weeknight dinners.
*—Bianca Noiseux, Bristol, CT*

**Takes:** 30 min. • **Makes:** 10 servings

- 1 large butternut squash (about 5 lbs.), peeled and cubed
- ¼ cup butter, cubed
- 3 Tbsp. half-and-half cream
- 2 Tbsp. honey
- 2 tsp. dried parsley flakes
- ½ tsp. salt
- ⅛ tsp. dried thyme
- ⅛ tsp. coarsely ground pepper

1. In a large saucepan, bring 1 in. of water to a boil. Add squash; cover and cook for 10-15 minutes or until tender.
2. Drain squash; mash with remaining ingredients.

**¾ CUP** 145 cal., 5g fat (3g sat. fat), 14mg chol., 161mg sod., 26g carb. (9g sugars, 7g fiber), 2g pro.

**APPLE BUTTERNUT SQUASH** Omit butter, honey, parsley, thyme and pepper. Cook squash as directed. Mash with cream, salt, ⅓ cup apple butter and ½ tsp. ground cinnamon.

**MAPLE-CINNAMON BUTTERNUT SQUASH** Omit cream, honey, parsley, salt, thyme and pepper. Cook squash as directed. Mash with butter, ⅓ cup maple syrup, 1 tsp. ground cinnamon and ¼ tsp. ground nutmeg.

## CREAMY CARROT CASSEROLE

My mom and I developed this recipe to see if there was a carrot dish that even people who don't care for carrots would enjoy. So far, I haven't met anyone who hasn't liked this casserole.
*—Laurie Heward, Fillmore, UT*

---

**Prep:** 15 min. • **Bake:** 30 min.
**Makes:** 8 servings

- 1½ lbs. carrots, sliced or 1 pkg. (20 oz.) frozen sliced carrots, thawed
- 1 cup mayonnaise
- 1 Tbsp. grated onion
- 1 Tbsp. prepared horseradish
- ¼ cup shredded cheddar cheese
- 2 Tbsp. crushed Ritz crackers

**1.** Preheat oven to 350°. Place 1 in. water in a large saucepan; add carrots. Bring to a boil. Reduce heat; cover and simmer until crisp-tender, 7-9 minutes. Drain, reserving ¼ cup cooking liquid. Transfer carrots to a 1½-qt. baking dish.
**2.** In a small bowl, combine the mayonnaise, onion, horseradish and reserved ¼ cup cooking liquid; spread mixture evenly over carrots. Sprinkle with shredded cheese; top with cracker crumbs. Bake, uncovered, for 30 minutes.
**¾ CUP** 238 cal., 22g fat (4g sat. fat), 6mg chol., 241mg sod., 10g carb. (4g sugars, 2g fiber), 2g pro.

## DISCO FRIES

Disco fries are New Jersey's version of poutine. You can find them at diners when you're in need of a late-night bite, or anytime you've got a craving for a hearty, savory snack.

*—Melissa Gaman, Jersey City, NJ*

**Prep:** 15 min. • **Cook:** 30 min.
**Makes:** 4 servings

- 4 cups frozen french-fried potatoes (about 1 lb.)
- 3 Tbsp. unsalted butter
- ¼ cup chopped shallot
- 3 Tbsp. all-purpose flour
- 1½ cups reduced-sodium beef broth
- 2 tsp. Worcestershire sauce
- ½ tsp. pepper
- ¼ tsp. salt
- 6 oz. mozzarella cheese
- 2 Tbsp. thinly sliced green onions

1. Bake french fries according to package directions; add 10-15 minutes to the baking time or bake until very crispy, tossing occasionally.
2. Meanwhile, melt butter in a small saucepan over medium heat. Add shallot; cook, stirring frequently, until softened and browned, about 2 minutes. Add flour; whisk until smooth. Cook until roux is lightly browned, 1-2 minutes. Reduce heat to medium-low; slowly whisk in beef broth until smooth. Add Worcestershire, pepper and salt. Simmer, whisking occasionally, until the gravy has thickened enough to coat the back of a spoon, about 6-8 minutes. Keep warm.
3. Grate 4 oz. mozzarella on the large holes of a box grater. Cut remaining mozzarella into small cubes. Top fries with shredded and cubed cheese. Return to the oven and bake until cheese is just melted, 4-5 minutes.
4. Divide fries among 4 plates; top generously with the gravy. Sprinkle with green onions. Serve extra gravy on the side if desired. Serve immediately.

**1 SERVING** 404 cal., 24g fat (12g sat. fat), 58mg chol., 1002mg sod., 34g carb. (3g sugars, 3g fiber), 14g pro.

## ZUCCHINI PARMESAN

You'll knock their socks off with this easy-to-prep side that's absolutely delicious. My favorite time to make it is when the veggies are fresh out of the garden.
*—Sandi Guettler, Bay City, MI*

**Takes:** 25 min. • **Makes:** 6 servings

- 4 medium zucchini, cut into ¼-in. slices
- 1 Tbsp. olive oil
- ½ to 1 tsp. minced garlic
- 1 can (14½ oz.) Italian diced tomatoes, undrained
- 1 tsp. seasoned salt
- ¼ tsp. pepper
- ¼ cup grated Parmesan cheese

1. In a large skillet, saute zucchini in oil until crisp-tender. Add garlic; cook 1 minute longer.
2. Stir in the tomatoes, seasoned salt and pepper. Simmer, uncovered, until liquid is evaporated, 9-10 minutes. Sprinkle with Parmesan cheese. Serve with a slotted spoon.

**½ CUP** 81 cal., 3g fat (1g sat. fat), 3mg chol., 581mg sod., 10g carb. (6g sugars, 2g fiber), 3g pro.

## BULGUR WITH PINE NUTS

Bulgur wheat is not only good for you ... it's great for your budget! A few simple ingredients flavor it wonderfully.
—Taste of Home *Test Kitchen*

**Takes:** 20 min. • **Makes:** 4 servings

- 1 cup uncooked bulgur
- 2 cups chicken broth
- 3 Tbsp. chopped green onions
- ¼ cup pine nuts, toasted

In a large saucepan, combine bulgur, broth and onions; bring to a boil over high heat. Reduce heat; cover and simmer for 15-18 minutes or until broth is absorbed. Add pine nuts; stir to combine.

**½ CUP** 177 cal., 5g fat (1g sat. fat), 0 chol., 472mg sod., 29g carb. (1g sugars, 7g fiber), 7g pro.

## HERB BISCUIT LOAF

These buttery, golden rolls are a sure way to make any meal special—from Thanksgiving dinner to a weekday supper. Their wonderful herb flavor seems complex but is simple to achieve.
*—Amy Smith, Maplewood, MN*

**Prep:** 15 min. • **Bake:** 30 min.
**Makes:** 20 servings

- ¼ cup butter, melted
- ½ tsp. dried minced onion
- ½ tsp. dried basil
- ¼ to ½ tsp. caraway seeds
- ⅛ tsp. garlic powder
- 2 tubes (12 oz. each) buttermilk biscuits

In a shallow bowl, combine the first 5 ingredients. Dip biscuits into butter mixture; fold in half and place in rows in a greased 8-in. square baking pan. Drizzle with remaining butter mixture. Bake at 350° until golden brown, 27-30 minutes.

**1 BISCUIT** 121 cal., 6g fat (3g sat. fat), 6mg chol., 298mg sod., 15g carb. (2g sugars, 0 fiber), 2g pro.

## MAPLE & BACON GLAZED BRUSSELS SPROUTS

Here's a side dish even the children will love! Maple syrup adds a bit of sweetness.

*—Jan Valdez, Chicago, IL*

**Prep:** 15 min. • **Cook:** 20 min.
**Makes:** 4 servings

- 5 bacon strips, chopped
- 1 lb. fresh Brussels sprouts, trimmed
- 3 Tbsp. butter
- ½ cup chicken broth
- ¼ cup chopped pecans
- ¼ cup maple syrup
- ¼ tsp. salt
- ¼ tsp. pepper

1. In a small skillet, cook bacon over medium heat until crisp. Remove to paper towels with a slotted spoon; drain.
2. Meanwhile, cut an "X" in the core of each Brussels sprout. In a large skillet, saute sprouts in butter until lightly browned, 4-5 minutes.
3. Stir in broth, pecans, maple syrup, salt and pepper. Bring mixture to a boil. Reduce heat; cover and simmer for 5 minutes. Uncover; cook and stir until Brussels sprouts are tender, 8-10 minutes longer. Sprinkle with bacon.

**¾ CUP** 273 cal., 18g fat (7g sat. fat), 32mg chol., 544mg sod., 25g carb. (15g sugars, 5g fiber), 8g pro.

## SMOKY CAULIFLOWER

The smoked Spanish paprika gives a simple side of cauliflower more depth of flavor. We're fans of roasted veggies of any kind, and this one is a definite winner.
*—Juliette Mulholland, Corvallis, OR*

**Takes:** 30 min. • **Makes:** 8 servings

- 1 large head cauliflower, broken into 1-in. florets (about 9 cups)
- 2 Tbsp. olive oil
- 1 tsp. smoked paprika
- ¾ tsp. salt
- 2 garlic cloves, minced
- 2 Tbsp. minced fresh parsley

1. Place cauliflower in a large bowl. Combine the oil, paprika and salt. Drizzle over cauliflower; toss to coat. Transfer to a 15x10x1-in. baking pan. Bake, uncovered, at 450° for 10 minutes.
2. Stir in garlic. Bake 10-15 minutes longer or until cauliflower is tender and lightly browned, stirring occasionally. Sprinkle with parsley.

**¾ CUP** 58 cal., 4g fat (0 sat. fat), 0 chol., 254mg sod., 6g carb. (3g sugars, 3g fiber), 2g pro.

### KEEP PARSLEY FRESH UP TO A MONTH

Trim stems; place parsley bunch in a tumbler with 1 in. of water. Be sure no loose leaves are in the water. Tie a produce bag around the tumbler to trap humidity; store in the refrigerator. Change the water and flip the bag inside out each time you use the parsley.

## CREAMED CORN

Five ingredients are all you'll need for my popular dinner accompaniment. It's wonderful no matter what the occasion is. Try it on a barbecue buffet or your holiday menu.
*—Barbara Brizendine, Harrisonville, MO*

**Prep:** 10 min. • **Cook:** 3 hours
**Makes:** 5 servings

- 2 pkg. (one 16 oz., one 10 oz.) frozen corn
- 1 pkg. (8 oz.) cream cheese, softened and cubed
- ¼ cup butter, cubed
- 1 Tbsp. sugar
- ½ tsp. salt

In a 3-qt. slow cooker coated with cooking spray, combine all ingredients. Cover and cook on low for 3-3½ hours or until cheese is melted and corn is tender. Stir just before serving.

**¾ CUP** 378 cal., 26g fat (16g sat. fat), 74mg chol., 439mg sod., 34g carb. (5g sugars, 4g fiber), 8g pro.

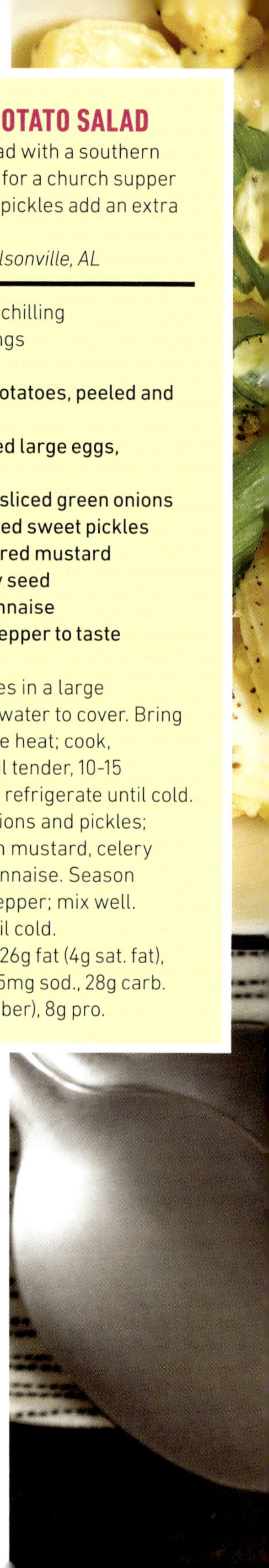

## SOUTHERN POTATO SALAD

This potato salad with a southern twist is perfect for a church supper or potluck. The pickles add an extra sweetness.

*—Gene Pitts, Wilsonville, AL*

**Prep:** 30 min. + chilling
**Makes:** 8 servings

- 5 medium potatoes, peeled and cubed
- 6 hard-boiled large eggs, chopped
- ½ cup thinly sliced green onions
- ¼ cup chopped sweet pickles
- 1 tsp. prepared mustard
- 1 tsp. celery seed
- 1 cup mayonnaise
- Salt and pepper to taste

1. Place potatoes in a large saucepan; add water to cover. Bring to a boil. Reduce heat; cook, uncovered, until tender, 10-15 minutes. Drain; refrigerate until cold.
2. Add eggs, onions and pickles; toss well. Stir in mustard, celery seed and mayonnaise. Season with salt and pepper; mix well. Refrigerate until cold.

**¾ CUP** 377 cal., 26g fat (4g sat. fat), 169mg chol., 275mg sod., 28g carb. (5g sugars, 2g fiber), 8g pro.

## CONFETTI QUINOA

If you have never tried quinoa, start with my easy side, brimming with colorful veggies. I serve it with orange-glazed chicken.

*—Kim Ciepluch, Kenosha, WI*

**Takes:** 30 min. • **Makes:** 4 servings

- 2 cups water
- 1 cup quinoa, rinsed
- ½ cup chopped fresh broccoli
- ½ cup coarsely chopped zucchini
- ¼ cup shredded carrots
- ½ tsp. salt
- 1 Tbsp. lemon juice
- 1 Tbsp. olive oil

1. In a large saucepan, bring the water to a boil. Add the next 5 ingredients. Reduce heat; simmer, covered, until liquid is absorbed, 12-15 minutes.
2. Stir in lemon juice and oil. Remove from heat; fluff with a fork.

**⅔ CUP** 196 cal., 6g fat (1g sat. fat), 0 chol., 307mg sod., 29g carb. (1g sugars, 4g fiber), 7g pro.

**POTATO SALAD TIPS**

**What potatoes and pickles work best?** Use waxy spuds—red, Yukon Gold or fingerlings. Sweet pickles are classic; dill pickles work too.

**How should I store leftovers?** Refrigerate in an airtight container for 3-4 days.

## RANCH BEANS

These beans are served at all of our barbecues. It seems most people who live here like spicy, flavorful food, and this is just right.
*—Wilma Ruth James, Ranger, TX*

**Prep:** 20 min. + standing • **Cook:** 3 hours
**Makes:** 8 servings

- 1 pkg. (16 oz.) dried pinto beans
- 1 qt. water
- 1 can (6 oz.) tomato paste
- ½ cup chopped onion
- 1 garlic clove, minced
- 1 to 2 Tbsp. chili powder
- 2 to 3 tsp. crushed red pepper flakes
- 1 tsp. salt
- 1 tsp. ground cumin
- ½ tsp. dried marjoram

1. Place beans in a Dutch oven; add water to cover by 2 in. Bring to a boil; boil for 2 minutes. Remove from the heat; cover and let stand for 1 hour.
2. Drain beans, discarding liquid. Return beans to pan; add 1 qt. water. Bring to boil. Reduce heat; cover and simmer until beans are tender, about 1½ hours. Stir in remaining ingredients; bring to a boil. Reduce heat; cover and simmer to allow flavors to blend, about 1½ hours longer.

**¾ CUP** 226 cal., 1g fat (0 sat. fat), 0 chol., 345mg sod., 41g carb. (4g sugars, 10g fiber), 14g pro.

### BEANS TIPS

**How can I serve ranch-style beans?** They're a classic BBQ side—serve with honey-chipotle ribs, barbecued chicken or burgers.

**Can I use canned beans instead of dried?** Yes. Use canned pintos, skip the initial boil, and simmer only until flavors meld and the liquid thickens.

## GRILLED CABBAGE

I don't really like cabbage, but I fixed this recipe and couldn't believe how good it was! We threw some burgers on the grill and our dinner was complete. I never thought I'd skip dessert because I was full from eating too much cabbage!
*—Elizabeth Wheeler, Thornville, OH*

**Takes:** 30 min. • **Makes:** 8 servings

- 1 medium head cabbage (about 1½ lbs.)
- ⅓ cup butter, softened
- ¼ cup chopped onion
- ½ tsp. garlic salt
- ¼ tsp. pepper
- Optional: Minced fresh parsley and salad dressing of choice

1. Cut cabbage into 8 wedges; place on a double thickness of heavy-duty foil (about 24x12 in.). Spread cut sides of cabbage with butter. Sprinkle with onion, garlic salt and pepper.
2. Fold foil around cabbage and seal tightly. Grill, covered, over medium heat until tender, about 20 minutes. Open foil carefully to allow steam to escape. If desired, garnish with parsley and salad dressing.

**1 WEDGE** 98 cal., 8g fat (5g sat. fat), 20mg chol., 188mg sod., 7g carb. (4g sugars, 3g fiber), 2g pro.

## SIMPLE WALDORF SALAD

This is my go-to salad when I need a quick little something for a meal. When I want a sweeter taste, I use whipped cream instead of yogurt.
*—Wendy Masters, East Garafraxa, ON*

**Takes:** 10 min. • **Makes:** 6 servings

- 2 large Gala or Honeycrisp apples, unpeeled and chopped (about 3 cups)
- 2 cups chopped celery
- ¼ cup raisins
- ¼ cup chopped walnuts, toasted
- ⅓ cup reduced-fat mayonnaise
- ⅓ cup plain yogurt

Combine apples, celery, raisins and walnuts. Add mayonnaise and yogurt; toss to coat. Refrigerate, covered, until serving.

**NOTE** To toast nuts, bake in a shallow pan at 350° for 5-10 minutes or cook in a skillet over low heat until lightly browned, stirring occasionally.

**¾ CUP** 140 cal., 8g fat (1g sat. fat), 6mg chol., 119mg sod., 17g carb. (12g sugars, 3g fiber), 2g pro.

## SLOW-COOKER CHEESY POTATOES

The slow cooker does most of the heavy lifting in this quick, cheesy side dish. Rather than requiring you to cut potatoes, this dump-and-go dish uses frozen hash browns for convenience.
—Taste of Home *Test Kitchen*

**Prep:** 15 min. • **Cook:** 2 hours
**Makes:** 10 servings

- 1 can (10½ oz.) condensed cream of chicken soup, undiluted
- 1 cup sour cream
- 1 cup whole milk
- ½ cup chopped onion
- ½ tsp. salt
- ½ tsp. pepper
- ½ tsp. garlic powder
- 1 pkg. (28 oz.) frozen shredded hash brown potatoes
- 2 cups shredded cheddar cheese, divided

1. In a large bowl, whisk together soup, sour cream and milk. Add onion, salt, pepper and garlic powder. Stir in hash browns and 1 cup shredded cheese until combined.

2. Transfer mixture to a 5- or 6-qt. slow cooker. Sprinkle remaining 1 cup shredded cheese on top. Cook, covered, until potatoes are tender and edge is bubbly, 2-3 hours on high or 4-6 hours on low.

**1 SERVING** 254 cal., 15g fat (8g sat. fat), 44mg chol., 531mg sod., 21g carb. (4g sugars, 3g fiber), 9g pro.

## PESTO QUINOA SALAD

My daughter-in-law got me hooked on quinoa, and I'm so glad she did! I've been substituting quinoa in some of my favorite pasta recipes, and this dish is the happy result of one of those experiments. I love using my garden tomatoes and peppers in this salad; however, sun-dried tomatoes and roasted red peppers are equally delicious.

*—Sue Gronholz, Beaver Dam, WI*

**Prep:** 25 min. + chilling
**Makes:** 4 servings

- ⅔ cup water
- ⅓ cup quinoa, rinsed
- 2 Tbsp. prepared pesto
- 1 Tbsp. finely chopped sweet onion
- 1 Tbsp. olive oil
- 1 tsp. balsamic vinegar
- ¼ tsp. salt
- 1 medium sweet red pepper, chopped
- 1 cup cherry tomatoes, quartered
- ⅔ cup fresh mozzarella cheese pearls (about 4 oz.)
- 2 Tbsp. minced fresh basil, optional

1. In a small saucepan, bring water to a boil; stir in quinoa. Reduce heat; simmer, covered, 10-12 minutes or until liquid is absorbed. Cool slightly.
2. Mix pesto, onion, oil, vinegar and salt; stir in pepper, tomatoes, cheese and quinoa. Refrigerate, covered, to allow flavors to blend, 1-2 hours. If desired, stir in basil.

**¾ CUP** 183 cal., 11g fat (4g sat. fat), 15mg chol., 268mg sod., 14g carb. (3g sugars, 2g fiber), 6g pro.

## SHAVED FENNEL SALAD

This salad tastes even more impressive than it looks. It has an incredible crunch thanks to the cucumbers, radishes and apples, and the fennel fronds add just the faintest hint of licorice flavor.

*—William Milton III, Clemson, SC*

**Takes:** 15 min. • **Makes:** 8 servings

- 1 large fennel bulb, fronds reserved
- 1 English cucumber
- 1 medium Honeycrisp apple
- 2 Tbsp. extra virgin olive oil
- ½ tsp. kosher salt
- ¼ tsp. coarsely ground pepper
- 2 radishes, thinly sliced

With a mandoline or vegetable peeler, cut the fennel, cucumber and apple into very thin slices. Transfer to a large bowl; toss with olive oil, salt and pepper. Top with radishes and reserved fennel fronds to serve.

**¾ CUP** 55 cal., 4g fat (1g sat. fat), 0 chol., 138mg sod., 6g carb. (4g sugars, 2g fiber), 1g pro.

# PARMESAN ROASTED BROCCOLI

Sure, it's simple and healthy but, this roasted broccoli is also delicious. Cutting the stalks into tall trees turns the ordinary veggie into a standout side dish.

*—Holly Sander, Lake Mary, FL*

**Takes:** 30 min. • **Makes:** 4 servings

- 2 small broccoli crowns (about 8 oz. each)
- 3 Tbsp. olive oil
- ½ tsp. salt
- ½ tsp. pepper
- ¼ tsp. crushed red pepper flakes
- 4 garlic cloves, thinly sliced
- 2 Tbsp. grated Parmesan cheese
- 1 tsp. grated lemon zest

1. Preheat oven to 425°. Cut broccoli crowns into quarters from top to bottom. Drizzle with oil; sprinkle with salt, pepper and pepper flakes. Place in a parchment-lined 15x10x1-in. pan.
2. Roast until crisp-tender, 10-12 minutes. Sprinkle with garlic; roast 5 minutes longer. Sprinkle with cheese; roast until cheese is toasted and stalks of broccoli are tender, 2-4 minutes longer. Sprinkle with lemon zest.

**2 BROCCOLI PIECES** 144 cal., 11g fat (2g sat. fat), 2mg chol., 378mg sod., 9g carb. (2g sugars, 3g fiber), 4g pro.

## ZUCCHINI PATTIES

My sister gave me this recipe and I, in turn, have given it to many of my friends. These patties have a nice flavor and are compatible with just about any entree. *—Annabelle Cripe, Goshen, IN*

**Prep:** 15 min. • **Cook:** 20 min.
**Makes:** 4 servings

- 2 cups shredded zucchini, squeezed to remove excess liquid
- ½ cup biscuit/baking mix
- ½ cup shredded cheddar cheese
- 2 Tbsp. grated onion
- ½ tsp. salt
- ½ tsp. dried basil
- ¼ tsp. pepper
- 2 large eggs, lightly beaten
- 2 Tbsp. butter

In a bowl, combine the first 7 ingredients. Stir in eggs; mix well. Shape the mixture into 6 patties, using about ¼ cup zucchini mixture for each patty. In a skillet over medium-high heat, melt butter; cook patties until lightly browned, 4-5 minutes on each side.

**2 PATTIES** 214 cal., 14g fat (8g sat. fat), 122mg chol., 618mg sod., 14g carb. (3g sugars, 1g fiber), 8g pro.

**"I added 1 tsp. of Old Bay seafood seasoning to this, and it was amazing."**
—MS11145, TASTEOFHOME.COM

## CONTEST-WINNING GRILLED MUSHROOMS

Mushrooms cooked over hot coals always taste good, but this easy recipe makes them taste fantastic. As a mother of two children, I love to cook entire meals on the grill. It's fun spending time outdoors with the kids. *—Melanie Knoll, Marshalltown, IA*

**Takes:** 15 min. • **Makes:** 4 servings

- ½ lb. medium fresh mushrooms
- ¼ cup butter, melted
- ½ tsp. dill weed
- ½ tsp. garlic salt
- Grilled lemon wedges, optional

1. Thread mushrooms on 4 metal or soaked wooden skewers. Combine butter, dill and garlic salt; brush over mushrooms.
2. Grill, covered, over medium-high heat until tender, 10-15 minutes, basting and turning every 5 minutes. Serve with grilled lemon wedges if desired.

**1 SKEWER** 77 cal., 8g fat (5g sat. fat), 20mg chol., 230mg sod., 2g carb. (1g sugars, 0 fiber), 1g pro.

## HOMEMADE JIFFY CINNAMON ROLLS

I got this recipe from my mom. I like to refrigerate the dough overnight to quickly bake first thing in the morning.
*—Heather Maldaner, Rolling Hills, AB*

**Prep:** 30 min. • **Bake:** 20 min.
**Makes:** 6 rolls

- 1¼ cups all-purpose flour
- 1 Tbsp. sugar
- 1 tsp. baking powder
- ½ tsp. salt
- 2 Tbsp. cold butter
- 7 to 8 Tbsp. 2% milk

FILLING

- 2 Tbsp. plus 2 tsp. butter, softened, divided
- ⅓ cup packed brown sugar
- 1 tsp. ground cinnamon

1. In a bowl, combine flour, sugar, baking powder and salt. Cut in cold butter until crumbly. Stir in milk, 1 Tbsp. at a time, and toss with a fork until mixture forms a ball. Turn dough onto a lightly floured surface; roll into a 7-in. square. Spread with 2 Tbsp. softened butter.

2. Combine the brown sugar and cinnamon; sprinkle over butter. Roll up jelly-roll style. Cut into 6 even slices. Place cut side up in greased muffin cups. Bake at 400° for 18-20 minutes or until golden brown. Melt remaining 2 Tbsp. butter; brush over rolls. Serve warm.

**1 SERVING** 239 cal., 10g fat (6g sat. fat), 26mg chol., 367mg sod., 35g carb. (15g sugars, 1g fiber), 3g pro.

BLUEBERRY PIE WITH GRAHAM CRACKER CRUST, PAGE 287

# QUICK & EASY SWEETS

GRANDMA KRAUSE'S COCONUT COOKIES, PAGE 297

## AMISH SUGAR COOKIES

These easy-to-make cookies simply melt in your mouth! I've passed the recipe around to many friends. After I gave the recipe to my sister, she entered the cookies in a local fair and won the best of show prize!
*—Sylvia Ford, Kennett, MO*

**Prep:** 15 min. • **Bake:** 10 min./batch
**Makes:** about 5 dozen

- 1 cup butter, softened
- 1 cup canola oil
- 1 cup sugar
- 1 cup confectioners' sugar
- 2 large eggs, room temperature
- 1 tsp. vanilla extract
- 4½ cups all-purpose flour
- 1 tsp. baking soda
- 1 tsp. cream of tartar

1. Preheat oven to 375°. In a large bowl, beat butter, oil and sugars. Beat in eggs until well blended. Beat in vanilla. Combine the flour, baking soda and cream of tartar; gradually add to creamed mixture.
2. Drop by small teaspoonfuls onto ungreased baking sheets. Bake for 8-10 minutes or until lightly browned. Remove to wire racks to cool.

**1 COOKIE** 117 cal., 7g fat (2g sat. fat), 14mg chol., 48mg sod., 13g carb. (5g sugars, 0 fiber), 1g pro.

## BLACKBERRY COBBLER

In summer, blackberries abound in fields and along country roads around here. It's fun to pick them, especially when we know this dessert will be the result.
*—Tina Hankins, Laconia, NH*

**Prep:** 10 min. • **Bake:** 45 min.
**Makes:** 6 servings

- ¼ cup butter, softened
- ½ cup sugar
- 1 cup all-purpose flour
- 2 tsp. baking powder
- ½ cup 2% milk
- 2 cups fresh or frozen blackberries
- ¾ cup unsweetened apple juice
- Optional: Vanilla ice cream or whipped cream

1. Preheat oven to 350°. In a small bowl, cream butter and sugar until light and fluffy, 5-7 minutes. Combine flour and baking powder; add to the creamed mixture alternately with milk; stir just until moistened.
2. Pour into a greased 1½-qt. baking dish. Sprinkle with blackberries. Pour apple juice over top. Bake until golden brown, 45-50 minutes. Serve warm. Top with ice cream or whipped cream if desired.

**1 SERVING** 197 cal., 6g fat (4g sat. fat), 17mg chol., 169mg sod., 33g carb. (19g sugars, 2g fiber), 2g pro.

## ADD A GLAZE

To give these cookies a fancy twist, drizzle them with a simple glaze of confectioners' sugar and a few teaspoons of water, milk or juice. Add a little almond extract, vanilla or food coloring if desired.

## STRAWBERRY TRIFLE

I won first prize in a dairy recipe contest with this gorgeous strawberry trifle. You can double the recipe and make two for large groups.
*—Norma Steiner, Monroe, WI*

**Prep:** 20 min. + chilling
**Makes:** 10 servings

- 1 cup 2% milk
- 1 cup sour cream
- 1 pkg. (3.4 oz.) instant vanilla pudding mix
- 1 tsp. grated orange zest
- 2 cups heavy whipping cream, whipped
- 8 cups cubed angel food cake
- 4 cups sliced fresh strawberries
- Additional whipped cream, optional

1. In a large bowl, beat the milk, sour cream, pudding mix and orange zest on low speed until thickened. Fold in whipped cream.
2. Place half the cake cubes in a 3-qt. glass bowl. Arrange one-third of the strawberries around side of bowl and over cake; top with half the pudding mixture. Repeat layers once. Top with the remaining berries. Refrigerate for 2 hours. If desired, top with additional whipped cream just before serving.

**1 SERVING** 376 cal., 23g fat (14g sat. fat), 62mg chol., 360mg sod., 38g carb. (30g sugars, 2g fiber), 6g pro.

### SUCCESS TIPS

To avoid squishing the light-as-air angel food cake, freeze it overnight, then cut it with a serrated knife, using a back-and-forth sawing motion. For a special touch, add 1 Tbsp. orange liqueur to the sour cream mixture.

## GRANDMA'S RICE PUDDING

You can whip up this classic dessert on short notice if you keep cooked rice on hand. Cooked rice can be frozen in an airtight container for up to three months. Just thaw it in the refrigerator or microwave when you're ready to use it.
*—Margaret DeChant, Newberry, MI*

**Prep:** 10 min. • **Bake:** 45 min.
**Makes:** 6 servings

- 1½ cups cooked rice
- ¼ cup raisins
- 2 large eggs
- 1½ cups whole milk
- ½ cup sugar
- ½ tsp. ground nutmeg
- Additional milk, optional

1. Place cooked rice and raisins in a greased 1-qt. casserole. In a small bowl, whisk eggs, milk, sugar and nutmeg; pour over rice.
2. Bake, uncovered, at 375° until a knife inserted in the center comes out clean, 45-50 minutes. Cool slightly before serving. Pour milk over each serving if desired. Refrigerate leftovers.

**1 CUP** 197 cal., 4g fat (2g sat. fat), 79mg chol., 52mg sod., 36g carb. (23g sugars, 0 fiber), 5g pro.

## PINEAPPLE UPSIDE-DOWN DUMP CAKE

No matter the season, this dump cake recipe is wonderful! It works well with gluten-free and sugar-free cake mixes too.
*—Karin Gatewood, Josephine, TX*

**Prep:** 10 min.
**Cook:** 2 hours + standing
**Makes:** 10 servings

- ¾ cup butter, divided
- ⅔ cup packed brown sugar
- 1 jar (6 oz.) maraschino cherries, drained
- ½ cup chopped pecans, toasted
- 1 can (20 oz.) unsweetened pineapple tidbits or crushed pineapple, undrained
- 1 pkg. yellow cake mix (regular size)
- Vanilla ice cream, optional

**1.** In a microwave, melt ½ cup butter; stir in brown sugar. Spread evenly onto bottom of a greased 5-qt. slow cooker. Sprinkle with cherries and pecans; top with pineapple. Sprinkle evenly with dry cake mix. Melt the remaining butter; drizzle over top.
**2.** Cook, covered, on high 2 hours or until fruit mixture is bubbly. (To avoid scorching, rotate slow-cooker insert a half turn midway through cooking, lifting carefully with oven mitts.)
**3.** Turn off slow cooker; let stand, uncovered, for 30 minutes before serving. If desired, serve with ice cream.

**NOTE** To toast nuts, bake in a shallow pan in a 350° oven for 5-10 minutes or cook in a skillet over low heat until lightly browned, stirring occasionally.

**½ CUP** 455 cal., 22g fat (10g sat. fat), 37mg chol., 418mg sod., 66g carb. (47g sugars, 1g fiber), 3g pro.

## PEANUT BUTTER PUDDING PIE

This pie is pretty enough for company—if your family doesn't get to it first! No one will be able to resist a sweet piece of this creamy chocolate and peanut butter dessert.

*—Valerie Sisson, Norton, OH*

**Prep:** 20 min. + chilling
**Makes:** 8 servings

- 2 cups 2% milk
- 1 pkg. (3 oz.) cook-and-serve vanilla pudding mix
- 1 cup peanut butter chips
- 1 graham cracker crust (9 in.)
- 2½ cups whipped topping
- ⅓ cup milk chocolate chips
- 1 tsp. shortening

1. In a saucepan, whisk milk and pudding mix. Cook and stir over medium heat until mixture comes to a boil. Reduce heat; stir in peanut butter chips until melted. Pour into crust. Cover and refrigerate until set, 3-4 hours.
2. Spread whipped topping over pie. In a microwave-safe bowl, melt chocolate chips and shortening; cool for 5 minutes. Drizzle over topping. Refrigerate until serving.

**1 PIECE** 388 cal., 20g fat (10g sat. fat), 10mg chol., 275mg sod., 45g carb. (33g sugars, 2g fiber), 7g pro.

### MAKE IT AHEAD

Since it needs at least 3–4 hours to set, you can easily prep the pudding layer in advance—even the night before. Wait to add whipped topping and chocolate drizzle until soon before serving, though.

## PUDDING TIPS

**How do I avoid lumpy pudding?** Whisk dry ingredients first, then slowly add milk while whisking. Keep whisking as it boils and thickens.

**Can I use a different milk?** Whole milk is best—lighter or plant-based milks won't won't taste as rich. If you only have low-fat milk, you can enrich it with cream.

**Is there a different way to serve this pudding?** Pour pudding into a baked pastry shell, chill overnight and top with whipped cream for an easy pie.

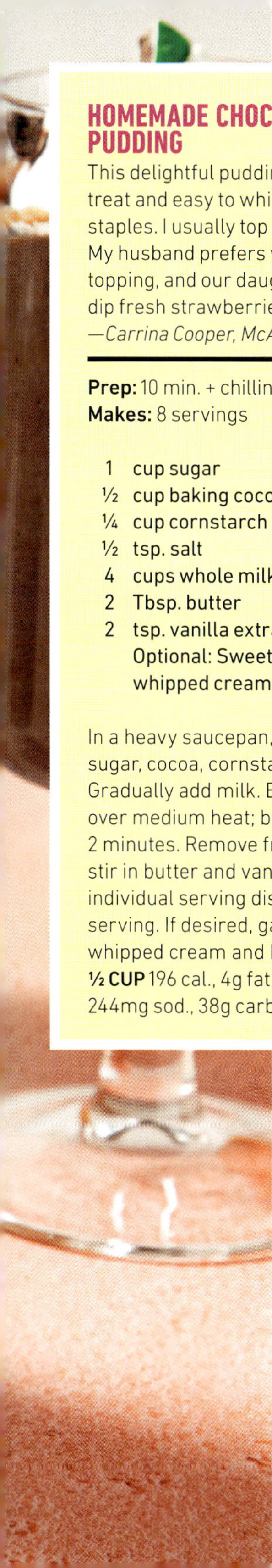

## HOMEMADE CHOCOLATE PUDDING

This delightful pudding is always a treat and easy to whip up with pantry staples. I usually top it with M&M's. My husband prefers whipped topping, and our daughter loves to dip fresh strawberries in hers.
*—Carrina Cooper, McAlpin, FL*

**Prep:** 10 min. + chilling
**Makes:** 8 servings

- 1 cup sugar
- ½ cup baking cocoa
- ¼ cup cornstarch
- ½ tsp. salt
- 4 cups whole milk
- 2 Tbsp. butter
- 2 tsp. vanilla extract
- Optional: Sweetened whipped cream and M&M's

In a heavy saucepan, combine the sugar, cocoa, cornstarch and salt. Gradually add milk. Bring to a boil over medium heat; boil and stir for 2 minutes. Remove from the heat; stir in butter and vanilla. Spoon into individual serving dishes. Chill until serving. If desired, garnish with whipped cream and M&M's.
**½ CUP** 196 cal., 4g fat, 2mg chol., 244mg sod., 38g carb., 5g pro.

## CHERRY DREAM CAKE

I serve this because it's so festive and easy. No one will know your secret is adding a package of gelatin to a boxed cake mix!
*—Margaret McNeil, Germantown, TN*

**Prep:** 15 min. + chilling
**Bake:** 30 min. + cooling
**Makes:** 20 servings

- 1 pkg. white cake mix (regular size)
- 1 pkg. (3 oz.) cherry gelatin
- 1½ cups boiling water
- 1 pkg. (8 oz.) cream cheese, softened
- 2 cups thawed whipped topping
- 1 can (21 oz.) cherry pie filling

1. Prepare the cake mix according to package directions, using a greased 13x9-in. baking pan. Bake at 350° until a toothpick inserted in center comes out clean, 30-35 minutes.
2. Dissolve gelatin in boiling water. Cool the cake on a wire rack for 3-5 minutes. Poke holes in cake with a meat fork or wooden skewer; gradually pour gelatin over cake. Cool for 15 minutes. Cover and refrigerate for 30 minutes.
3. In a large bowl, beat cream cheese until fluffy. Fold in the whipped topping. Carefully spread over cake. Top with pie filling. Cover and refrigerate for at least 2 hours before serving.

**1 PIECE** 245 cal., 11g fat (5g sat. fat), 39mg chol., 242mg sod., 34g carb. (22g sugars, 1g fiber), 3g pro.

## APPLE CRUMB BARS

This apple bar recipe has been a favorite of mine for many years—it's always a hit at parties and with family.

*—Barbara Pickard, Union Lake, MI*

**Prep:** 15 min. • **Bake:** 35 min.
**Makes:** 3 dozen

- 3 cups all-purpose flour
- 1½ cups old-fashioned oats
- 1½ cups packed brown sugar
- ¾ tsp. baking soda
- 1¼ cups cold butter, divided
- 5 to 6 cups thinly sliced peeled apples
- 1 cup sugar
- 3 Tbsp. cornstarch
- 1 cup cold water
- 1 tsp. vanilla extract
- Vanilla ice cream, optional

1. Preheat oven to 350°. In a large bowl, combine flour, oats, brown sugar and baking soda; cut in 1 cup plus 2 Tbsp. butter until mixture resembles coarse crumbs. Set aside 2 cups for topping. Press remaining oat mixture into a greased 13x9-in. baking pan. Arrange apples over the top.
2. In a small saucepan, combine sugar, cornstarch, water, vanilla and remaining 2 Tbsp. butter. Bring to a boil. Cook and stir until thickened, 1-2 minutes; pour over the apples. Sprinkle with reserved oat mixture.
3. Bake for 35-45 minutes or until the top is lightly browned. Cool in pan on a wire rack. Serve with ice cream if desired.

**1 BAR** 174 cal., 7g fat (4g sat. fat), 17mg chol., 94mg sod., 28g carb. (16g sugars, 1g fiber), 2g pro.

## GRILLED NECTARINES WITH BURRATA & HONEY

The classic Caprese gets a sweet makeover with this inspired summer starter. Burrata, mint and honey are served over nectarine halves—or any stone fruit you like—in this creamy, dreamy dish.
*—Anthony Gans, Hawthorne, CA*

**Takes:** 15 min. • **Makes:** 6 servings

- 3 medium ripe nectarines, halved and pitted
- Cooking spray
- 8 oz. burrata cheese
- 2 Tbsp. honey
- 12 fresh mint leaves
- Flaky sea salt, such as Maldon

1. Heat a grill pan over medium-high heat. Spritz cut sides of nectarines with cooking spray. Place cut sides down on pan. Grill until just tender, 4-5 minutes. Meanwhile, drain the burrata; cut into 6 slices.
2. Arrange the grilled nectarine halves, cut side up, on a serving platter. Top with burrata, honey and mint; sprinkle with sea salt.

**1 SERVING** 160 cal., 8g fat (5g sat. fat), 27mg chol., 60mg sod., 15g carb. (13g sugars, 1g fiber), 7g pro.

**"This was a really interesting combination of flavors. The burrata and honey pair so well together. The nectarines need to have the perfect sweetness and ripeness to make this dish. I loved it—just make sure you get good fruit to make it pop."**
—AUG2295, TASTEOFHOME.COM

## OLD-FASHIONED BANANA CREAM PIE

This fluffy no-bake pie is full of old-fashioned flavor, with only a fraction of the work. Because it uses instant pudding, it's ready in just minutes.
*—Perlene Hoekema, Lynden, WA*

**Takes:** 10 min. • **Makes:** 8 servings

- 1 cup cold 2% milk
- 1 pkg. (3.4 oz.) instant vanilla pudding mix
- ½ tsp. vanilla extract
- 1 carton (12 oz.) frozen whipped topping, thawed, divided
- 1 graham cracker crust (9 in.)
- 2 medium firm bananas, sliced
- Additional banana slices, optional

1. In a large bowl, whisk milk, pudding mix and vanilla for 2 minutes (mixture will be thick). Fold in 3 cups whipped topping.
2. Pour 1⅓ cups pudding mixture into pie crust. Layer with banana slices and remaining pudding mixture. Top with remaining whipped topping. If desired, garnish with additional banana slices. Refrigerate until serving.

**1 PIECE** 311 cal., 13g fat (9g sat. fat), 2mg chol., 213mg sod., 43g carb. (34g sugars, 1g fiber), 2g pro.

**CHOCOLATE & PEANUT BUTTER BANANA CREAM PIE** Substitute a 9-in. chocolate crumb crust for the graham cracker crust. Arrange banana slices in crust. In a microwave-safe bowl, mix ¾ cup peanut butter and 2 oz. chopped chocolate; microwave on high until blended and smooth, 1-1½ minutes, stirring every 30 seconds. Spoon over bananas. Prepare pudding mix filling as directed; pour over the top. Layer with remaining whipped topping. Just before serving, garnish with chopped salted peanuts or chopped peanut butter cups.

## GINGER PLUM TART

Sweet cravings, begone: This free-form plum tart is done in only 35 minutes. Plus, it's extra-awesome when served warm.
—Taste of Home *Test Kitchen*

**Prep:** 15 min. • **Bake:** 20 min.
**Makes:** 8 servings

- 1 sheet refrigerated pie crust
- 3½ cups sliced fresh plums (about 10 medium)
- 3 Tbsp. plus 1 tsp. coarse sugar, divided
- 1 Tbsp. cornstarch
- 2 tsp. finely chopped crystallized ginger
- 1 large egg white
- 1 Tbsp. water

1. Preheat oven to 400°. On a clean work surface, unroll dough. Roll out to a 12-in. circle. Transfer to a parchment-lined baking sheet.
2. In a large bowl, toss plums with 3 Tbsp. sugar and cornstarch. Arrange plums on crust to within 2 in. of edge; sprinkle with ginger. Fold crust edge over plums, pleating as you go.
3. In a small bowl, whisk egg white and water; brush over folded crust. Sprinkle with remaining 1 tsp. sugar.
4. Bake for 20-25 minutes or until the crust is golden brown. Cool in pan on a wire rack. Serve warm or at room temperature.

**1 PIECE** 190 cal., 7g fat (3g sat. fat), 5mg chol., 108mg sod., 30g carb. (14g sugars, 1g fiber), 2g pro.

## FLORIDA ORANGE CAKE

This recipe is a perfect showcase for our Florida oranges, with juice in the cake and marmalade in the frosting. Everyone comments on how luscious the cake tastes.

*—Terry Bray, Auburndale, FL*

**Prep:** 10 min. • **Bake:** 30 min. + cooling
**Makes:** 16 servings

- 1 pkg. yellow cake mix (regular size)
- 1 cup orange juice
- 3 large eggs, room temperature
- ⅓ cup water
- ⅓ cup canola oil

FROSTING

- 1 pkg. (8 oz.) cream cheese, softened
- ¼ cup butter, softened
- 1 Tbsp. orange marmalade
- 3 cups confectioners' sugar

1. Preheat the oven to 350°. In a large bowl, combine cake mix, orange juice, eggs, water and oil; beat on low speed for 30 seconds. Beat on medium for 2 minutes.
2. Pour into a greased 9x9-in. baking pan. Bake until a toothpick inserted in center comes out clean, 30-35 minutes. Cool completely on a wire rack.
3. For frosting, in a small bowl, beat cream cheese and butter until smooth. Beat in the orange marmalade and confectioners' sugar. Spread over cake. If desired, swirl with additional orange marmalade. Store in the refrigerator.

**1 PIECE** 347 cal., 14g fat (6g sat. fat), 57mg chol., 315mg sod., 53g carb. (39g sugars, 0 fiber), 3g pro.

### SUBSTITUTE ORANGE ZEST

If you don't have orange marmalade for the frosting, you can use 1-2 tsp. grated orange zest instead. The orange flavor will be just as punchy. For a pretty garnish, you can grate some extra zest on top of the cake.

5i

## CHOCOLATE & PEANUT BUTTER CRISPY BARS

I created these dairy-free chocolaty peanut bars, and my kids and their friends can't get enough!
*—Dawn Pasco, Overland Park, KS*

**Prep:** 15 min. + chilling
**Bake:** 25 min. + cooling
**Makes:** 2 dozen

- 1 pkg. fudge brownie mix (13x9-in. pan size)
- 1½ cups chunky peanut butter
- 2 cups semisweet chocolate chips
- 1 cup creamy peanut butter
- 3 cups Rice Krispies

1. Line a 13x9-in. baking pan with parchment, letting ends extend up sides. Prepare and bake brownie mix according to package directions, using prepared pan. Cool in pan on a wire rack 30 minutes. Refrigerate until cold.
2. Spread chunky peanut butter over brownies. Place chocolate chips and creamy peanut butter in a large microwave-safe bowl. Microwave in 30-second intervals until melted; stir until smooth. Stir in Rice Krispies; spread over chunky peanut butter layer. Refrigerate, covered, at least 30 minutes or until set.
3. Lifting with parchment, remove brownies from pan. Cut into bars and store in an airtight container in the refrigerator.

**1 BAR** 390 cal., 27g fat (6g sat. fat), 16mg chol., 234mg sod., 35g carb. (21g sugars, 3g fiber), 9g pro.

5i

## BLUEBERRY PIE WITH GRAHAM CRACKER CRUST

We live in blueberry country and this pie is a perfect way to showcase the luscious berries. A neighbor made this pie for us when we had a death in the family several years ago. Our whole family enjoys it.
*—R. Ricks, Kalamazoo, MI*

**Prep:** 20 min. + chilling
**Makes:** 8 servings

- ¾ cup sugar
- 3 Tbsp. cornstarch
- ⅛ tsp. salt
- ¼ cup water
- 4 cups fresh blueberries, divided
- 1 graham cracker crust (9 in.)
- Whipped cream

1. In a large saucepan, combine sugar, cornstarch and salt. Gradually add water, stirring until smooth. Stir in 2 cups blueberries. Bring to a boil; cook and stir until thickened, 1-2 minutes. Remove from heat; cool to room temperature.
2. Gently stir the remaining 2 cups blueberries into the cooled blueberry mixture. Spoon into crust. Refrigerate, covered, until chilled, 1-2 hours. Serve with whipped cream.

**GRAHAM CRACKER CRUST (9 IN.)** Combine 1½ cups crushed graham cracker crumbs (24 squares), ¼ sugar and ⅓ cup melted butter. Press onto the bottom and up the side of an ungreased 9-in. pie plate. Bake at 375° until lightly browned, 8-10 minutes. Cool on a wire rack before filling.

**1 PIECE** 230 cal., 6g fat (1g sat. fat), 0 chol., 159mg sod., 46g carb. (35g sugars, 2g fiber), 1g pro.

## QUICK & EASY TIRAMISU

No one can resist this classic creamy dessert. It's quick to prepare but can be made ahead for added mealtime convenience.
—Taste of Home *Test Kitchen*

**Prep:** 20 min. + chilling
**Makes:** 6 servings

- 2 cups cold 2% milk
- 1 pkg. (3.4 oz.) instant vanilla pudding mix
- 1 cup heavy whipping cream
- 3 Tbsp. confectioners' sugar
- 28 soft ladyfingers, split
- 2½ tsp. instant coffee granules
- ½ cup boiling water
- 1 Tbsp. baking cocoa

1. In a large bowl, whisk milk and pudding mix for 2 minutes. Let stand until soft-set, about 2 minutes. In a small bowl, beat cream until it begins to thicken. Add confectioners' sugar; beat until soft peaks form. Fold into pudding; cover and refrigerate.
2. Arrange half the ladyfingers cut side up in an 11x7-in. dish. Dissolve coffee granules in boiling water; drizzle half over the ladyfingers. Spread with half the pudding mixture. Repeat layers. Sprinkle with cocoa. Refrigerate until serving.

**1 PIECE** 384 cal., 19g fat (11g sat. fat), 123mg chol., 379mg sod., 47g carb. (33g sugars, 1g fiber), 7g pro.

## TENNESSEE PEACH PUDDING

This out-of-this-world dessert is one of our favorite peach recipes. I was raised in Oklahoma, and we used Elberta peaches right off our trees when we made this outstanding cobbler.
—*Virginia Crowell, Lyons, OR*

**Prep:** 20 min. • **Bake:** 40 min.
**Makes:** 8 servings

- 1 cup all-purpose flour
- ½ cup sugar
- 2 tsp. baking powder
- ½ tsp. salt
- ½ tsp. ground cinnamon, optional
- ½ cup 2% milk
- 3 cups sliced peeled fresh or frozen peaches

TOPPING

- 1½ cups water
- ½ cup sugar
- ½ cup packed brown sugar
- 1 Tbsp. butter
- ¼ tsp. ground nutmeg
- Vanilla ice cream, optional

1. Preheat the oven to 400°. Combine flour, sugar, baking powder, salt and, if desired, cinnamon. Stir in milk just until combined; fold in peaches. Spread into a greased 8-in. square baking dish.
2. For topping, combine water, sugars, butter and nutmeg in a large saucepan. Bring to a boil, stirring until sugars are dissolved. Pour over the peach mixture. Bake until filling is bubbly and a toothpick inserted in the topping comes out clean, 40-50 minutes. Serve warm or cold, with ice cream if desired.

**1 SERVING** 253 cal., 2g fat (1g sat. fat), 5mg chol., 269mg sod., 57g carb. (44g sugars, 1g fiber), 3g pro.

**PLUM COBBLER** Substitute plums for the peaches.

> **"This recipe is fantastic! I cut both sugars to ⅓ cup, as we're trying to reduce our sugar intake. It was plenty sweet and yummy with ice cream or cold milk."**
> —LINDA226, TASTEOFHOME.COM

## ROCKY ROAD FREEZER PIE

Whip up this simple chocolaty pie the day before, and you'll feel like a champ when you serve it on party day.
*—Addrenne Roth, Donna, TX*

**Prep:** 15 min. + freezing
**Makes:** 8 servings

- 1½ cups half-and-half cream
- 1 pkg. (3.9 oz.) instant chocolate pudding mix
- 1 carton (8 oz.) frozen whipped topping, thawed
- ⅓ cup semisweet chocolate chips
- ⅓ cup miniature marshmallows
- ⅓ cup chopped pecans
- 1 graham cracker crust (9 in.)
- Optional: Miniature marshmallows, chopped pecans and chocolate sauce

In a large bowl, whisk cream and pudding mix for 2 minutes. Fold in whipped topping. Stir in chocolate chips, marshmallows and pecans. Transfer to pie crust. Freeze until firm, about 6 hours. Remove from freezer 10 minutes before serving. If desired, top with marshmallows, pecans and chocolate sauce.

**1 PIECE** 184 cal., 10g fat (5g sat. fat), 11mg chol., 175mg sod., 20g carb. (15g sugars, 1g fiber), 2g pro.

5i

## HEALTHY PEANUT BUTTER COOKIES

You'll need only four ingredients and one bowl for these peanut butter cookies. For a gluten-free recipe, ensure the oat bran is made in a certified gluten-free facility.
—Taste of Home *Test Kitchen*

**Prep:** 15 min. • **Bake:** 15 min./batch
**Makes:** 2 dozen

- 1 large egg, room temperature, beaten
- 1 cup creamy peanut butter
- ¼ cup oat bran
- ¼ cup maple syrup

1. Preheat the oven to 350°. In a large bowl, mix all ingredients. Roll level tablespoonfuls into balls. Place on ungreased baking sheets; flatten with a fork.
2. Bake for 15 minutes. Remove to a wire rack to cool.

**1 COOKIE** 78 cal., 6g fat (1g sat. fat), 8mg chol., 49mg sod., 5g carb. (3g sugars, 1g fiber), 3g pro.

### PEANUT BUTTER COOKIES TIPS

**Can I use natural peanut butter?** Yes, but expect slight changes in taste and texture compared to regular peanut butter.

**What makes these cookies healthier?** They use oat bran instead of flour, which adds fiber and protein.

## LEMON OLIVE OIL CAKE

Olive oil cakes stay tender and moist longer than butter-based cakes, so they are wonderful if you need to make dessert ahead of time. Serve with your favorite seasonal berries.
*—Nicole Gackowski, Antioch, CA*

**Prep:** 15 min. • **Bake:** 30 min. + cooling
**Makes:** 8 servings

- 2 large eggs, room temperature
- ⅔ cup sugar
- ½ cup extra virgin olive oil
- ⅓ cup 2% milk
- 1 Tbsp. grated lemon zest
- 3 Tbsp. lemon juice
- 1 cup all-purpose flour
- 1 tsp. baking powder
- ¼ tsp. salt
- Confectioners' sugar

1. Preheat the oven to 350°. Line a greased 8-in. round baking pan with parchment. In a large bowl, beat the eggs on high speed for 3 minutes. Gradually add sugar, beating until thickened. Gradually beat in oil. Beat in milk, lemon zest and lemon juice.
2. In another bowl, whisk flour, baking powder and salt; fold into egg mixture. Transfer batter to prepared pan, spreading evenly. Bake for 30-35 minutes or until a toothpick inserted in center comes out clean. Cool in pan for 15 minutes before removing to a wire rack; remove parchment. Cool completely. Dust with confectioners' sugar.

**1 PIECE** 266 cal., 15g fat (2g sat. fat), 47mg chol., 157mg sod., 30g carb. (18g sugars, 1g fiber), 4g pro.

## AIR-FRYER MOCHA PUDDING CAKES

These mouthwatering mini cakes make the perfect treat for two. My mom used to make these when I was a little girl. Now I whip them up and pop them in my air fryer for a speedy dessert.
*—Debora Simmons, Eglon, WV*

**Takes:** 30 min. • **Makes:** 2 servings

- ¼ cup all-purpose flour
- 3 Tbsp. sugar
- 1½ tsp. baking cocoa
- ½ tsp. baking powder
- ⅛ tsp. salt
- 3 Tbsp. 2% milk
- 1½ tsp. butter, melted
- ¼ tsp. vanilla extract

TOPPING

- 2 Tbsp. brown sugar
- 1½ tsp. baking cocoa
- 3 Tbsp. hot brewed coffee
- 1 Tbsp. hot water
- Whipped topping, optional

1. Preheat air fryer to 350°. In a small bowl, combine flour, sugar, cocoa, baking powder and salt. Stir in the milk, butter and vanilla until smooth. Spoon into 2 lightly greased 4-oz. ramekins. Combine brown sugar and cocoa; sprinkle over batter. Combine coffee and water; pour over topping.
2. Place ramekins on tray in air-fryer basket. Cook 15-20 minutes or until a knife inserted in the center comes out clean. Serve warm or at room temperature, with whipped topping if desired.

**1 PUDDING CAKE** 229 cal., 4g fat (2g sat. fat), 9mg chol., 306mg sod., 47g carb. (33g sugars, 1g fiber), 3g pro.

## VANILLA WAFER COOKIES

These buttery cookies bake up chewy and crispy at the same time. Sprinkle with colored sugar or leave them as-is. Their simplicity is beauty enough!
—*Edith MacBeath, Gaines, PA*

**Prep:** 20 min. • **Bake:** 15 min.
**Makes:** about 3½ dozen

- ½ cup butter, softened
- 1 cup sugar
- 1 egg
- 1 Tbsp. vanilla extract
- 1⅓ cups all-purpose flour
- ¾ tsp. baking powder
- ¼ tsp. salt

1. In a large bowl, cream butter and sugar until light and fluffy. Beat in egg and vanilla. Combine dry ingredients; add to creamed mixture and mix well.
2. Drop by teaspoonfuls 2 in. apart onto ungreased baking sheets. Bake at 350° for 12-15 minutes or until the edges are golden brown. Remove to wire racks to cool.

**2 COOKIES** 109 cal., 5g fat (3g sat. fat), 22mg chol., 90mg sod., 16g carb. (9g sugars, 0 fiber), 1g pro.

> **"Buttery and delicious! They are crispy and very tasty. I made them for a banana pudding, but I also enjoyed a few on their own."**
> —TAMMYCOOKBLOGSBOOKS, TASTEOFHOME.COM

## APPLE DUMPLING BAKE

I received this recipe from a friend, and I tweaked it to suit my family's tastes. Mountain Dew is the secret ingredient in this rich apple dessert that's a snap to make.
—*Chris Shields, Monrovia, IN*

**Prep:** 15 min. • **Bake:** 35 min.
**Makes:** 8 servings

- 2 medium Granny Smith apples
- 2 tubes (8 oz. each) refrigerated crescent rolls
- 1 cup sugar
- ⅓ cup butter, softened
- ½ tsp. ground cinnamon
- ¾ cup Mountain Dew soda
- Vanilla ice cream

1. Preheat oven to 350°. Peel, core and cut each apple into 8 wedges. Unroll both tubes of crescent dough; separate each into 8 triangles. Wrap a triangle around each wedge. Place in a greased 13x9-in. baking dish.
2. In a bowl, mix the sugar, butter and cinnamon until blended; sprinkle over dumplings. Slowly pour soda around rolls (do not stir).
3. Bake, uncovered, until golden brown and apples are tender, 35-40 minutes. Serve warm with ice cream.

**2 DUMPLINGS** 414 cal., 20g fat (9g sat. fat), 20mg chol., 510mg sod., 55g carb. (35g sugars, 1g fiber), 4g pro.

### LAYERED LEMON PIE

This is a great ending for almost any meal that kids and adults all enjoy. The creamy lemon filling is always a hit with my husband.
*—Elizabeth Yoder, Belcourt, ND*

**Prep:** 20 min. + chilling
**Makes:** 8 servings

- 1 pkg. (8 oz.) cream cheese, softened
- ½ cup sugar
- 1 can (15¾ oz.) lemon pie filling, divided
- 1 carton (8 oz.) frozen whipped topping, thawed
- 1 graham cracker crust (9 in.)

In a small bowl, beat cream cheese and sugar until smooth. Beat in half the pie filling. Fold in whipped topping. Spoon into crust. Spread remaining pie filling over cream cheese layer. Refrigerate for at least 15 minutes before serving.
**1 PIECE** 526 cal., 24g fat (13g sat. fat), 104mg chol., 251mg sod., 72g carb. (61g sugars, 1g fiber), 6g pro.

**TEST KITCHEN TIP**
**For the most attractive, easy-to-cut pieces, give the pie lots of time to chill—overnight, if possible.**

### SLOW-COOKER PINA COLADA BANANAS FOSTER

I took bananas Foster one step further and combined it with the flavors of my favorite tropical drink—pina colada. Make sure your bananas are not super ripe.
*—Trisha Kruse, Eagle, ID*

**Prep:** 10 min. • **Cook:** 2 hours
**Makes:** 6 servings (3 cups)

- 4 medium firm bananas
- 1 can (8 oz.) pineapple tidbits, drained
- ¼ cup butter, melted
- 1 cup packed brown sugar
- ¼ cup rum
- ½ tsp. coconut extract
- ½ cup sweetened shredded coconut, toasted
- Optional: Coconut ice cream, vanilla wafers and cream-filled wafer cookies

1. Cut bananas in half lengthwise, then widthwise. Layer sliced bananas and pineapple in bottom of a 1½-qt. slow cooker. Combine butter, brown sugar, rum and coconut extract in a small bowl; pour over fruit. Cook, covered, on low until heated through, about 2 hours.
2. Sprinkle individual servings with toasted coconut. Serve with optional ingredients as desired.
**½ CUP** 358 cal., 11g fat (7g sat. fat), 20mg chol., 95mg sod., 63g carb. (53g sugars, 3g fiber), 1g pro.

## MISSISSIPPI MUD PIE

This southern favorite is one my family can never get enough. My grandmother, mother and aunts always made this dish for family gatherings. Now I make it for just about every event because it's so easy to prepare and everyone loves it! There are never any leftovers.
*—Elizabeth Williston, Thibodaux, LA*

**Prep:** 30 min. • **Bake:** 15 min. + cooling
**Makes:** 12 servings

- 1 cup all-purpose flour
- 1 cup chopped pecans
- ½ cup butter, softened
- 1 pkg. (5.9 oz.) instant chocolate pudding mix
- 1 pkg. (8 oz.) cream cheese, softened
- 1 cup confectioners' sugar
- 1 container (16 oz.) frozen whipped topping, thawed, divided
- Optional: Toasted chopped pecans and chocolate curls

1. Preheat oven to 350°. In a large bowl, beat the flour, pecans and butter until blended. Press into bottom of a 13x9-in. baking dish. Bake until golden brown, about 15 minutes. Remove to a wire rack; cool completely.

2. Make chocolate pudding according to package directions; let stand 5 minutes. In a bowl, beat cream cheese and confectioners' sugar until smooth; fold in 1 cup whipped topping. Spread cream cheese mixture over the cooled crust. Spread pudding over cream cheese layer; top with the remaining whipped topping. If desired, top with additional pecans and chocolate curls.

**1 PIECE** 466 cal., 29g fat (17g sat. fat), 46mg chol., 214mg sod., 44g carb. (28g sugars, 2g fiber), 5g pro.

## COCONUT COOKIES TIPS

**Can I use toasted coconut?** Yes—toast all or part of the coconut for extra flavor. Sweetened coconut is moist and rich, while unsweetened is drier and subtler.

**Can I prep these cookies ahead?** Freeze unbaked dough for up to a month, or baked cookies for up to 6 months. At room temperature, they keep about 3 days.

## GRANDMA KRAUSE'S COCONUT COOKIES

When my daughters were young, their great-grandma made them cookies with oats and coconut. Thankfully, she shared the recipe.
*—Debra J. Dorn, Dunnellon, FL*

**Prep:** 40 min. + freezing
**Bake:** 10 min./batch
**Makes:** about 3½ dozen

- 1 cup shortening
- 1 cup sugar
- 1 cup packed brown sugar
- 2 large eggs, room temperature
- 1 tsp. vanilla extract
- 2 cups all-purpose flour
- 1 tsp. baking powder
- 1 tsp. baking soda
- ¼ tsp. salt
- 1 cup old-fashioned oats
- 1 cup sweetened shredded coconut

1. In a large bowl, beat shortening and sugars until blended. Beat in eggs and vanilla. In another bowl, whisk flour, baking powder, baking soda and salt; gradually beat into sugar mixture. Stir in oats and coconut.
2. Divide dough into 4 portions. On a lightly floured surface, shape each into a 6-in.-long log. Wrap in waxed paper; freeze 2 hours or until firm.
3. Preheat the oven to 350°. Unwrap and cut dough crosswise into ½-in. slices, reshaping as needed. Place 2 in. apart on ungreased baking sheets. Bake until golden brown, 10-12 minutes. Cool on pans for 5 minutes. Remove to wire racks to cool completely.

**1 COOKIE** 124 cal., 6g fat (2g sat. fat), 9mg chol., 66mg sod., 17g carb. (11g sugars, 0 fiber), 1g pro.

## FLUFFY KEY LIME PIE

For a taste of paradise, try this light and creamy confection. It's low in fat, sugar and fuss. Dessert doesn't get any better than that!
*—Frances VanFossan, Warren, MI*

**Prep:** 20 min. + chilling
**Makes:** 8 servings

- ¼ cup boiling water
- 1 pkg. (3 oz.) lime gelatin
- 2 cartons (6 oz. each) Key lime yogurt
- 1 carton (8 oz.) frozen whipped topping, thawed
- 1 9-in. graham cracker crust

1. In a large bowl, add boiling water to gelatin; stir for 2 minutes to completely dissolve. Whisk in yogurt. Fold in the whipped topping. Pour into crust.
2. Refrigerate, covered, until set, about 2 hours.

**1 PIECE** 194 cal., 3g fat (1g sat. fat), 2mg chol., 159mg sod., 33g carb. (18g sugars, 0 fiber), 3g pro.

## GRILLED STONE FRUITS WITH BALSAMIC SYRUP

Get ready to experience another side of stone fruits. Hot off the grill, this late-summer dessert practically melts in your mouth.
*—Sonya Labbe, West Hollywood, CA*

**Takes:** 20 min. • **Makes:** 4 servings

- ½ **cup balsamic vinegar**
- 2 **Tbsp. brown sugar**
- 2 **medium peaches, peeled and halved**
- 2 **medium nectarines, peeled and halved**
- 2 **medium plums, peeled and halved**

1. In a small saucepan, combine vinegar and brown sugar. Bring to a boil; cook until liquid is reduced by half.
2. On a lightly oiled grill rack, grill peaches, nectarines and plums, covered, over medium heat or broil 4 in. from heat 3-4 minutes on each side or until tender.
3. Slice fruit; arrange on a serving plate. Drizzle with sauce.

**1 SERVING** 114 cal., 1g fat (0 sat. fat), 0 chol., 10mg sod., 28g carb. (24g sugars, 2g fiber), 2g pro.

## CLASSIC LEMON BARS

These delicious bars are simple enough for no-fuss dinners yet elegant, too, for special celebrations. They'll be a hit at your home regardless of when you serve them.

*—Melissa Mosness, Loveland, CO*

---

**Prep:** 15 min. • **Bake:** 25 min. + cooling
**Makes:** 9 servings

- ½ cup butter, softened
- ¼ cup sugar
- 1 cup all-purpose flour

FILLING

- ¾ cup sugar
- 2 large eggs
- 3 Tbsp. lemon juice
- 2 Tbsp. all-purpose flour
- 1 tsp. grated lemon zest
- ¼ tsp. baking powder
- Confectioners' sugar

1. Preheat oven to 350°. In a small bowl, cream butter and sugar until light and fluffy, 5-7 minutes; gradually beat in flour until blended.
2. Press into an ungreased 8-in. square baking dish. Bake for 15-20 minutes or until edges are lightly browned.
3. For the filling, in a small bowl, beat sugar, eggs, lemon juice, flour, lemon zest and baking powder until frothy. Pour over crust.
4. Bake 10-15 minutes longer or until set and lightly browned. Cool on a wire rack. Sprinkle with confectioners' sugar. Cut into squares.

**1 PIECE** 250 cal., 11g fat (7g sat. fat), 74mg chol., 99mg sod., 35g carb. (23g sugars, 0 fiber), 3g pro.

## OLD-TIME BUTTERMILK PIE

This old-fashioned family recipe dates back to the 1800s. My mother and grandmother made it with buttermilk and eggs from our farm and set it on the tables at church meetings and social gatherings. I did the same. Now my grown children make the pie too!
*—Kate Mathews, Shreveport, LA*

**Prep:** 15 min. • **Bake:** 45 min. + cooling
**Makes:** 10 servings

CRUST
- 1½ cups all-purpose flour
- 1 tsp. salt
- ½ cup shortening
- ¼ cup cold 2% milk
- 1 large egg, lightly beaten

FILLING
- ½ cup butter, softened
- 2 cups sugar
- 3 Tbsp. all-purpose flour
- 3 large eggs
- 1 cup buttermilk
- 1 tsp. vanilla extract
- 1 tsp. ground cinnamon
- ¼ cup lemon juice
- Optional: Whipped cream and fresh berries

1. Preheat oven to 350°. In a large bowl, mix flour and salt. Cut in shortening until crumbly. Gradually stir in milk and egg. On a lightly floured surface, roll dough to a ⅛-in.-thick circle; transfer to a 9-in. pie plate. Trim crust to ½ in. beyond rim of plate; flute edge.
2. For the filling, in a large bowl, cream butter and sugar; beat in flour. Add the eggs, 1 at a time, beating well after each addition. Stir in the buttermilk, vanilla, cinnamon and lemon juice; mix well. Pour into crust.
3. Bake until center is set, 45-50 minutes. Cool completely on a wire rack. Serve or refrigerate within 2 hours. If desired, top servings with whipped cream and fresh berries.

**1 PIECE** 448 cal., 21g fat (9g sat. fat), 100mg chol., 388mg sod., 59g carb. (42g sugars, 1g fiber), 6g pro.

## RASPBERRY CUSTARD KUCHEN

Back where I grew up in Wisconsin, people have been baking this treat, a German cake, for generations. We love it for breakfast or as a special dessert. It's no fuss to fix and impressive to serve.
*—Virginia Arndt, Sequim, WA*

**Prep:** 20 min. • **Bake:** 40 min.
**Makes:** 12 servings

- 1½ cups all-purpose flour, divided
- ½ tsp. salt
- ½ cup cold butter
- 2 Tbsp. heavy whipping cream
- ½ cup sugar

FILLING

- 3 cups fresh raspberries
- 1 cup sugar
- 1 Tbsp. all-purpose flour
- 2 large eggs, beaten
- 1 cup heavy whipping cream
- 1 tsp. vanilla extract
- Confectioners' sugar, optional

1. In a bowl, combine 1 cup flour and salt; cut in butter until the mixture resembles coarse crumbs. Stir in cream; pat onto bottom of a greased 13x9-in. baking dish. Combine the sugar and remaining flour; sprinkle over crust.
2. Arrange raspberries over crust. In a large bowl, combine sugar and flour. Stir in eggs, cream and vanilla; pour over berries.
3. Bake at 375° for 40-45 minutes or until lightly browned. Serve warm or cold. Store in the refrigerator. Top with confectioners' sugar when serving, if desired.

**1 PIECE** 328 cal., 17g fat (10g sat. fat), 86mg chol., 195mg sod., 42g carb. (27g sugars, 3g fiber), 4g pro.

## NEW ENGLAND INDIAN PUDDING

This recipe was inspired by traditional New England Indian pudding. My version is made in the slow cooker instead of being baked for hours in the oven. If the molasses flavor is too strong, cut the amount to 1/3 cup.
*—Susan Bickta, Kutztown, PA*

**Prep:** 15 min. • **Cook:** 3½ hours
**Makes:** 8 servings

- 1 pkg. (8½ oz.) cornbread/muffin mix
- 1 pkg. (3.4 oz.) instant butterscotch pudding mix
- 4 cups whole milk
- 3 large eggs, room temperature, lightly beaten
- ½ cup molasses
- 1 tsp. ground cinnamon
- ¼ tsp. ground cloves
- ¼ tsp. ground ginger
- Optional: Vanilla ice cream or sweetened whipped cream

1. In a large bowl, whisk cornbread mix, pudding mix and milk until blended. Add eggs, molasses and spices; whisk until combined. Transfer to a greased 4- or 5-qt. slow cooker. Cover and cook on high for 1 hour.
2. Reduce the heat to low. Stir pudding, making sure to scrape the side of slow cooker well. Cover and cook until very thick, 2½-3 hours longer, stirring once per hour. Serve warm, with ice cream or whipped cream if desired.

**⅔ CUP** 330 cal., 9g fat (4g sat. fat), 83mg chol., 526mg sod., 51g carb. (36g sugars, 2g fiber), 8g pro.

## EASY COCONUT PIE

This old-fashioned dessert is easy to assemble, so it's the one I rely on when dinnertime is fast approaching. I sometimes sprinkle slices with cinnamon or nutmeg.
*—Virginia Krites, Cridersville, OH*

**Prep:** 10 min. • **Bake:** 50 min.
**Makes:** 6 servings

- 2 cups 2% milk
- 1 cup sugar
- 4 large eggs, room temperature
- ½ cup all-purpose flour
- 6 Tbsp. butter, melted
- 1 tsp. vanilla extract
- ½ tsp. salt
- 1 cup sweetened shredded coconut
- Whipped cream, optional

1. Preheat the oven to 350°. In a blender, combine first 7 ingredients. Cover and process for 10 seconds; scrape side. Process for another 10 seconds. Add coconut; process until blended, about 2 seconds. Pour into a greased 10-in. pie plate.
2. Bake for 50-55 minutes or until a knife inserted in center comes out clean. Serve warm and, if desired, top with whipped cream.

**1 PIECE** 446 cal., 23g fat (15g sat. fat), 183mg chol., 435mg sod., 53g carb. (42g sugars, 1g fiber), 8g pro.

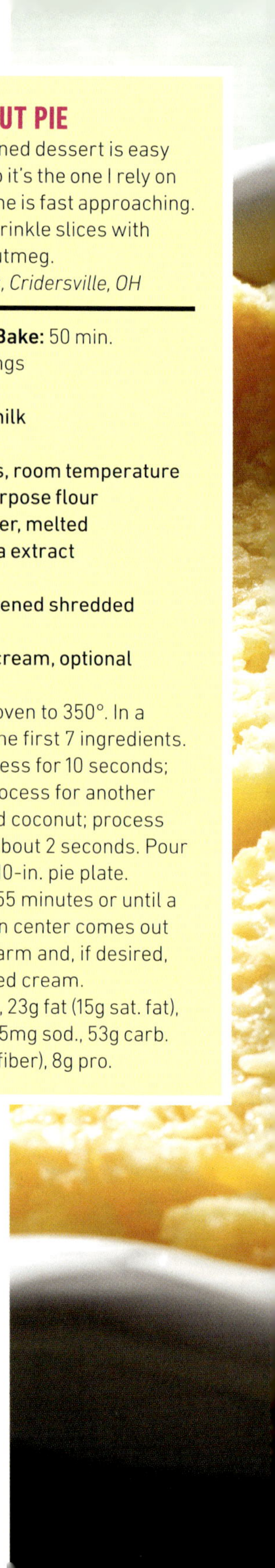

## PEACH COBBLER DUMP CAKE

This recipe gives you the best of both worlds: sweet, tender cake with a beautifully crisp cobbler topping. Add a scoop of vanilla ice cream on the side, and dessert's golden.
*—Keri Sparks, Little Elm, TX*

**Prep:** 10 min. • **Bake:** 35 min.
**Makes:** 15 servings

- 2 cans (15 oz. each) sliced peaches in extra-light syrup
- 2 Tbsp. brown sugar
- 1 tsp. ground cinnamon
- 1 pkg. yellow cake mix (regular size)
- ¾ cup sliced almonds
- ½ cup cold butter

1. Preheat oven to 350°. Pour 1 can of peaches into a greased 13x9-in. baking dish. Drain remaining can of peaches and add to baking dish; sprinkle with brown sugar and cinnamon. Sprinkle with cake mix and almonds.
2. Cut butter into very thin slices; arrange over top, spacing evenly. Bake until golden brown and fruit is bubbly, 35-40 minutes. Serve warm.

**1 PIECE** 234 cal., 11g fat (5g sat. fat), 16mg chol., 242mg sod., 34g carb. (22g sugars, 1g fiber), 2g pro.

## AIR-FRYER S'MORES

File this recipe for a rainy summer day, or as an amazing use No. 101 for your air fryer: crunchy, gooey, melty s'mores ready in two minutes. If you know, you know!
*—Megan Taylor, Greenfield, WI*

**Takes:** 10 min. • **Makes:** 2 servings

- 2 whole graham crackers, broken in half
- 2 large marshmallows, cut in half horizontally
- ½ milk chocolate candy bar, broken into 2 pieces

Preheat air fryer to 400°. Place 4 graham cracker halves in air fryer. Place halved marshmallows in the center of each, sticky side down. Cook for 2-3 minutes or until marshmallows are melted and slightly browned. Remove from the air fryer; place a chocolate piece on top of 2 marshmallows. Place the other cooked halves on top of the chocolate to make 2 s'mores. Let chocolate slightly melt; serve immediately.

**1 S'MORE** 147 cal., 5g fat (2g sat. fat), 3mg chol., 109mg sod., 25g carb. (14g sugars, 1g fiber), 2g pro.

### CUSTOMIZE 'EM

- Swap in gingersnaps, shortbread or other crisp cookies.
- Add peanut butter, caramel, Nutella, jam or Biscoff.
- Slip in strawberry or banana slices.
- Use any chocolate—dark, milk, white—or candy bars.

# ICON INDEX

## FAST FIX

### Soups & Stews


Bean Counter Chowder....35
Chicken Ramen Noodle Bowl....25
Chickpea Tortilla Soup....23
Creamy Taco Soup....10
Easy Spinach Bisque....17
Easy White Chicken Chili....13
Egg Drop Soup....27
Gumbo in a Jiffy....15
Kids' Favorite Chili....19
Shrimp Bisque....16
Spinach & Tortellini Soup....31
Spinach & White Bean Soup....26
Spring Salmon Chowder....10
Watermelon Gazpacho....23

ALL-AMERICAN HAMBURGERS, PAGE 42

### Beef


Air-Fryer Cowboy Casserole....75
Air-Fryer Salisbury Steak....65
All-American Hamburgers....42
Bacon Cheeseburger Pasta....73
Beef Broccoli Stir-Fry....49
Beef Tenderloin in Mushroom Sauce....59
Black Bean & Beef Tostadas....70
Catalina Taco Salad....69
Cheeseburger Cups....38
Garlic-Butter Steak....62
Greek-Style Ribeye Steaks....43
Hearty Meatball Sub Sandwiches....55
Quick Beef & Noodles....80
Saucy Beef with Broccoli....56
Skillet Steak Supper....69
So-Easy Sloppy Joes....70
Spinach Flank Steak Pinwheels....60
Stovetop Italian Macaroni....63
Tacos in a Bowl....44
Tangy Sweet & Sour Meatballs....64
Zesty Steak Salad....51


### Pork


Air-Fryer Jamaican Jerk Pork Chops....101
Breaded Pork Cutlets....113
Chili Spaghetti with Hot Dogs....101
Garlic Toast Pizzas....108
Grilled Pork & Poblano Peppers....106
Ham & Swiss with a Twist....90
Hoisin Pork Tenderloin....109
Kielbasa Bow Tie Skillet....105
Lemon-Caper Pork Medallions....116
Oven-Fried Green Tomato BLT....104
Pasta & Broccoli Sausage Simmer....125
Pasta with Chorizo & Spinach....96
Pork Chops with Honey-Balsamic Glaze....114

Pork Medallions with Garlic-Strawberry Sauce....94
Pork Tenderloin Diane....111
Sausage Potato Supper....105
Savory Beer Pork Chops....92
Skillet Ham & Rice....102
Skillet Pork Chops with Apples & Onion....89
Smoked Sausage & Veggie Sheet-Pan Supper....110
Spicy Mac & Cheese....123
Taco Pork Chops....110
Tender Sweet & Sour Pork Chops....121
Tenderloin with Herb Sauce....86
Tuscan Pork....115

**Poultry**

Air-Fryer Chicken Taco Pockets....150
Artichoke Chicken Pesto Pizza....128
Buffalo Sloppy Joes....167
Cherry Chicken Croissants....131
Chicken Pasta Caesar Salad....163
Creamy Dijon Chicken....147
Crumb-Coated Chicken & Blackberry Salsa....151
Crunchy Asian Chicken Salad....145
Easy Asian-Style Chicken Slaw....169
Hawaiian Turkey Burgers....149
Mediterranean Turkey Panini....152
Mediterranean Turkey Skillet....156
Nectarine Chicken Salad....152
Sausage-Stuffed Butternut Squash....141
Spicy Buffalo Chicken Wraps....139
Super Quick Chicken Fried Rice....158
Turkey Breast Tenderloins with Raspberry Sauce....168
Turkey Cutlets with Pan Gravy....135
Turkey Tostadas....134
White Wine Garlic Chicken....128

**Seafood**

Air-Fryer Tilapia Fillets....185
Breaded Baked Tilapia....188
Broiled Cod....197
Brown Sugar-Glazed Salmon....177
Cajun Baked Catfish....190

SEARED SALMON WITH STRAWBERRY BASIL RELISH, PAGE 181

Creamy Tomato Shrimp with Penne....183
Crumb-Coated Red Snapper....182
Feta Salmon Salad....206
Feta Shrimp Skillet....175
Herbed Tuna Sandwiches....206
Homemade Fish Sticks....174
Honey Walleye....186
Lobster Rolls....205
Mediterranean Shrimp Orzo Salad....195
Parmesan Baked Cod....176
Parsley-Crusted Cod....182
Pesto Corn Salad with Shrimp....180
Quick Moroccan Shrimp Skillet....187
Salmon Pasta Salad....188
Seared Salmon with Strawberry Basil Relish....181
Shrimp & Noodle Bowls....198
Shrimp Fried Rice....179
Shrimp Orzo with Feta....172
Shrimp Pomodoro....204
Shrimp Quesadillas....202
Shrimp Salad-Stuffed Avocados....189
Shrimp Scampi Spinach Salad....197
Simple Herbed Scallops....184
Southwest Fish Tacos....193
Special Scallop Salad....172
Speedy Salmon Patties....194
Tilapia & Lemon Sauce....179
Tilapia with Jasmine Rice....198
Tuna Burgers....201
Tuna Melt Sandwiches....192
Tuna Zucchini Cakes....174
Tuscan Salmon Pasta....185

**Meatless**

Avocado Egg Salad Toast....224
Bean Burritos....228
Black Bean & Sweet Potato Rice Bowls....212
Crispy Tofu with Black Pepper Sauce....223
Curried Egg Salad....231

MUFFIN-TIN LASAGNAS, PAGE 223

## FAST FIX

### Meatless (continued)


Edamame Salad with Sesame Ginger Dressing .... 210
Feta Garbanzo Bean Salad .... 234
Fresh Veggie Pockets .... 239
Gnocchi with Pesto Sauce .... 238
Italian Grilled Cheese Sandwiches .... 226
Lazy Lasagna for 2 .... 232
Mediterranean Chickpeas .... 214
Muffin-Tin Lasagnas .... 223
Peanut Butter Ramen .... 221
Portobello Melts .... 236
Sage & Browned Butter Ravioli .... 217
Salsa Black Bean Burgers .... 233
Speedy Hummus Pizza .... 217
Spinach Feta Turnovers .... 220
Spinach Pizza Quesadillas .... 213
Three-Cheese Quesadillas .... 233
Tortellini with Tomato Spinach Cream Sauce .... 219
Tropical Squash & Black Bean Burritos .... 218
Vegetarian Hummus Wraps .... 230


### Dinner Add-Ons


Air-Fryer Buffalo Cauliflower .... 249
Air-Fryer Carrots .... 242
Air-Fryer Cornbread .... 244
Au Gratin Peas & Potatoes .... 250
Bulgur with Pine Nuts .... 258
Confetti Quinoa .... 262
Contest-Winning Grilled Mushrooms .... 270
Glazed Ranch Carrots .... 250
Grilled Cabbage .... 265
Honey-Thyme Butternut Squash .... 255
Parmesan Roasted Broccoli .... 269
Peach & Burrata Salad .... 248
Quick Ambrosia Fruit Salad .... 255
Quick Green Beans with Bacon .... 242
Roquefort Pear Salad .... 252
Shaved Fennel Salad .... 268
Simple Waldorf Salad .... 266
Smoky Cauliflower .... 261
Spinach-Parm Casserole .... 244
Sunflower Noodle Coleslaw .... 253
Zucchini Parmesan .... 258


### Sweets


Air-Fryer Mocha Pudding Cakes .... 292
Air-Fryer S'mores .... 305
Grilled Nectarines with Burrata & Honey .... 283
Grilled Stone Fruits with Balsamic Syrup .... 298
Old-Fashioned Banana Cream Pie .... 284


## AIR FRYER


Air-Fried Butternut Squash Tacos .... 225
Air-Fryer Buffalo Cauliflower .... 249
Air-Fryer Carrots .... 242
Air-Fryer Chicken Taco Pockets .... 150
Air-Fryer Cornbread .... 244
Air-Fryer Cowboy Casserole .... 75
Air-Fryer Crispy Curry Drumsticks .... 157
Air-Fryer Jamaican Jerk Pork Chops .... 101
Air-Fryer Mocha Pudding Cakes .... 292
Air-Fryer Reuben Calzones .... 49
Air-Fryer S'mores .... 305
Air-Fryer Salisbury Steak .... 65
Air-Fryer Shrimp .... 190
Air-Fryer Southern-Style Chicken .... 167
Air-Fryer Tilapia Fillets .... 185


## PRESSURE COOKER


Pressure-Cooker Beef Tips .... 78
Pressure-Cooker Corn Chowder .... 14
Pressure-Cooker Philly Cheesesteak Sandwiches .... 81
Pressure-Cooker Saucy Italian Chicken .... 164
Pressure-Cooker Smoky White Beans & Ham .... 96


## SLOW COOKER

### Soups & Stews


Ginger Chicken Noodle Soup .... 21
Greek-Style Lentil Soup .... 27
Saucy Indian-Style Chicken & Vegetables .... 18
Slow-Cooker Beef Stew .... 28
Slow-Cooker Chicken & Rice Soup .... 8

Slow-Cooker Sweet Potato Soup.......29
Southwest Chicken Stew.......17
Vegetable Lentil Soup.......18

**Beef**
Brisket for a Bunch.......43
California Tamale Pie.......48
Chili Coney Dogs.......66
Cube Steaks with Gravy.......41
Easy Corned Beef & Cabbage.......79
Easy Slow-Cooked Swiss Steak.......83
Easy Slow-Cooker Pot Roast.......54
Flavorful Pot Roast.......63
French Dip.......58
Garlic Beef Stroganoff.......46
Mexican Bubble Pizza.......41
Roast Beef & Gravy.......45
Slow-Cooker Asian Short Ribs.......66
Slow-Cooker Beef au Jus.......73
Slow-Cooker Pot Roast.......82

**Pork**
Polish Kraut & Apples.......119
"Secret's in the Sauce" BBQ Ribs.......98
Slow-Cooked Mesquite Ribs.......91
Slow-Cooker Cubano Sandwiches.......95
Slow-Cooker Pizza Casserole.......115
Slow-Cooker Pork Chops.......102
Tangy Pulled Pork Sandwiches.......86

**Poultry**
Slow-Cooked Chicken a la King.......145
Slow-Cooked Turkey Sloppy Joes.......143
Slow-Cooked Turkey Stroganoff.......136
Slow-Cooker Buffalo Chicken Lasagna.......155
Slow-Cooker Luau Chicken.......161
Slow-Cooker Roast Chicken.......138
Slow-Cooker Turkey Breast.......148
Teriyaki Chicken Thighs.......148

**Meatless**
Slow-Cooker Chickpea Tagine.......230
Slow-Cooker Mac & Cheese.......237

**Dinner Add-Ons**
Creamy Polenta with Balsamic Glaze.......247
Slow-Cooked Apple Cider.......245
Slow-Cooker Cheesy Potatoes.......267
Slow-Cooker Mac & Cheese.......37

**Sweets**
New England Indian Pudding.......302
Pineapple Upside-Down Dump Cake.......278
Slow-Cooker Pina Colada Bananas Foster.......294


## 5 INGREDIENTS 5i


**Soups & Stews**
Egg Drop Soup.......27
Gumbo in a Jiffy.......15
Hearty Navy Bean Soup.......22
Spinach & White Bean Soup.......26

**Beef**
Air-Fryer Reuben Calzones.......49
Bacon Cheeseburger Pasta.......73
Black Bean & Beef Tostadas.......70
Cast-Iron Skillet Steak.......44
Easy Slow-Cooked Swiss Steak.......83
Flavorful Pot Roast.......63
Garlic-Butter Steak.......62
Mexican Bubble Pizza.......41
Quick Beef & Noodles.......80
Roast Beef & Gravy.......45
Slow-Cooker Beef au Jus.......73
Spinach Flank Steak Pinwheels.......60

**Pork**
Au Gratin Sausage Skillet.......92
Breaded Pork Cutlets.......113

BREADED PORK CUTLETS, PAGE 113

## 5 INGREDIENTS


**Pork (continued)**

Cabbage Sausage Supper ... 89
Garlic Toast Pizzas ... 108
Polish Kraut & Apples ... 119
Sausage Manicotti ... 121
Sausage Potato Supper ... 105
Savory Beer Pork Chops ... 92
"Secret's in the Sauce" BBQ Ribs ... 98
Simple Marinated Grilled Pork Chops ... 122
Skillet Pork Chops with Apples & Onion ... 89
Slow-Cooked Mesquite Ribs ... 91
Spaghetti with Bacon ... 112
Taco Pork Chops ... 110

**Poultry**

Air-Fryer Crispy Curry Drumsticks ... 157
Artichoke Chicken Pesto Pizza ... 128
Easy Asian-Style Chicken Slaw ... 169
Favorite Lasagna Roll-Ups ... 169
Juicy Air-Fryer Cornish Hens ... 136
Sausage & Pepper Sheet-Pan Sandwiches ... 164
Sausage-Stuffed Butternut Squash ... 141
Sheet-Pan Sausage & Potato Dinner ... 132
Slow-Cooker Luau Chicken ... 161
Slow-Cooker Turkey Breast ... 148
Super Quick Chicken Fried Rice ... 158
White Wine Garlic Chicken ... 128

**Seafood**

Air-Fryer Shrimp ... 190
Breaded Baked Tilapia ... 188
Crumb-Coated Red Snapper ... 182
Honey Walleye ... 186
Parmesan Baked Cod ... 176
Pesto Corn Salad with Shrimp ... 180
Shrimp & Noodle Bowls ... 198
Shrimp Fried Rice ... 179

**Meatless**

Avocado Egg Salad Toast ... 224
Bean Burritos ... 228
Gnocchi with Pesto Sauce ... 238
Italian Grilled Cheese Sandwiches ... 226
Lazy Lasagna for 2 ... 232
Muffin-Tin Lasagnas ... 223
Roasted Curried Chickpeas & Cauliflower ... 227
Sage & Browned Butter Ravioli ... 217
Spinach Feta Turnovers ... 220
Spinach Pizza Quesadillas ... 213

**Dinner Add-Ons**

Air-Fryer Buffalo Cauliflower ... 249
Air-Fryer Carrots ... 242
Bulgur with Pine Nuts ... 258
Confetti Quinoa ... 262
Contest-Winning Grilled Mushrooms ... 270
Creamed Corn ... 261
Glazed Ranch Carrots ... 250
Grilled Cabbage ... 265
Parmesan Roasted Broccoli ... 269
Quick Green Beans with Bacon ... 242
Smoky Cauliflower ... 261
Spinach-Parm Casserole ... 244
Zucchini Parmesan ... 258

**Sweets**

Air-Fryer S'mores ... 305
Blueberry Pie with Graham Cracker Crust ... 287
Cherry Dream Cake ... 281
Chocolate & Peanut Butter Crispy Bars ... 287
Fluffy Key Lime Pie ... 297
Grilled Stone Fruits with Balsamic Syrup ... 298
Healthy Peanut Butter Cookies ... 290
Layered Lemon Pie ... 294

CHOCOLATE & PEANUT BUTTER CRISPY BARS, PAGE 287

# INDEX BY PROTEIN SOURCE

GARLIC-BUTTER STEAK, PAGE 62

## BEEF

### Beef Roasts


Easy Slow-Cooker Pot Roast...............54
Flavorful Pot Roast...............63
Roast Beef & Gravy...............45
Slow-Cooker Beef au Jus...............73
Slow-Cooker Pot Roast...............82


### Ground Beef


Air-Fryer Cowboy Casserole...............75
Air-Fryer Salisbury Steak...............65
Bacon Cheeseburger Pasta...............73
Beef & Tater Bake...............52
Black Bean & Beef Tostadas...............70
Burrito Bake...............76
Cabbage Roll Casserole...............72
California Tamale Pie...............48
Cheeseburger Cups...............38
Creamy Taco Soup...............10
Favorite Hamburger Stew...............8


Favorite Hamburger Stew...............8


Favorite Mexican Lasagna...............58
Freezer Burritos...............53
Grilled Meat Loaf...............46
Li'l Cheddar Meat Loaves...............38
Mexican Bubble Pizza...............41
Mom's Meat Loaf...............75
One-Skillet Lasagna...............76
Refried Bean-Taco Pizza...............51
Slow-Cooker Pizza Casserole...............115
Stovetop Italian Macaroni...............63
Stuffed Peppers for Two...............61
Tacos in a Bowl...............44


### Other Beef


Beef Broccoli Stir-Fry...............49
Beef Tenderloin in Mushroom Sauce...............59
Cast-Iron Skillet Steak...............44
Cube Steaks with Gravy...............41
Easy Corned Beef & Cabbage...............79
Easy Slow-Cooked Swiss Steak...............83
Garlic Beef Stroganoff...............46
Garlic-Butter Steak...............62
Greek-Style Ribeye Steaks...............43
Layered Reuben Casserole...............54
Pressure-Cooker Beef Tips...............78
Quick Beef & Noodles...............80
Saucy Beef with Broccoli...............56
Skillet Steak Supper...............69
Slow-Cooker Asian Short Ribs...............66
Slow-Cooker Beef Stew...............28
Spinach Flank Steak Pinwheels...............60
Tangy Sweet & Sour Meatballs...............64


## PORK

### Bacon


BLT Quinoa Bowls...............107
Oven-Fried Green Tomato BLT...............104
Pressure-Cooker Corn Chowder...............14
Shortcut Minestrone...............34
Spaghetti with Bacon...............112
Spicy Mac & Cheese...............123


### Ham


Skillet Ham & Rice...............102
Ham & Swiss with a Twist...............90

LEMON-CAPER PORK MEDALLIONS, PAGE 116


## PORK

**Ham (continued)**

Hearty Navy Bean Soup .......22
Old-Fashioned Ham & Bean Soup .....30
Pressure-Cooker Smoky White Beans & Ham .......96

**Other Pork**

"Secret's in the Sauce" BBQ Ribs .......98
Slow-Cooked Mesquite Ribs .......91
Slow-Cooker Cubano Sandwiches .......95
Slow-Cooker Pizza Casserole .......115

**Pork Chops**

Air-Fryer Jamaican Jerk Pork Chops .......101
Favorite Grilled Pork Chops .......118
Greek Pork Chops .......97
One-Skillet Pork Chop Supper .......125
Pork Chops with Honey-Balsamic Glaze .......114
Savory Beer Pork Chops .......92
Simple Marinated Grilled Pork Chops .......122
Skillet Pork Chops with Apples & Onion .......89
Slow-Cooker Pork Chops .......102
Southern Fried Pork Chops .......98
Taco Pork Chops .......110
Tender Sweet & Sour Pork Chops .......121

**Pork Sausage**

Au Gratin Sausage Skillet .......92
Cabbage Sausage Supper .......89
Chili Spaghetti with Hot Dogs .......101
Garlic Toast Pizzas .......108
Gumbo in a Jiffy .......15
Kielbasa Bow Tie Skillet .......105
Mama's Spaghetti Pie .......108
Pasta & Broccoli Sausage Simmer .......125
Pasta with Chorizo & Spinach .......96
Polish Kraut & Apples .......119
Potato & Pepper Sausage Bake .......117
Sausage Manicotti .......121
Sausage Potato Supper .......105
Smoked Sausage & Veggie Sheet-Pan Supper .......110
Spinach & Sausage Lentil Soup .......21

**Pork Tenderloin**

Breaded Pork Cutlets .......113
Grilled Pork & Poblano Peppers .......106
Hoisin Pork Tenderloin .......109
Lemon-Caper Pork Medallions .......116
Pork Medallions with Garlic-Strawberry Sauce .......94
Pork Tenderloin Diane .......111
Pork Tenderloin with Peach Honey Mustard .......95
Tangy Pulled Pork Sandwiches .......86
Tenderloin with Herb Sauce .......86
Tuscan Pork .......115

## POULTRY

**Boneless Skinless Chicken Breasts**

Chicken Gyros .......161
Chicken Veronique .......159
Copycat Fried Chicken Sandwich .......133
Creamy Dijon Chicken .......147
Crumb-Coated Chicken & Blackberry Salsa .......151
Ginger Chicken Noodle Soup .......21
Southwest Chicken Stew .......17
Goat Cheese-Stuffed Chicken with Apricot Glaze .......134
Pressure-Cooker Saucy Italian Chicken .......164
Slow-Cooked Chicken a la King .......145
Spicy Buffalo Chicken Wraps .......139
White Wine Garlic Chicken .......128

**Boneless Skinless Chicken Thighs**

Grilled Huli Huli Chicken .......155
Saucy Indian-Style Chicken & Vegetables .......18
Slow-Cooker Luau Chicken .......161
Teriyaki Chicken Thighs .......148

### Cooked Chicken

Air-Fryer Chicken Taco Pockets...... 150
Artichoke Chicken Pesto Pizza........ 128
Cherry Chicken Croissants................131
Chicken Biscuit Potpie.........................147
Chicken Broccoli Casserole.............. 140
Chicken Pasta Caesar Salad............ 163
Easy Asian-Style Chicken Slaw........169
Nectarine Chicken Salad................... 152
Super Quick Chicken Fried Rice...... 158

### Other Chicken

Air-Fryer Crispy Curry
Drumsticks........................................ 157
Air-Fryer Southern-Style
Chicken..................................................167
Amish Chicken Corn Soup...................32
Cazuela.........................................................11
Chicken Ramen Noodle Bowl..............25
Cornflake "Fried" Chicken................. 157
Crunchy Asian Chicken Salad.......... 145
Delicious Oven Barbecued
Chicken.............................................. 163
Easy White Chicken Chili......................13
Juicy Air-Fryer Cornish Hens.......... 136
Lemony Chicken & Rice..................... 150
Nutty Oven-Fried Chicken................ 160
Sheet-Pan Pineapple
Chicken Fajitas................................ 142
Sheet-Pan Sausage &
Potato Dinner.................................... 132
Slow-Cooker Buffalo Chicken
Lasagna.............................................. 155
Slow-Cooker Chicken & Rice Soup......8

### Turkey

Buffalo Sloppy Joes.............................167
Favorite Lasagna Roll-Ups................169
Italian Sausage-Stuffed
Zucchini............................................. 130
Kids' Favorite Chili.................................19
Mediterranean Turkey Skillet.......... 156
Sausage-Stuffed Butternut
Squash................................................141
Slow-Cooked Turkey Stroganoff..... 136
Slow-Cooker Turkey Breast............. 148
Turkey Breast Tenderloins with
Raspberry Sauce............................. 168
Turkey Cutlets with Pan Gravy......... 135
Turkey Tostadas.................................. 134

### Whole Chicken

Country Roasted Chicken................. 144
Slow-Cooker Roast Chicken............ 138

## SEAFOOD

### Fish

Air-Fryer Tilapia Fillets..................... 185
Breaded Baked Tilapia.................. 188
Broiled Cod......................................... 197
Brown Sugar-Glazed Salmon.......... 177
Cajun Baked Catfish.......................... 190
Crumb-Coated Red Snapper........... 182
Feta Salmon Salad.........................206
Herbed Tuna Sandwiches.................206
Homemade Fish Sticks......................174
Honey Walleye.................................... 186
Parmesan Baked Cod.........................176
Parsley-Crusted Cod......................... 182
Rustic Fish Chowder.............................25
Salmon Pasta Salad.......................... 188
Seared Salmon with Strawberry
Basil Relish....................................... 181
Southwest Fish Tacos....................... 193
Speedy Salmon Patties......................194
Spring Salmon Chowder......................10
Tilapia & Lemon Sauce...................... 179
Tilapia with Jasmine Rice................. 198
Tuna Burgers....................................... 201
Tuna Melt Sandwiches....................... 192
Tuna Mushroom Bake........................ 177
Tuna Zucchini Cakes...........................174
Tuscan Salmon Pasta........................ 185

CHERRY CHICKEN CROISSANTS, PAGE 131

## SEAFOOD (CONTINUED)

### Other Seafood


Lobster Rolls ... 205
Mini Scallop Casseroles ... 202
Special Scallop Salad ... 172


### Shrimp


Air-Fryer Shrimp ... 190
Creamy Tomato Shrimp with Penne ... 183
Feta Shrimp Skillet ... 175
Mediterranean Shrimp Orzo Salad ... 195
Pesto Corn Salad with Shrimp ... 180
Quick Moroccan Shrimp Skillet ... 187
Shrimp & Macaroni Casserole ... 201
Shrimp & Noodle Bowls ... 198
Shrimp Bisque ... 16
Shrimp Fried Rice ... 179
Shrimp Orzo with Feta ... 172
Shrimp Pomodoro ... 204
Shrimp Quesadillas ... 202
Shrimp Salad-Stuffed Avocados ... 189
Shrimp Scampi Spinach Salad ... 197
Simple Herbed Scallops ... 184

CHICKPEA TACOS, PAGE 210

## MEATLESS

### Beans & Lentils


Bean Burritos ... 228
Bean Counter Chowder ... 35
Black Bean & Sweet Potato Rice Bowls ... 212
Black Beans with Brown Rice ... 236
Chickpea Tacos ... 210
Feta Garbanzo Bean Salad ... 234
Mediterranean Chickpeas ... 214
Roasted Curried Chickpeas & Cauliflower ... 227
Salsa Black Bean Burgers ... 233
Slow-Cooker Chickpea Tagine ... 230
Speedy Hummus Pizza ... 217
Tropical Squash & Black Bean Burritos ... 218
Vegetarian Hummus Wraps ... 230
Chickpea Tortilla Soup ... 23
Greek-Style Lentil Soup ... 27
One-Pot Coconut Curry Lentil Soup ... 29
Spinach & White Bean Soup ... 26
Vegetable Lentil Soup ... 18


### Dairy


Grilled Cheese & Tomato Soup Bake ... 235
Italian Grilled Cheese Sandwiches ... 226
Lazy Lasagna for 2 ... 232
Meatless Chili Mac ... 228
Muffin-Tin Lasagnas ... 223
Slow-Cooker Mac & Cheese ... 237
Three-Cheese Quesadillas ... 233
Spinach & Tortellini Soup ... 31


### Eggs


Avocado Egg Salad Toast ... 224
Chiles Rellenos Quiche ... 226
Curried Egg Salad ... 231


### Other Meatless


Air-Fried Butternut Squash Tacos ... 225
Caprese Eggplant Hero ... 216
Crispy Tofu with Black Pepper Sauce ... 223
Edamame Salad with Sesame Ginger Dressing ... 210
Fresh Veggie Pockets ... 239
Gnocchi with Pesto Sauce ... 238
Peanut Butter Ramen ... 221
Portobello Melts ... 236
Sage & Browned Butter Ravioli ... 217
Spinach Feta Turnovers ... 220
Spinach Pizza Quesadillas ... 213
Tortellini with Tomato Spinach Cream Sauce ... 219
Vegan Butter Cauliflower ... 215

# ALPHABETICAL INDEX


## A

Air-Fried Butternut Squash Tacos .......... 225
Air-Fryer Buffalo Cauliflower .......... 249
Air-Fryer Carrots .......... 242
Air-Fryer Chicken Taco Pockets .......... 150
Air-Fryer Cornbread .......... 244
Air-Fryer Cowboy Casserole .......... 75
Air-Fryer Crispy Curry Drumsticks .......... 157
Air-Fryer Jamaican Jerk Pork Chops .......... 101
Air-Fryer Mocha Pudding Cakes .......... 292
Air-Fryer Reuben Calzones .......... 49
Air-Fryer S'mores .......... 305
Air-Fryer Salisbury Steak .......... 65
Air-Fryer Shrimp .......... 190
Air-Fryer Southern-Style Chicken .......... 167
Air-Fryer Tilapia Fillets .......... 185
All-American Hamburgers .......... 42
Amish Chicken Corn Soup .......... 32
Amish Sugar Cookies .......... 274
Apple Crumb Bars .......... 282
Apple Dumpling Bake .......... 293
Artichoke Chicken Pesto Pizza .......... 128
Au Gratin Peas & Potatoes .......... 250
Au Gratin Sausage Skillet .......... 92
Avocado Egg Salad Toast .......... 224

## B

Bacon Cheeseburger Pasta .......... 73
Bean Burritos .......... 228
Bean Counter Chowder .......... 35
Beef & Cheese Wraps .......... 56
Beef & Tater Bake .......... 52
Beef Broccoli Stir-Fry .......... 49
Beef Tenderloin in Mushroom Sauce .......... 59
Black Bean & Beef Tostadas .......... 70

AIR-FRYER SHRIMP, PAGE 190

Black Bean & Sweet Potato Rice Bowls ... 212
Black Beans with Brown Rice ... 236
Blackberry Cobbler ... 274
BLT Quinoa Bowls ... 107
Blueberry Pie with Graham Cracker Crust ... 287
Breaded Baked Tilapia ... 188
Breaded Pork Cutlets ... 113
Brisket for a Bunch ... 43
Broiled Cod ... 197
Brown Sugar-Glazed Salmon ... 177
Buffalo Sloppy Joes ... 167
Bulgur with Pine Nuts ... 258
Burrito Bake ... 76

## C

Cabbage Roll Casserole ... 72
Cabbage Sausage Supper ... 89
Cajun Baked Catfish ... 190
California Tamale Pie ... 48
Caprese Eggplant Hero ... 216
Cast-Iron Skillet Steak ... 44
Catalina Taco Salad ... 69
Cazuela ... 11
Cheeseburger Cups ... 38
Cherry Chicken Croissants ... 131
Cherry Dream Cake ... 281
Chicken Biscuit Potpie ... 147
Chicken Broccoli Casserole ... 140
Chicken Gyros ... 161
Chicken Pasta Caesar Salad ... 163
Chicken Ramen Noodle Bowl ... 25
Chicken Veronique ... 159
Chickpea Tacos ... 210
Chickpea Tortilla Soup ... 23
Chiles Rellenos Quiche ... 226
Chili Coney Dogs ... 66
Chili Spaghetti with Hot Dogs ... 101
Chocolate & Peanut Butter Crispy Bars ... 287
Classic Lemon Bars ... 299
Confetti Quinoa ... 262
Contest-Winning Grilled Mushrooms ... 270
Cool as a Cucumber Soup ... 32
Copycat Fried Chicken Sandwich ... 133
Cornflake "Fried" Chicken ... 157
Country Roasted Chicken ... 144
Creamed Corn ... 261
Creamy Carrot Casserole ... 256
Creamy Dijon Chicken ... 147
Creamy Polenta with Balsamic Glaze ... 247
Creamy Taco Soup ... 10
Creamy Tomato Shrimp with Penne ... 183
Crispy Tofu with Black Pepper Sauce ... 223
Crumb-Coated Chicken & Blackberry Salsa ... 151
Crumb-Coated Red Snapper ... 182
Crunchy Asian Chicken Salad ... 145
Cube Steaks with Gravy ... 41
Curried Egg Salad ... 231

## D

Delicious Oven Barbecued Chicken ... 163
Disco Fries ... 257

## E

Easy Asian-Style Chicken Slaw ... 169
Easy Coconut Pie ... 302
Easy Corned Beef & Cabbage ... 79
Easy Slow-Cooked Swiss Steak ... 83
Easy Slow-Cooker Pot Roast ... 54
Easy Spinach Bisque ... 17
Easy White Chicken Chili ... 13
Edamame Salad with Sesame Ginger Dressing ... 210
Egg Drop Soup ... 27

## F

Farmhouse Apple Coleslaw ... 247
Favorite Grilled Pork Chops ... 118
Favorite Hamburger Stew ... 8
Favorite Lasagna Roll-Ups ... 169
Favorite Mexican Lasagna ... 58
Feta Garbanzo Bean Salad ... 234
Feta Salmon Salad ... 206

Feta Shrimp Skillet ... 175
Flavorful Pot Roast ... 63
Florida Orange Cake ... 285
Fluffy Key Lime Pie ... 297
Freezer Burritos ... 53
French Dip ... 58
Fresh Veggie Pockets ... 239

**G**

Garden Shell Salad ... 246
Garlic Beef Stroganoff ... 46
Garlic-Butter Steak ... 62
Garlic Toast Pizzas ... 108
Ginger Chicken Noodle Soup ... 21
Ginger Plum Tart ... 284
Glazed Ranch Carrots ... 250
Gnocchi with Pesto Sauce ... 238
Goat Cheese-Stuffed Chicken with Apricot Glaze ... 134
Grandma Krause's Coconut Cookies ... 297
Grandma's Rice Pudding ... 277
Greek Pork Chops ... 97
Greek-Style Lentil Soup ... 27
Greek-Style Ribeye Steaks ... 43
Grilled Cabbage ... 265
Grilled Cheese & Tomato Soup Bake ... 235
Grilled Huli Huli Chicken ... 155
Grilled Meat Loaf ... 46
Grilled Nectarines with Burrata & Honey ... 283
Grilled Pork & Poblano Peppers ... 106
Grilled Stone Fruits with Balsamic Syrup ... 298
Gumbo in a Jiffy ... 15

**H**

Ham & Swiss with a Twist ... 90
Hawaiian Turkey Burgers ... 149
Healthy Peanut Butter Cookies ... 290
Hearty Meatball Sub Sandwiches ... 55
Hearty Navy Bean Soup ... 22
Herb Biscuit Loaf ... 259
Herbed Tuna Sandwiches ... 206
Hoisin Pork Tenderloin ... 109
Homemade Chocolate Pudding ... 281
Homemade Fish Sticks ... 174
Homemade Jiffy Cinnamon Rolls ... 271
Honey-Thyme Butternut Squash ... 255
Honey Walleye ... 186

**I**

Italian Grilled Cheese Sandwiches ... 226
Italian Sausage-Stuffed Zucchini ... 130

**J**

Juicy Air-Fryer Cornish Hens ... 136
Juicy Watermelon Salad ... 251

**K**

Kids' Favorite Chili ... 19
Kielbasa Bow Tie Skillet ... 105

**L**

Layered Lemon Pie ... 294
Layered Reuben Casserole ... 54
Lazy Lasagna for 2 ... 232
Lemon-Caper Pork Medallions ... 116
Lemon Olive Oil Cake ... 291
Lemony Chicken & Rice ... 150
Li'l Cheddar Meat Loaves ... 38
Lobster Rolls ... 205

**M**

Mama's Spaghetti Pie ... 108
Maple & Bacon Glazed Brussels Sprouts ... 260
Meatless Chili Mac ... 228

Mediterranean Chickpeas ................ 214
Mediterranean Shrimp Orzo Salad ................ 195
Mediterranean Turkey Panini ................ 152
Mediterranean Turkey Skillet ................ 156
Mexican Bubble Pizza ................ 41
Mini Scallop Casseroles ................ 202
Mississippi Mud Pie ................ 295
Mom's Meat Loaf ................ 75
Muffin-Tin Lasagnas ................ 223

## N

Nectarine Chicken Salad ................ 152
New England Indian Pudding ................ 302
No-Knead Honey Oatmeal Bread ................ 253
Nutty Oven-Fried Chicken ................ 160

## O

Old-Fashioned Banana Cream Pie ................ 284
Old-Fashioned Ham & Bean Soup ................ 30
Old-Time Buttermilk Pie ................ 300
One-Pot Coconut Curry Lentil Soup ................ 29
One-Skillet Lasagna ................ 76
One-Skillet Pork Chop Supper ................ 125
Oven-Fried Green Tomato BLT ................ 104

## P

Parmesan Baked Cod ................ 176
Parmesan Roasted Broccoli ................ 269
Parsley-Crusted Cod ................ 182
Pasta & Broccoli Sausage Simmer ................ 125

ONE-SKILLET LASAGNA, PAGE 76

Pasta with Chorizo & Spinach ................ 96
Peach & Burrata Salad ................ 248
Peach Cobbler Dump Cake ................ 304
Peanut Butter Pudding Pie ................ 279
Peanut Butter Ramen ................ 221
Pesto Corn Salad with Shrimp ................ 180
Pesto Quinoa Salad ................ 268
Pineapple Upside-Down Dump Cake ................ 278
Polish Kraut & Apples ................ 119
Pork Chops with Honey-Balsamic Glaze ................ 14
Pork Medallions with Garlic-Strawberry Sauce ................ 94
Pork Tenderloin Diane ................ 111
Pork Tenderloin with Peach Honey Mustard ................ 95
Portobello Melts ................ 236
Potato & Pepper Sausage Bake ................ 117
Pressure-Cooker Beef Tips ................ 78
Pressure-Cooker Corn Chowder ................ 14
Pressure-Cooker Philly Cheesesteak Sandwiches ................ 81
Pressure-Cooker Saucy Italian Chicken ................ 164
Pressure-Cooker Smoky White Beans & Ham ................ 96

## Q

Quick & Easy Tiramisu ................ 288
Quick Ambrosia Fruit Salad ................ 255
Quick Beef & Noodles ................ 80
Quick Green Beans with Bacon ................ 242
Quick Moroccan Shrimp Skillet ................ 187

## R

Ranch Beans ................ 264
Raspberry Custard Kuchen ................ 301
Refried Bean-Taco Pizza ................ 51
Roast Beef & Gravy ................ 45
Roasted Curried Chickpeas & Cauliflower ................ 227
Rocky Road Freezer Pie ................ 290
Roquefort Pear Salad ................ 252
Rustic Fish Chowder ................ 25

## S

Sage & Browned Butter Ravioli ................ 217
Salmon Pasta Salad ................ 188
Salsa Black Bean Burgers ................ 233

Saucy Beef with Broccoli....56
Saucy Indian-Style Chicken & Vegetables....18
Sausage & Pepper Sheet-Pan Sandwiches....164
Sausage Manicotti....121
Sausage Potato Supper....105
Sausage-Stuffed Butternut Squash....141
Savory Beer Pork Chops....92
Seared Salmon with Strawberry Basil Relish....181
"Secret's in the Sauce" BBQ Ribs....98
Shaved Fennel Salad....268
Sheet-Pan Pineapple Chicken Fajitas....142
Sheet-Pan Sausage & Potato Dinner....132
Shortcut Minestrone....34
Shrimp & Macaroni Casserole....201
Shrimp & Noodle Bowls....198
Shrimp Bisque....16
Shrimp Fried Rice....179
Shrimp Orzo with Feta....172
Shrimp Pomodoro....204
Shrimp Quesadillas....202
Shrimp Salad-Stuffed Avocados....189
Shrimp Scampi Spinach Salad....197
Simple Herbed Scallops....184
Simple Marinated Grilled Pork Chops....122
Simple Waldorf Salad....266
Skillet Ham & Rice....102
Skillet Pork Chops with Apples & Onion....89
Skillet Steak Supper....69
Slow-Cooked Apple Cider....245
Slow-Cooked Chicken a la King....145
Slow-Cooked Mesquite Ribs....91
Slow-Cooked Turkey Sloppy Joes....143
Slow-Cooked Turkey Stroganoff....136
Slow-Cooker Asian Short Ribs....66
Slow-Cooker Beef au Jus....73
Slow-Cooker Beef Stew....28
Slow-Cooker Buffalo Chicken Lasagna....155
Slow-Cooker Cheesy Potatoes....267
Slow-Cooker Chicken & Rice Soup....8
Slow-Cooker Chickpea Tagine....230

SHRIMP SCAMPI SPINACH SALAD, PAGE 197


Slow-Cooker Cubano Sandwiches....95
Slow-Cooker Luau Chicken....161
Slow-Cooker Mac & Cheese....237
Slow-Cooker Pina Colada Bananas Foster....294
Slow-Cooker Pizza Casserole....115
Slow-Cooker Pork Chops....102
Slow-Cooker Pot Roast....82
Slow-Cooker Roast Chicken....138
Slow-Cooker Sweet Potato Soup....29
Slow-Cooker Turkey Breast....148
Smoked Sausage & Veggie Sheet-Pan Supper....110
Smoky Cauliflower....261
So-Easy Gazpacho....12
So-Easy Sloppy Joes....70
Southern Fried Pork Chops....98
Southern Potato Salad....262
Southwest Chicken Stew....17
Southwest Fish Tacos....193
Spaghetti with Bacon....112
Special Scallop Salad....172
Speedy Hummus Pizza....217
Speedy Salmon Patties....194
Spicy Buffalo Chicken Wraps....139
Spicy Mac & Cheese....123
Spinach & Sausage Lentil Soup....21
Spinach & Tortellini Soup....31
Spinach & White Bean Soup....26
Spinach Feta Turnovers....220
Spinach Flank Steak Pinwheels....60
Spinach-Parm Casserole....244
Spinach Pizza Quesadillas....213

TURKEY CUTLETS WITH PAN GRAVY, PAGE 135


Spring Salmon Chowder....................10
Stovetop Italian Macaroni....................63
Strawberry Trifle....................276
Stuffed Peppers for Two....................61
Sunflower Noodle Coleslaw....................253
Super Quick Chicken Fried Rice....................158

## T

Taco Pork Chops....................110
Tacos in a Bowl....................44
Tangy Pulled Pork Sandwiches....................86
Tangy Sweet & Sour Meatballs....................64
Tender Sweet & Sour Pork Chops....................121
Tenderloin with Herb Sauce....................86
Tennessee Peach Pudding....................289
Teriyaki Chicken Thighs....................148
Three-Cheese Quesadillas....................233
Tilapia & Lemon Sauce....................179
Tilapia with Jasmine Rice....................198
Tortellini with Tomato Spinach Cream Sauce....................219
Tropical Squash & Black Bean Burritos....................218
Tuna Burgers....................201
Tuna Melt Sandwiches....................192
Tuna Mushroom Bake....................177
Tuna Zucchini Cakes....................174
Turkey Breast Tenderloins with Raspberry Sauce....................168
Turkey Cutlets with Pan Gravy....................135
Turkey Tostadas....................134
Tuscan Pork....................115
Tuscan Salmon Pasta....................185

## V

Vanilla Wafer Cookies....................293
Vegan Butter Cauliflower....................215
Vegetable Lentil Soup....................18
Vegetarian Hummus Wraps....................230

## W

Watermelon Gazpacho....................23
White Wine Garlic Chicken....................128

## Z

Zesty Steak Salad....................51
Zucchini Parmesan....................258
Zucchini Patties....................270